Orthodox psychotherapy

Original title: Orthodoxi Psichotherapia

Note: The third edition of the original text has been used
      for the translation

Original ©: Metropolitan of Nafpaktos Hierotheos

Translated by Esther Williams, 1994

Cover art: Yannis Yeremtzes

Published by: Birth of the Theotokos Monastery
             P.O. 107, 321 00 Levadia, Greece
             tel. & fax: 0268 31204

First edition 1994

Reprinted 1995, 1997

ISBN 960-7070-27-5

**Metropolitan of Nafpaktos
Hierotheos**

Orthodox psychotherapy

(The science of the Fathers)

**Translated by
Esther Williams**

Birth of the Theotokos Monastery

Abbreviations

BEPES	Bibliothiki Ellinon Pateron kai Ekklisiastikon Syggrapheon, Athens, 1955
CS	Cistercian Studies. Cistercian Publications, Kalamazoo, Michigan, 1982.
CWS	Classics of Western Spirituality. Paulist Press and London SPCK.
EF	Early Fathers from the Philokalia. London, Faber and Faber, 1954.
EPE	Ellines Pateres tis Ekklisias. Thessaloniki.
ET	English translation.
FC	Fathers of the Church. Washington DC., Catholic University.
LCC	Library of Christian Classics. Philadelphia, Westminster; London, SCM 1953-66.
NPNF	A Select Library of Nicene and Post-Nicene Fathers.
NPNFns	Ibid., new series.
PG	Patrologia Graeca, comp. Migne, J-P. Paris, 1857-66.
Philok.	Philokalia. Astir, Athens. ET London, Faber and Faber.
RR	Romaioi i Romioi Pateres tis Ekklisias. Pournara, Thessaloniki.
SC	Sources Chretiennes. Les Editions du Cerf, Paris.
SCM	Student Christian Movement.
SPCK	Society for Promotion of Christian Knowledge.
Writings	Writings from the Philokalia on Prayer of the Heart. London, Faber and Faber, 1954.

Contents

Translator's Note

Before embarking on this study, the reader is asked to absorb a few Greek terms for which there is no English word that would not be imprecise or misleading. Chief among these is NOUS, which refers to the 'eye of the heart' and is often translated as mind or intellect. Here we keep the Greek word NOUS throughout. The adjective related to it is NOETIC (noeros).

Another pair of words, PRAXIS (action) and THEORIA (vision) generally refer in the patristic writings to ascetic practice and the vision of God respectively. The use of 'contemplation' for THEORIA has been avoided.

NEPSIS is the kind of sober-minded vigilance that characterises the ascetic life of the Fathers. It is usually translated as watchfulness. The adjective is NEPTIC.

HESYCHIA means stillness, and the practice of stillness in the presence of God is called HESYCHASM.

I could not have undertaken this work without the help of the English translation of three volumes of the Greek Philokalia. In the bibliography and in the footnotes to our author's rich offering of quotations I have indicated these and other published translations of which I made use, sometimes altering the wording. I have also found helpful the many translations into modern Greek which are increasingly making their appearance.

I gratefully acknowledge the encouragement, help and advice given by the author and by Miss Effie Mavromichali, who has translated some of his other books into English. I hope very much that if there are mistakes, I will be forgiven and told about them so that they may be corrected in the future.

Esther Williams

110 Princess Court
Queensway, London W2 4RF

Preface to the English edition

At the beginning of this year Mrs Esther Williams of England presented me with an English translation of my book "Orthodox Psychotherapy" which she said just finished. I was indeed greatly surprised that a person unknown to me would show such an interest in the subject of this book and would engage herself in translation of it with admirable diligence and commitment. I feel the need to thank her deeply and pray to God to give her strength, to illumine her and grant her every perfect gift.

It should be noted that with its first publication in Greece, in 1986 "Orthodox Psychotherapy" gave rise to many discussions which result in the publication of three other books, all relevant in content. One of them has already been translated into English under the title "The Illness and Cure of the Soul in the Orthodox Tradition". Yet it is this first book that contains the important message that the church can heal an ailing personality.

The term "Orthodox Psychotherapy" does not refer to specific cases of people suffering from psychological problems of neurosis. Rather it refers to all people. According to Orthodox Tradition, after Adam's fall man became ill; his "nous" was darkened and lost communion with God. Death entered into the person's being and caused many anthropological, social, even ecological problems. In the tragedy of his fall man maintained the image of God within him but lost completely the likeness of Him, since his communion with God was disrupted. However the incarnation of Christ and the work of the Church aim at enabling the person to attain to the likeness of God, that is to reestablish communion with God. This passage way from a fallen state to divinization is called the healing of the person, because it is connected with his return from a state of being contrary to nature, to that of a state according to nature and above nature. By adhering to Orthodox therapeutic treatment as conceived by the Holy Fathers of the Church man can cope successfully with the thoughts (logismoi) and thus solve his problems completely and comprehensively.

I would like to reemphasize that the diagnoses of all neurotic and pathological states are not the subject of this book; for they belong to the domain of psychiatry and neurology. On the other hand many psychological illnesses are caused by the anxiety of death, the lack of meaning in life, a guilty conscience and the loss of communion with God on man's part. Surely the theology of the Church can help by either preventing or by healing people suffering from such existential dilemmas.

Thus psychiatry and neurology are called to cure pathological anomalies, whereas Orthodox theology cures the deeper causes that engender them.

The reader of this book will find in it the pathway by which a person arrives at communion with God, thus fulfilling the destiny of human existence as well as the method by which he can even protect himself from various physical illnesses.

Orthodox psychotherapy will therefore be more helpful to those who want to solve their existential problems; those who have realised that their nous has been dar-kened and for this reason they must be delivered from the tyranny of their passions and thoughts (logismoi) in order to attain to the illumination of their nous and communion with God.

All this therapeutic treatment or psychotherapy is closely connected with the neptic tradition of the Church and its hesychastic life, as it is preserved in the texts of the Philokalia, in the works of the Fathers of the Church and notably in the teaching of St. Gregory Palamas. Certainly one should not disregard the fact that the neptic and hesychastic life is the same life which one sees in the life of the Prophets and the Apostles as is described precisely in the texts of Holy Scripture. It will be made clear in the analysis of the chapters in this book that the neptic life is in fact the life of the Gospels.

I am pleased that this book will be read by an English speaking audience because I feel that the neptic and ascetic life had also existed in the western world before it was substituted by Scholastic theology. Scholasticism, indeed, connected knowledge with reason and has created serious problems when one considers that knowledge refers to the whole of human existence and is not simply exhausted by reason. I believe that the greatest problem of western philosophy is that it identifies the nous with reason and intellectual knowledge with existential knowledge. Even contemporary scholars in the West point to this fact. In truth the neptic tradition is the common tradition of both the East and the West, before the intrusion of scholasticism and the identification of theology with metaphysics. And it is this tradition which fully calms man's spirit which seeks fulfilment, inner peace and stillness. Within the turmoil and pain of today's world which distresses us and torments us; and which forsakes us to real hunger and thirst it is necessary that we find and live this therapeutical way, as recommended to us by the Holy Fathers of the Church it creates spiritual and solves the existential, social and ecological problems. Surely the holy Fathers of the Church preceeded contemporary psychologists and psychiatrists.

Persons who have been healed are the evidence that the Church intervenes in society in a salvific way. It is precisely this great purpose which the Orthodox Church serves through her theology and life.

Archimandrite Hierotheos S. Vlachos

Author's Prologue

Contemporary man, tired and discouraged by the various problems which torment him, is looking for rest and refreshment. Basically he is seeking a cure for his soul, as it is mainly there that he feels the problem. He is going through a 'mental depression'. For this reason psychiatric explanations are circulating broadly in our time. Psychotherapy in particular is widespread. While these things were almost unknown before, they are horribly prevalent now, and many people are turning to psychotherapists to find peace and comfort. For I repeat, contemporary man feels that he is in need of healing.

Along with realising this fundamental need, I notice every day that Christianity, and especially Orthodoxy, which preserves the essence of Christianity, is making much use of 'psychotherapy', or rather, that Orthodoxy is mainly a therapeutic science. Every means that it employs, and indeed its very aim, is to heal man and guide him to God. For in order to attain communion with God and achieve the blessed state of divinisation, we must first be healed. So, beyond all other interpretations, Orthodoxy is mainly a therapeutic science and treatment. It differs clearly from other psychiatric methods, because it is not anthropocentric but theanthropocentric and because it does not do its work with human methods, but with the help and energyof divine grace, essentially through the synergy of divine and human volition.

I have wanted to emphasise certain truths in this book. I have wished to point out the essence of Christianity and also the method which it employs for achieving this healing. My basic aim is to help contemporary man to find his cure within the Orthodox Church, as we too are struggling to attain it. I realise that we are all sick and seeking the Physician. We are ill and seeking a cure. The Orthodox Church is the inn and hospital in which every sick and distressed person can be cured.

If this book becomes the occasion for some people to turn for their healing to the Church and its teaching, I will praise God Who gave me the inspiration and strength to carry out this difficult undertaking, and I will ask Him to have mercy on me for my many weaknesses.

Written in Edessa on September 30, 1987,
the day of the Holy Martyr Gregory
the Enlightener, Bishop
of Great Armenia.   *Archimandrite Hierotheos S. Vlachos*

Introduction

I feel it my duty to give a few basic explanations for the study and understanding of the chapters which follow.

The title 'Orthodox Psychotherapy' has been given to the book as a whole because it presents the teaching of the Fathers on curing the soul. I know that the term 'psychotherapy' is almost modern and is used by many psychiatrists to indicate themethod which they follow for curing neurotics. But since many psychiatrists do not know the Church's teaching or do not wish to apply it, and since their anthropology is very different from the anthropology and soteriology of the Fathers, in using the term 'psychotherapy', I have not made use of their views. It would have been very easy at some points to set out their views, some of which agree with the teaching of the Fathers and others of which are in conflict with it, and to make the necessary comments, but I did not wish to do that. I thought that it would be better to follow the teaching of the Church through the Fathers without mingling them together. Therefore I have prefixed the word 'Orthodox' to the word 'Psychotherapy' (healing of the soul), to make the title "Orthodox Psychotherapy". It could also have been formulated as "Orthodox Therapeutic Treatment".

Many teachings of the Fathers are cited with their references to support the text as it develops. I am well aware that texts containing a large number of references are not easy to read. However, I preferred this safer method, rather than making the study easy to read. Unfortunately, books nowadays are often read in a sentimental way, and I did not wish this subject, so crucial today, to be written in that way.

We have made use of many Fathers in developing the sub-ject, most of all the so-called neptic Fathers, without of course overlooking the so-called social ones. I say "so-called" because I do not believe that this distinction exists in essence. In Ortho-dox theology those called neptics are eminently social and those called social are essentially neptic. The Three Hierarchs, for example, lived a watchful, ascetic life, they purified their minds, and thus they shepherded the people of God. I believe firmly that the social quality of the saints is a dimension of asceticism.

There is a great deal of neptic teaching in the works of the Three Hierarchs. But I have made greater use of the Fathers of the "Philokalia" since they have abundant material and since the "Philokalia" is a collection of mystical theological texts and "constitutes a highly inspired effulgence of the hallowed ascetic experience of divine patristic figures on whom shone the holy and life-giving spirit" (Gk. Philokalia I, editors' pro-logue, p. 9). According to the editors of the Greek edition of the Philokalia, after the cessation of the hesychastic conflicts of the fourteenth century the need arose for a collection of the principle works of the Fathers concerning hesychastic life and noetic prayer. They wrote: "There is every indication that the collection was made by highly spiritual monks of Mount Athos from the library of the Holy Mountain, and begun in the second half of the fourteenth century, from 1350 on. This period coincides with the cessation of the famous hesychastic controversies. Concretely it ends with the triumphant Synodic justification of the Athonite Fathers. At that time it had be-come clear that there was need of a statement of the view of the Eastern Orthodox Fathers concerning hesychastic asceticism and noetic prayer. These had been a target of rationalising and socially active Roman Catholicism with the appearance of the slandererous monk Barlaam from Calabria, afterwards a bishop of the Roman Catholic Church (Gk. Philokalia I, p. 1-11).

The final elaboration of the texts of the Philokalia was made by St. Makarios, former Bishop of Corinth, and St. Nikodimos of the Holy Mountain and so "the Philokalia in a way takes on the dimensions of a Synodal presentation of the Mystical Theology of the Eastern Orthodox Church..." (p. 11). For this reason the texts of the Fathers of the Philokalia have been used, with a view to describing and presenting the Church's teaching about the illness and cure of the soul, nous, heart, and thoughts. However, where there was need I have not hesitated to turn to the texts of other great Fathers, such as St. Gregory the Theologian, St. Gregory Palamas (especially his 'Triads'), St. John Chrysostom, St. Basil the Great, St. Symeon the New Theologian, etc.

It is true that there is not a special chapter devoted to the sacraments of Holy Baptism and Holy Communion. In many places the great value of the sacramental life of our Church is emphasised. However, there is no special word about Baptism because I know that I am speaking to people who have already been baptised and so there is presumably no need for it. On the other hand, the sacrament of the Divine Eucharist is the centre of the spiritual and sacramental life of the Church. Holy Communion is what differentiates the asceticism of the Orthodox Church from all other "asceticism". I regard it as very necessary for man's spiritual life and for his salvation. But preparation is needed in order to be able worthily to have communion of the Body and Blood of Christ. For Holy Communion, according to the liturgical prayers, is for those who are prepared a light which enlightens, and for those not prepared it is a consuming fire. The Apostle Paul says: "Whoever eats the bread or drinks the cup of the Lord in an unworthy manner will be guilty of profaning the body and blood of the Lord. Let a man examine himself, and so eat of the bread and drink of the cup. For any one who eats and drinks without discerning the body eats and drinks judgment upon himself. That is why many of you are weak and ill, and some have died" (1 Cor. 11, 27-30).

We are living in a time when much is being said about

*ecclesiology, eucharistiology and eschatology. We have no ob-
jection to this. We believe that these are the essential elements
of the spiritual life. But the Church, the holy Eucharistand
eschatology are closely connected with the ascetic life. I firmly
believe that priority must be given to the subject of the ascetic
life, which is the path of preparation for Holy Communion.
And because this aspect is being disregarded, it has been
necessary to give special emphasis to these matters. Holy Communion helps to cure if all the other religious treatment which
is the basis of Orthodox asceticism is followed.*

*Much is being said today about psychological problems. I
believe that the so-called psychological problems are mainly
problems of thoughts, a darkened mind, and an impure heart.
The impure heart as described by the Fathers, the dark and
gloomy mind and impure thoughts are the source of all the
so-called psychological problems. When a man is inwardly
healed, when he has discovered the place of his heart, when he
has purified the noetic part of his soul and freed his intelligence, he has no psychological problems. He lives in the
blessed and undisturbed peace of Christ. We say these things
with the reservation that the body, of course, can be made sick
by fatigue, exhaustion, weakening, and decay.*

*The first chapter, entitled "Orthodoxy as a therapeutic
science", can be characterised as a summary of the whole book.
In fact it includes the main points in all the chapters. I confess
that the third chapter, entitled "Orthodox psychotherapy", is
difficult in some places. I could not avoid this because I had to
analyse the terms soul, nous, heart and intelligence and consider their interrelationships and differences.*

*A seventh chapter, entitled "Noetic prayer as a method of
healing", could perhaps have been written. But since there
were places in all the chapters in which the value and necessity of prayer were emphasised, especially in the chapter on
hesychia as a method of therapy, and since there are excellent
books describing the method and value of noetic prayer, I have
preferred not to include this chapter, in spite of the original*

intention. I recommend a study of other books which are in circulation.

I would ask that this book be not only read but also studied. It might need to be studied for a second and third time, with the particular purpose of being applied. May the holy Fathers whose teaching is presented here enlighten both me and the readers so that we may proceed on the path of the healing and salvation of our souls.

I sincerely ask God that any mistakes which I may have made should be corrected and that they should not do harm to the souls of the readers, since these chapters were written in order to help and not to harm. Likewise I beg the readers who find any mistakes to let me know so that they can be corrected.

In conclusion I would like to thank all who have helped with this publication. The benefit which may result will be due to them as well. "May the Lord grant them their hearts' desire".

Archim. H.S.V.

1. Orthodoxy as a therapeutic science

Many interpretations of Christianity have been formulated and many answers given to the questions: What is Christianity and what is its mission in the world? Most are not true. In what follows we shall seek to make it quite clear that Christianity, and especially Orthodoxy, is therapy. We shall also try to describe what therapy is and how it is attained.

1. What Christianity is

Many people interpreting the character of Christianity see it as one of the numerous philosophies and religions known from antiquity. Certainly Christianity is not a philosophy in the sense that prevails today. Philosophy sets up a system of thought which in most cases bears no relationship to life. The main difference between Christianity and philosophy is that the latter is human thinking, while Christianity is a revelation of God. It is not a discovery by man but a revelation by God Himself to man. It was impossible for human logic to find the truths of Christianity. Where the human word was powerless, there came the divine-human Word, or Christ the Godman, the Word of God. This divine revelation was formulated in the philosophical terms of the time, but again it must be emphasised that it is not a philosophy. The garments of the divine-human Word are taken from the philosophy of that time.

St. John Chrysostom, interpreting Isaiah 3,1: "Behold the

Lord, the Lord of Hosts, takes away from Jerusalem and from Judah... the mighty man and the soldier, the judge and the prophet, the diviner...", observes: "He seems here to be calling a diviner a person who is capable of conjecturing the future through profound intelligence and experience of things. Divining and prophesying are indeed two different things: the prophet, setting self aside, speaks under divine inspiration; the diviner for his part starts from what has already happened, puts his own intelligence to work and foresees many future events, as an intelligent person normally does. But the difference between them is great: it is the distance that separates human intelligence from divine grace"[1].

So speculation (or philosophy) is one thing, and prophecy, or the word of the prophet who theologises, is another. The former is a human activity while the latter is a revelation of the Holy Spirit.

In the patristic writings, and especially in the teaching of St. Maximus, philosophy is referred to as the beginning of the spiritual life. However, he used the term 'practical philosophy' to mean cleansing the heart from passions, which really is the first stage of the soul's journey towards God.

Yet Christianity cannot be regarded as a religion, at least not as religion presents itself today. God is usually visualised as dwelling in heaven and directing human history from there: He is extremely exacting, seeking satisfaction from man, who has fallen to earth in his sickness and weakness. There is a wall of separation between God and man. This has to be surmounted by man, and religion is a very effective help. Various religious rites are employed for this purpose.

According to another view, man feels powerless in the universe and needs a mighty God to help him in his weakness. In this view God does not create man, but man creates God. Again, religion is conceived as man's relationship to the Absolute God, that is to say, the "relationship of the 'I' to the

---

1. Commentary on Isaiah. SC 304 p. 154

Absolute Thou". Yet again, many regard religion as a means whereby the people are deluded into transferring their hopes to the future life. In this way strong powers put pressure on the people by means of religion.

But Christianity is something higher than these interpretations and theories; it cannot be contained within the usual conception and definition of religion given in the "natural" religions. God is not the Absolute Thou, but a living Person Who is in organic communion with man. Moreover Christianity does not simply transfer the problem to the future or await the delight of the kingdom of heaven after history and after the end of time. In Christianity the future is lived in the present and the kingdom of God begins in this life. According to the patristic interpretation, the kingdom of God is the grace of the Triune God, it is vision of the uncreated Light.

We Orthodox are not waiting for the end of history and the end of time, but through living in Christ we are running to meet the end of history and thus already living the life expected after the Second Coming. St. Symeon the New Theologian says that he who has seen the uncreated light and united with God is not awaiting the Second Coming of the Lord but living it. So the eternal embraces us at every moment of time. Therefore past, present and future are essentially lived in one unbroken unity. This is so-called condensed time.

Thus Orthodoxy cannot be characterised as the 'opium of the people', precisely because it does not postpone the problem. It offers life, transforms biological life, sanctifies and transforms societies. Where Orthodoxy is lived in the right way and in the Holy Spirit, it is a communion of God and men, of heavenly and earthly, of the living and the dead. In this communion all the problems which present themselves in our life are truly resolved.

Yet since the membership of the Church includes sick people and beginners in the spiritual life, it is to be expected that some of them understand Christianity as religion in the sense referred to above. Moreover, the spiritual life is a dynamic journey. It begins with baptism, which is purification of the 'image', and continues through ascetic living aimed at attaining 'likeness', which is to say communion with God. Anyway it must be made clear that even when we still speak of Christianity as a religion we must do it with certain necessary presuppositions.

The first is that Christianity is mainly a Church. 'Church' means 'Body of Christ'. There are many places in the New Testament where Christianity is called the Church. We shall only mention Christ's words: "You are Peter, and on this rock I will build my church" (Matt. 16:18) and the words of the Apostle Paul to the Colossians: "And he is the head of the body, the church" (1:18) and to his disciple Timothy: "...so that you may know how you ought to conduct yourself in the house of God, which is the church of the living God, the pillar and ground of the truth" (1 Tim., 3, 15). This means that Christ does not simply dwell in heaven and direct history and the lives of men from there, but He is united with us. He assumed human nature and deified it; thus in Christ deified human nature is at the right hand of the Father. So Christ is our life and we are 'members of Christ'.

The second presupposition is that the aim of the Christian is to attain the blessed state of deification. Deification is identical with 'likeness', that is, to be like God. However, in order to reach the likeness, to attain the vision of God, and for this vision not to be a consuming fire but a life-giving light, purification must previously have taken place. This purification and healing is the Church's work. When the Christian participates in worship without undergoing life-giving purification - and moreover these acts of worship also aim towards man's purification - then he is not really living within the Church. Christianity without purification is utopia. So when we are being purified, especially when we are seeing to our healing, we can speak of religion. And this accords with the words of the Lord's brother James: "If anyone among you thinks he is religious, and does not bridle his tongue but deceives his own heart, this one's religion is useless. Pure and undefiled religion before God and the Father is this: to visit orphans and widows in their trouble, and to keep oneself unspotted from the world" (Jas. 1:26-27).

This abstinence gives us the right to claim that Christianity is neither philosophy nor 'natural' religion, but mainly healing. It is the healing of a person's passions so that he may attain communion and union with God.

In the parable of the Good Samaritan the Lord showed us several truths. As soon as the Samaritan saw the man who had fallen among thieves who had wounded him and left him half dead, he "had compassion on him and went to him and bandaged his wounds, pouring on oil and wine; and he set him on his own animal, brought him to an inn and took care of him" (Luk. 10:33f). Christ treated the wounded man and brought him to the inn, to the Hospital which is the Church. Here Christ is presented as a physician who heals man's illnesses, and the Church as a Hospital.

It is very characteristic that in analysing this parable St. John Chrysostom presents the truths which we have just emphasised. Man went down "from the heavenly state to the state of the devil's deception, and he fell among thieves, that is, the devil and the hostile powers". The wounds which he sustained are the various sins. As David says, "My wounds are foul and festering because of my foolishness" (Ps. 38:5). For "every sin brings bruises and wounds". The Samaritan is Christ Himself, who came down from heaven to earth to heal wounded man. He used wine and oil for the wounds. That is to say, "by mixing the Holy Spirit with his blood, he brought life to man". According to another interpretation, "oil brings the comforting word, wine provides the astringent lotion, the instruction which brings concentration to the scattered mind". He set him upon his own animal: "Taking flesh upon his own divine shoulders, he lifted it towards the Father in Heaven". Thereupon the good Samaritan, Christ, led the man "into the wonderful and spacious inn, this universal Church". He gave him to the innkeeper, who is the Apostle Paul and "through Paul to the high priests and teachers and ministers of each church", saying: "Take care of the people of the Gentiles whom I have given to you in the Church. Since men are sick, wounded by sin, heal them, putting on them a stone plaster, that is, the prophetic sayings and the gospel teachings, making them whole through the admonitions and exhortations of the Old and New Testaments." So according to St. John Chrysostom, Paul is the one who upholds the churches of God "and heals all men through spiritual admonitions, distributing the bread of offering to each one..."[2].

In St. John Chrysostom's interpretation of this parable it is clearly evident that the Church is a Hospital which heals those sick with sin, while the bishops and priests, like the Apostle Paul, are the healers of the people of God.

These truths also appear in many other places in the New Testament. The Lord said: "Those who are well have no need of a physician, but those who are sick" (Matt. 9:12). Likewise Christ, as a physician of souls and bodies, was "...healing all kinds of sickness and all kinds of disease among the people... and they brought to him all sick people who were afflicted with various diseases and torments, and those who were demon-possessed, epileptics, and paralytics; and he healed them" (Matt. 4:23f). The Apostle Paul is well aware that the conscience of men, especially of simple ones, is weak: "When you thus sin against the brethren, and wound their weak conscience, you sin against Christ" (I Cor. 8:12). The Book of Revelation says that John the Evangelist saw a river of the water of life proceeding from the throne of God and of the Lamb. "On either side of the river was the tree of life... and the leaves of the tree were for the healing of the nations" (Rev. 22:1f).

So the work of the Church is therapeutic. It seeks to heal

---

2. PG 62, col.755-757

men's sicknesses, mainly those of the soul, which torment them. This is the basic teaching of the New Testament and of the Fathers of the Church. In what follows in this chapter as well as in other chapters many passages from the Fathers will bring out this truth.

Here again I want to emphasise the indispensability of the Church. I am very grateful to the priest and professor John Romanides for laying stress on this in his writings. I am convinced that he is very well read in the neptic Fathers -especially in the writings contained in the Philokalia - and has therefore grasped the real meaning of Christianity. I believe that this is his great contribution. For in this era when Christianity is being presented as a philosophy or intellectual theology or a culture and popular tradition - customs and manners - he presents this teaching about a therapeutic discipline and treatment.

Concretely, he says: "Having faith in Christ without undergoing healing in Christ is not faith at all. Here is the same contradiction that we find when a sick person who has great confidence in his doctor never carries out the treatment which he recommends. If Judaism and its successor, Christianity, had appeared in the twentieth century for the first time, they would most likely have been characterised not as religions but as medical sciences related to psychiatry. They would have a wide influence on society owing to their considerable successes in healing the ills of the partially functioning personality. In no way can prophetic Judaism and Christianity be construed as religions that use various magical methods and beliefs to promise escape from a supposed world of matter and evil or hypocrisy into a supposed spiritual world of security and success" [3].

In another work the same professor says: "The patristic tradition is neither a social philosophy nor an ethical system,

---

3. J. Romanides: Jesus Christ the life of the world. (A talk in Greek translation), p. 28f

nor is it religious dogmatism: it is a therapeutic treatment. In this respect it closely resembles medicine, especially psychiatry. The spiritual energy of the soul that prays unceasingly in the heart is a physiological instrument which everyone has and which requires healing. Neither philosophy nor any of the known positive or social sciences is capable of healing this instrument. That can only be done through the Fathers' neptic and ascetic teaching. Therefore those who are not healed usually do not even know of the existence of this instrument"[4] .

So in the Church we are divided into the sick, those undergoing therapeutic treatment, and those - saints - who have already been healed. "The Fathers do not categorise people as moral and immoral or good and bad on the basis of moral laws. This division is superficial. At depth humanity is differentiated into the sick in soul, those being healed and those healed. All who are not in a state of illumination are sick in soul... It is not only good will, good resolve, moral practice and devotion to the Orthodox Tradition which make an Orthodox, but also purification, illumination and deification. These stages of healing are the purpose of the mystical life of the Church, as the liturgical texts bear witness"[5].

2. Theology as a Therapeutic Science

From what has been said so far it is clear that Christianity is principally a science which cures, that is to say, a psychotherapeutic method and treatment. The same should be said of theology. It is not a philosophy but mainly a therapeutic treatment. Orthodox theology shows clearly that on the one hand it is a fruit of therapy and on the other hand it points the way to therapy. In other words, only those who have been cured and have attained communion with God are theologi-

---

4. J. Romanides: Romaioi i Romioi Pateres tis Ekklisias. Vol.1, p. 22f. In Greek
5. Ibid. p. 27

ans, and they alone can show Christians the true way to reach the 'place' of cure. So theology is both a fruit and a method of therapy.

Here we need to enlarge on what has been said in order to see these truths more clearly. We shall cite teachings of the Holy Fathers relating to theology and theologians.

I think that we should begin with St. Gregory Nazianzen, for it was not by chance that the Church gave him the title of Theologian. In the beginning of his famous theological texts he writes that it is not for everyone to theologise, to speak about God, because the subject is not so cheap and low. This work is not for all men but "for those who have been examined and are passed masters in the vision of God and who have previously been purified in soul and body, or at the very least are being purified". Only those who have passed from praxis to theoria, from purification to illumination, can speak about God. And when is this? "It is when we are free from all external defilement or disturbance, and when that which rules within us is not confused with vexations or erring images." Therefore the saint advises: "For it is necessary to be truly at ease to know God"[6].

Neilos the Ascetic links theology with prayer, principally with noetic prayer. We know very well from the teaching of the Holy Fathers that anyone who has acquired the grace of prayer of the heart has entered the first stages of the vision of God, for this type of prayer is a form of theoria. Therefore all who pray with the nous have communion with God, and this communion is man's spiritual knowledge of God. So St. Neilos says: "If you are a theologian, you will pray truly. And if you pray truly, you are a theologian"[7].

St. John Climacus introduces true theology in many places in his spiritually delightful 'Ladder'. "Total purity is the foundation for theology." "When a man's senses are perfectly

6. Gregory the Theologian. Or.27, 3. NPNFns, vol.7, p. 285
7. Evagrius. Philokalia 1, p. 62, 61

united to God, then what God has said is somehow mysteriously clarified. But where there is no union of this kind, then it is extremely difficult to speak about God"[8]. On the contrary, the man who does not actually know God speaks about Him only "in probabilities"[9]. Indeed according to patristic teaching it is very bad to speak in conjectures about God, because it leads a person to delusion. This saint knows how "the theology of the demons" develops in us. In vainglorious hearts which have not previously been purified by the operation of the Holy Spirit, the unclean demons "give us lessons in the interpretation of scripture"[10]. Therefore a slave of passion should not "dabble in theology"[11].

The saints received "divine things without thought", and according to the Fathers, they theologised not in an Aristotelian way through thinking, but "in the manner of the Apostles", that is to say through the operation of the Holy Spirit. If a person has not been cleansed of passions, especially fantasy, beforehand, he is unable to converse with God or to speak about God, since a nous "forming notions is incapable of theology". The saints lived a theology "written by the Spirit".

We find the same teaching in the works of St. Maximus the Confessor. When a person lives by practical philosophy, which is repentance and cleansing from passions, "he advances in moral understanding". When he experiences theoria, "he advances in spiritual knowledge". In the first case he can discriminate between virtues and vices; the second case, theoria, "leads the participant to the inner qualities of incorporeal and corporeal things". St. Maximus goes on to say that man is "granted the grace of theology when, carried on wings of love" in theoria and "with the help of the Holy Spirit, he discerns -

---

8. Ladder. Step 30. CWS p. 288
9. Ibid.
10. Ibid. p. 250
11. Ibid. p. 262

as far as this is possible for the human nous - the qualities of God"[12]. Theology, the knowledge of God, is unfolded to the person who has attained theoria. Indeed in another place the same Father says that a person who always "concentrates on the inner life" not only becomes restrained, long-suffering, kind and humble, but "he will also be able to contemplate, theologise and pray"[13]. Here too theology is closely connected with theoria and prayer.

It must be emphasised that a theology that is not the result of purification, that is, of 'praxis', is demonic. According to St. Maximus, "knowledge without praxis is the demons' theology"[14].

St. Thalassios, who had the same perspective, wrote that when man's nous begins with simple faith, it "will eventually attain a theology that transcends the nous and that is characterised by unremitting faith of the highest type and the vision of the invisible"[15]. Theology is beyond logic, it is a revelation of God to man, and the Fathers define it as theoria. Here too theology is chiefly vision of God. In another place the same saint wrote that genuine love gives birth to spiritual knowledge, and "this is succeeded by the desire of all desires: the grace of theology"[16].

In the teaching of St. Diadochos of Photiki theology is presented as the greatest gift offered to man by the Holy Spirit. All God's gifts of grace are "flawless", "but the gift which inflames our heart and moves it to the love of His goodness more than any other is theology". For theology, as "the early offspring of God's grace", "bestows on the soul the greatest gifts"[17].

According to the Apostle Paul, the Holy Spirit gives spir-

---

12. Philok.2, p. 69, 26
13. Ibid. p. 108, 64
14. PG 91, 601 C. Letter 20, to Marinos the Monk
15. Philok.2, p. 330, 80
16. Ibid. p. 328f, 62
17. Philok.1, p. 275, 67

itual knowledge to one person and wisdom to another (I Cor. 12, 8). Interpreting this, St. Diadochos says that spiritual knowledge unites man to God but does not move him to express outwardly what he knows. There are monks who love hesychia and are illuminated by the grace of God "yet do not speak about God". Wisdom is one of the rarest gifts, one which God gives to the person who has both expression and a capacious intellect. Therefore knowledge of God "comes through prayer, deep stillness and complete detachment, while wisdom comes through humble meditation on Holy Scripture and, above all, through grace given by God"[18]. The gift of theology is a work of the Holy Spirit but in cooperation with man, since the Holy Spirit does not actualise in man a spiritual knowledge of the mysteries "apart from that faculty in him which naturally searches out such knowledge"[19].

In the teaching of St. Gregory Palamas it is those who see God who are properly theologians, and theology is theoria. "For there is a knowledge about God and His doctrines, a theoria which we call theology..."[20]. Anyone who without knowledge and experience of matters of faith offers teaching about them "according to his own reasonings, trying with words to show the Good that transcends all words, has plainly lost all sense." And in his folly "he has become an enemy of God"[21]. Moreover there are cases in which people without having works, that is to say, without having undergone purification, have met and listened to holy men, but then they "try to form their own conceptions" and both reject the holy man and puff themselves up with pride[22].

All these things show that theology is properly the fruit of man's healing and not a rational discipline. Only a person

---

18. Ibid. p. 254f, 9
19. St. Maximus the Confessor. Philok.2, p. 239, 16
20. Triads. 1.3, 15
21. Ibid. 1, 3, 12
22. Ibid. 3, 1, 32. CWS p. 87

who has been purified or at least is being purified can be initiated into the ineffable mysteries and great truths, can receive revelations and afterwards convey them to the people. Therefore in the Orthodox patristic tradition theology is linked and identified with the spiritual father, and the spiritual father is the theologian par excellence - that is to say, the one who experiences the things of God and so can lead his spiritual children unerringly.

Father John Romanides writes characteristically: "The true Orthodox theologian is the one who has direct knowledge of some of God's energies through illumination or knows them more through vision. Or he knows them indirectly through prophets, apostles and saints or through scripture, the writings of the Fathers and the decisions and acts of their Ecumenical and Local Councils. The theologian is the one who through this direct or mediated spiritual knowledge and vision knows clearly how to distinguish between the actions of God and those of creatures and especially the works of the devil and the demons. Without the gift of discernment of spirits it is not possible to test spirits to see whether something is the action of the Holy Spirit or of the devil and the demons.

Therefore the theologian and the spiritual father are the same thing. A person who thinks and talks in search of a conceptual understanding of the doctrines of the faith after the Franco-Latin pattern certainly is not a spiritual father, nor can he be called a theologian in the proper sense of the word. Theology is not abstract knowledge or practice, like logic, mathematics, astronomy and chemistry, but on the contrary, it has a polemical character like logistics and medicine. The former is concerned with matters of defence and attack through bodily drill and strategies for the deployment of weapons, fortifications and defensive and offensive schemes, while the latter is fighting against mental and physical illnesses for the sake of health and the means of restoring health.

A theologian who is not acquainted with the methods of the

enemy nor with perfection in Christ is not only unable to struggle against the enemy for his own perfection, but is also in no position to guide and heal others. It is like being called a general, or even being one, without ever having been trained or fought, or studied the art of war, having only given attention to the beautiful, glorious appearance of the army in its splendid, bright uniforms at receptions and displays. It is like a butcher posing as a surgeon or like holding the position of a physician without knowing the causes of illnesses or the methods of curing them, or the state of health to which the patient should be restored"[23].

3. What Therapy is

Since we have said that Christianity and theology are primarily a therapeutic science, we must now outline briefly what therapy is. What does Orthodoxy with its theology and worship cure in us?

Therapy of the soul essentially means therapy and freeing of the nous. Human nature became 'sick' through its fall away from God. This sickness is mainly the captivity and fall of the nous. The ancestral sin is that man withdrew from God, lost divine grace, and this resulted in blindness, darkness and death of the nous. We can say more accurately that "the fall of man or the state of having inherited sin is: a) the failure of his noetic power to function soundly or even to function at all, b) the confusion of this power with the functions of the brain and of the body in general, and c) its resulting subjection to mental anguish and to the surrounding conditions. Every person has experience of the fall of his own noetic power to varying degrees, as he is exposed to an environment in which this power is not functioning or is below par... Malfunctioning of the noetic power results in bad relations between man and

---

23. Romanides: Dogmatic and Symbolic Theology... p. 85f. In Greek.

God and between people. It also results in the individual's
making use of both God and fallen man to fortify his personal
safety and happiness"[24].

This loss of the grace of God deadened man's nous; his
whole nature sickened, and he handed this sickness on to his
descendants as well. In Orthodox teaching this is how we
understand the inheritance of sin. The Fathers interpret St.
Paul's "as by one man's disobedience many were made sinners" (Rom. 5,19) not in legal terms but 'medically'. That is to
say, human nature became sick. St. Cyril of Alexandria interprets the situation thus: "After Adam fell by sin and sank into
corruption, at once impure pleasures rushed in, and the law
of the jungle sprang up in our members. So nature became
sick with sin through the disobedience of one, Adam. Then
the many became sinners, not as fellow transgressors with
Adam, for they did not even exist, but as being of that nature
which had fallen under the law of sin.... Human nature in
Adam became sick through the corruption of disobedience,
and thus the passions entered into it"[25]. In another place the
same Father uses the image of the root. Death came to the
whole human race by Adam, "just as when the root of a plant
is injured, all the young shoots that come from it must
wither"[26].

St. Gregory Palamas says characteristically: "The nous
which has rebelled against God becomes either bestial or
demonic and, after having rebelled against the laws of nature, lusts after what belongs to others..."[27]

Through the "rite of birth in God", holy baptism, man's
nous is illuminated, freed from slavery to sin and the devil,
and is united with God. That is why baptism is called illumination. But after that, because of sin, the nous is again

---

24. Romanides. Jesus Christ the Life of the World, p. 23. In Gk.
25. Commentary on Epistle to the Romans. PG 74, 788f
26. Ibid. 785
27. Homily 51, 10. EPE 11, p. 114f. In Gk.

darkened and deadened. The patristic writings make it clear
that every sin and every passion deadens the nous.

St. John of the Ladder writes that the evil demons strive
"to darken our spirit". Especially the demon of unchastity "by
darkening our minds, which guide us, pushes people "to do
things that only the mad would think of"[28].

In another chapter attention will be given to the nature of
man's nous. Here we are mainly concerned with the subject of
darkening. St. Maximus teaches: "As the world of the body
consists of things, so the world of the nous consists of conceptual images. And as the body fornicates with the body of a
woman, so the nous, forming a picture of its own body, fornicates with the conceptual image of a woman"[29]. This is the
darkness and fall of the nous.

In another connection the same holy Father teaches that
"when the body sins through material things and has the
bodily virtues to teach it self-restraint, so too when the nous
sins through impassioned conceptual images, it has the virtues of the soul to instruct it"[30]. This truth shows that the fall
of the nous creates confusion in the whole spiritual organism.
It creates anguish and agitation and in general makes the
person live the fall in all its tragicalness. Thus many problems which plague us come from this inner sickness. That is
why the psychotherapists cannot help very much, since it is
only Christ who can restore the nous deadened by passions.

Again St. Maximus, trying to define more clearly what is
impurity of the nous and hence its fall, writes that it consists
in four things: "first in having false knowledge; secondly in
being ignorant of any of the universals...; thirdly in having
impassioned thoughts; and fourthly in assenting to sin"[31].

---

28. Ladder. Step 15. CWS p. 185
29. Philok. 2, p. 91, 53
30. Ibid. p. 76, 64
31. Ibid. p. 88, 34

So the nous needs therapy, a therapy which the Fathers call quickening and purifying the nous.

A great deal is said about purity of mind and heart in the teachings of the Lord and the Apostles. The Lord, referring to the Pharisees of his time who were careful of external purity and neglected inner purity, said: "Blind Pharisee, first cleanse the inside of the cup and dish, that the outside of them may be clean also" (Matt. 23, 26). At the Apostles' meeting in Jerusalem Peter, confronting the problem of the Christian Gentiles as to whether they must first be circumcised and keep the law of the Old Testament, said: "God, who knows the heart, acknowledged them, by giving them the Holy Spirit just as he did to us, and made no distinction between us and them, purifying their hearts by faith" (Acts 15, 8f). The Apostle Paul recommended to the Christians of Corinth: "Let us cleanse ourselves from all filthiness of the flesh and spirit, perfecting holiness in the fear of God" (2 Cor. 7, 1). The blood of Christ shall "purge your conscience from dead works" (Heb. 9, 14). Likewise the same Apostle, writing to his disciple Timothy, affirms that we hold the mystery of the faith "with a pure conscience" (1 Tim. 3, 9). And the Apostle Peter is well aware that love for one another is the fruit of a pure heart, so he says: "Love one another fervently with a pure heart" (1 Pet. 1, 22).

So purification of the nous and heart is essential. We write about the nous and the heart even though we know that in patristic theology these two are joined together. We shall come back to that, however, in another chapter.

St. Maximus divides the spiritual life into three stages. They are practical philosophy natural theoria and mystical theology. According to a study of Maximus, "his teaching about a personal approach to salvation, is divided into three basic parts: 1) 'practical philosophy' or praxis 2) 'natural theoria' or simply theoria and 3) 'mystical theology' or simply theology. The first purifies a person of passions and adorns him with virtues; the second illuminates his nous with true knowledge; and the third crowns him with the highest mystical experience, which St. Maximus calls 'ecstasy'. These three parts constitute the basic stages on the path of man's personal salvation[32].

Indeed it must be noted that many Fathers distinguish these three stages in the spiritual life: practical philosophy or purification of the heart, natural theoria or illumination of the nous, and mystical theology or communion with God through theoria.

According to another division which appears in the patristic writings, the spiritual life is separated into praxis and theoria. This is not a distinction clearly opposed to the preceding one, but really the same thing. For praxis is purification, and theoria is illumination of the nous and communion with God. In any case praxis precedes theoria, the vision of God. "Praxis is the patron of theoria"[33]. More analytically, "praxis where the body is concerned consists of fasting and vigil, where the mouth is concerned it consists of psalmody. But prayer is better than psalmody, and silence more valuable than speech. In the case of the hands, praxis is what they do uncomplainingly..."[34]. And: "Theoria is the nous's vision; it is to be amazed and to understand all that has been and is to be."[35].

Certainly according to St. Maximus' teaching, theoria is not independent of praxis. "Praxis is not safe without theoria, nor is theoria true without praxis. For praxis must be intelligent and theoria must be efficacious...". Maximus does emphasise that "in the case of the more learned, theoria precedes praxis, whereas with simpler people praxis comes first". In both cases however, the outcome is good, they lead to the same result, the purification and salvation of man[36].

---

32. The monk A.Rantosavlievits: The Mystery of Salvation according to St. Maximus the Confessor. p. 122. In Gk.

33. Gregory the Theologian. Or.40, 37. NPNFns, vol.7, p. 374, 37

34. Ilias the Presbyter. Philok. 3, p. 34, 4

35. Isaac the Syrian. Epistle 4. Gk.ed.Spanos, p. 384 (not in ET)

36. PG 90, 1433-1437

Actually when we speak of purifying the soul, we mean principally releasing it from the passions[37], or rather transforming the passions. Furthermore, purification is also the "uniform development" of the human being, which leads to illumination of the nous. So purification is not only negative but also positive. The qualities of a pure soul are "intelligence devoid of envy, ambition free from malice, and unceasing love for the Lord of glory"[38]. In other words, if we are motivated by envy and our ambition contains malice and our love for God is not unceasing, it means that our heart has not yet been purified.

The nous is that which is in the image of God. We have defiled this image with sin and it must now be cleansed. Therefore Abba Dorotheos requests: "Let us make our image pure as we received it..."[39]. We shall have to suffer toil and intolerable bitterness until we have purified our nous, that "cur sniffing around the meat market and revelling in the uproar"[40]. If a man struggles not to commit sin and battles against passionate thoughts, he is humiliated and shattered in the fight, "but the sufferings of combat purify him little by little and bring him back to the natural state"[41].

Yet beside man's effort, if the Holy Spirit does not descend, the dead nous cannot be purified and brought to life, because "only the Holy Spirit can purify the nous"[42].

In any case, when, through the working together of divine grace and the human will, the nous has been purified, then it is illuminated, since "where there is purifying there is illumination"[43]. After purification, if a person guards his nous from defilement by sin, his nous is illuminating and illuminated.

---

37. St. Thalassios. Philok.2, p. 317, 78
38. St. Diadochos of Photike. Philok.1, p. 258, 19
39. Instructions 16, 171. SC p.466. CS p. 223
40. Ladder. Step 1. CWS p. 75
41. Dorotheos. SC p.412, 144. CS p. 197
42. Diadochos of Photike. Philok.1, p. 260, 28
43. Gregory the Theologian. Or.39, 8. NPNFns, vol.7, p. 354

That is why guarding the nous can be called "light-producing, lightning-producing, light-giving and fire-bearing"[44].

Briefly, we can affirm that man's cure is in fact purification of the nous, heart, and image, the restoration of the nous to its primordial and original beauty, and something more: his communion with God. When he becomes a temple of the Holy Spirit, we say that the cure has succeeded. Those cured are the saints of God.

4. Method of Therapy-Therapeutic Treatment

Having seen what Christianity is, what the character of Orthodox theology is, what therapy is, we shall now look at the method of therapeutic treatment, which is the method of the Orthodox faith. If we have so far located the problem, we must now do our best to make an inventory of the methods for achieving purity of heart, that is, the cure. For there is no great point in listing the higher states unless we go on to bring them to awareness and apply them.

How then is the soul cured?

First we must emphasise **right faith**. We Orthodox attach great importance to preserving the faith, just because we know that when faith is distorted, the cure is automatically distorted. We have previously emphasised that theology should be interpreted as medicine. Medical science has the healthy person in view when it tries to guide the sick person to health by various therapeutic methods. We can say the same thing about theology. Theology is the teaching of the Church about spiritual health, but also about the path which we sick must follow in order to be healed. That is why we

---

44. Hesychios the Priest. Philok.1, p. 192, 171

Orthodox give great weight to keeping the doctrine intact, not only because we fear the impairment of a teaching, but because we could lose the possibility of a cure and therefore of salvation. Furthermore, "the conflict between Palamas and Barlaam was not so much about the type of doctrine as about its methodological foundation. Barlaam based himself on metaphysics and metaphysical epistemology and logic, while Palamas took as his basis empirical verification and confirmation and their demonstrable results"[45].

Now in order to be cured it is essential **to feel that one is ill**. When a sick person is not aware of his illness, he cannot turn to a doctor. Self-knowledge is one of the first steps to a cure. St. Maximus teaches: "The person who has come to know the weakness of human nature has gained experience of divine power", and he is eager to achieve some things and has achieved other things through this divine power[46]. Peter of Damascus, describing the great value of prayer at night, says: "Practice of the moral virtues is effectuated by meditating on what has happened during the day", when we meditate on the lapses that occurred "in the confusion of the day", "so that during the stillness of the night we can become aware of the sins we have committed and can grieve over them"[47]. Only when we know our state can we grieve about it.

It is an indisputable fact that most Christians today are unaware of their spiritual condition. We are "dead in trespasses" and not only do not perceive it but even have the feeling that we are filled with the gifts of the Holy Spirit, adorned with virtues. Unfortunately, this self-satisfaction which plagues us is destroying the work of salvation. How can Christ speak to a person who justifies himself? We are like the Pharisee in the time of the Lord who did not feel the need of a physician. How can the great gift of repentance and

---

45. J. Romanides: RR vol.1, p. 18. In Gk.
46. Philok.2, p. 72, 39
47. Philok.3, p. 261

mourning unfold in a heart which does not feel its desolation, when the inner life is unable to develop?

In connection with the sense of being ill there should also be "self-condemnation", that is, the great gift of self-reproach. It shows that there is humility in the soul, since "self-reproach is always associated with humility"[48]. This self-reproach is a spiritual burden which, when placed upon the soul, "crushes and presses and squeezes out the salutary wine that rejoices the heart of man, that is, our inner man. Compunction is such a wine." Self-reproach, with the mourning which characterises it, also crushes the passions and fills the heart with most blissful joy[49]. "We must always condemn and criticise ourselves in order that by means of deliberately chosen humiliations we may protect ourselves from unwitting sin"[50].

But the sense of being ill is not enough in itself. In any case a therapist is required as well. This therapist is the priest, the spiritual father. He has first been cured of his own ailments or at least is struggling to be cured, and then he also cures his spiritual children. We have said before that the spiritual father must be a theologian, and vice versa. So in this case the saying applies "Physician, heal yourself" (Lk. 4, 23). One who has come through the devil's devices can safely guide his spiritual children. One who has come to know the great treasure called spiritual health can help others too to be cured. Anyone who has found his nous can help others too to find it. "The truly physician-like nous is one that first heals itself and then heals others of the diseases of which it has been cured"[51].

Many contemporary Christians regard priests as ministers of the Most High and as church officials who are helpful in various bureaucratic dealings, who perform the different

48. St. Gregory Palamas. To Xeni. Gk.Philok.4, p. 108, line 27
49. Ibid. p.109, lines 10-14
50. Ladder. Step 25, CWS p. 226
51. Thalassios. Philok. 2, p. 328, 44

sacraments when they are needed or celebrate the Divine Liturgy, and in this way can satisfy the need of their souls or fulfil a traditional duty. They are regarded as magicians who work magic! We know, however, that the grace of God is not transmitted magically or mechanically, but sacramentally. It is true that even an unworthy priest performs sacraments, but he cannot cure. For remission of sins is one thing but curing is another. Most Christians are satisfied with a formal confession or formal attendance at the Liturgy or even with a formal Communion and nothing more. They do not proceed to the cure of their souls. But the priests, the spiritual fathers, not only celebrate Communion but they cure people. They have a sound knowledge of the path of healing from passions and they make it known to their spiritual children. They show them how they can be freed from captivity, how their nous will be freed from slavery.

Here is how the holy Fathers view spiritual fatherhood. The pastor is also a physician. "A physician is one whose body and soul are sound, needing no plasters on them"[52]. St. John of the Ladder is very characteristic on what the priest should do in order to give healing:

"O wondrous man, acquire plasters, potions, razors, eye salves, sponges, instruments for blood-letting and cauterisation, ointments, sleeping draughts, a knife, bandages, and something against nausea (disgust at the stench of wounds). If we do not put these things to use, how are we to practise our science? There is no way, because physicians receive payment not for words but for deeds.

"A plaster is a cure for passions which are external, that is, bodily passions. A potion is a cure for inner passions and to drain off invisible uncleanness. A razor is humiliation which bites, but purifies the rot of conceit. An eye salve is for cleansing the eye of the soul which has been clouded by anger. An eye salve is a caustic chastisement which speedily brings

---

52. St. John of the Ladder. To the Shepherd. Moore 1979, p. 232f

healing. Blood-letting is a draining of unseen stench. Again, the blood-letting instrument is pre-eminently an intensive and brief remedy for the salvation of the sick. A sponge is used after the blood-letting to heal and refresh the patient with the gentle, meek and tender words of the physician. Cauterisation is a rule and a penance given with love to the sinner for a definite period of time for his repentance. An ointment is the soothing offered to the patient with a few words or some small consolation after cauterisation.

"A sleeping draught is that we lift the person's burden, and through an obedience give him rest and waking sleep and holy blindness to his own virtues. Bandages are for binding and strengthening those who are enervated and enfeebled by vainglory. The last instrument is the knife, which is a sentence and a decree to cut off a putrid member and a body dead in soul lest he spread his contagion among the rest.

"Blessed and praiseworthy are the 'non-disgust' of the physicians and the dispassion among shepherds. The former, not suffering from nausea, untiringly strive to dispel the stench. The latter will be able to restore to life every dead soul"[53].

Fr. John Romanides writes: "The successful repetition of the experience of confirmation, which in medical and patristic science is cure, is the truth of every science. Just as it is absurd to say that one who does not cure and does not know how to cure is a physician, so it is senseless to regard as a theologian one who is not at least in the state of illumination, who does not know what illumination and deification are, and who does not know how these things are achieved and therefore does not cure"[54].

Father John also writes: "It is assumed that above all others the therapists who guide the sick into these stages of therapy are the bishops and priests, the former having mostly come from monasticism. Today, however, after a century and

---

53. Ibid.
54. J. Romanides: RR vol.1, p. 18f In Gk.

a half of catastrophic neo-hellenic propaganda against hesy-chasm, such clergy are rare. There are few hesychast monks. The priesthood as described by Dionysios the Areopagite has almost disappeared"[55].

The therapist priest also recommends to his spiritual children an **orthodox way**, which is a way of orthodox devotion. Therefore in what follows we want to turn to that point, to describe the method which the sick person should follow under the guidance of his spiritual father in order to attain spiritual healing.

We want particularly to point to **asceticism**. "The forceful practice of self control and love, patience and stillness, will destroy the passions hidden within us"[56]. Nicetas St. Stethatos, disciple of St. Symeon the New Theologian, describes this ascetic practice. Man has five senses, so the ascetic practices are five in number: vigils, study, prayer, self-control and hesychia. The ascetic should combine the five senses with these five practices: sight with vigils, hearing with study, smell with prayer, taste with self-control and touch with hesychia. When he succeeds in making these links, "he quickly purifies the nous of his soul and by this refining makes it dispassionate and clear-sighted"[57].

We can say briefly that to practise asceticism is to apply God's law, to keep His commandments. The effort which we make to subordinate the will of man to the will of God, and to be changed by this, is called ascesis. We are well aware from the teaching of our holy Fathers that the whole Gospel consists of "precepts of salvation". What is contained in Scripture is God's commandment, which must be kept by those who seek their salvation. This is seen clearly in the Beatitudes (Matt. 5, 1-12).

---

55. Ibid. p. 27
56. Thalassios. Philok.2, p. 319, 8
57. Practical chapters, Ch. 91

"Blessed are the poor in spirit" is the Lord's commandment that we should look for our spiritual poverty, that is, that we should experience our wretchedness. "Blessed are those who mourn" is the Lord's commandment to weep over the passions which we have in us, over our desolation. "Blessed are those who hunger and thirst after righteousness" is the Lord's commandment to hunger and thirst after communion with God. "Blessed are the pure in heart" is Christ's commandment to purify our hearts. When He says "blessed" it is as if He said: "Become poor, mournful, thirsting for righteousness", and so forth.

So Christ's commandment is unceasing prayer, celebration of the Divine Liturgy, watchfulness, that is attention of the nous, purity of heart, and so forth. "The law is holy and the commandment holy and just and good" (Rom. 7, 12). John the Evangelist, the disciple of love, emphasises to the Christians: "Now by this we know that we know Him, if we keep His commandments. He who says, 'I know Him,' and does not keep His commandments is a liar, and the truth is not in him. But whoever keeps His word, truly the love of God is perfected in him. By this we know that we are in Him" (1 Jn. 2, 3-5). The same Evangelist emphasises authoritatively: "For this is the love of God, that we keep His commandments" (1 Jn .5, 3).

"The aim of our hierarchy is to make us as much like God as possible and to unite us to Him. But Scripture teaches us that we will only attain this through the most loving obser-vance of the commandments and the performance of divine services," according to St. Dionysios the Areopagite[58]. St. Gregory Palamas teaches that knowledge of created things comes from doing virtuous deeds. And when asked what is the aim of virtuous deeds, he writes: "Union with God and becoming like Him"[59]. Doing virtuous deeds is connected with keeping the commandments. This hesychast saint remarks

---

58. Ecclesiastical Hierarchies, ch.2. CWS p. 200
59. Gregory Palamas. Triads. 2, 3, 74

further that love for God "comes only through the sacred performance of the divine commandments"[60].

In what follows I would like to mention some sayings of the Fathers about the value of God's commandments.

"The whole purpose of the Saviour's commandments is to free the nous from dissipation and hatred"[61].

God's commandments "excel all the treasures of the world". A man who has gained inward possession of them finds the Lord in them"[62].

The keeping of God's commandments generates dispassion. The soul's dispassion preserves spiritual knowledge"[63].

Obedience to God's commandment "is the resurrection of the dead"[64].

St. Gregory of Sinai, describing the two basic ways of operation of the Holy Spirit, which we receive secretly in Holy Baptism, regards keeping the commandments as one of them. "The more we keep the commandments, the more manifestly the Holy Spirit sheds its brilliant light on us"[65].

All these things show how essential the ascetic life is for healing and restoring the soul. And as we have said, this ascetic life is primarily the keeping of the commandments of Christ the Saviour.

The basic commandments which effect our spiritual healing -as we also say in the troparia that we sing in the Church - are "fasting, vigils and prayer".

If almsgiving heals the soul's incensive power and prayer purifies the nous, fasting withers sensual desire[66] and thus the whole soul is offered to God healed. Fasting also humbles

---

60. Ibid. 2, 3, 77
61. Maximus. Philok.2, p. 107, 56
62. Isaac the Syrian. Ascetical Homilies. p. 42
63. Thalassios. Philok.2, p. 314, 25
64. Ibid. p. 328, 48
65. Gk.Philok.4, p. 67, 3
66. Maximus. Philok.2, p. 61, 79

the body: "Privation of food mortifies the body of the monk"[67].
Yet excessive fasting not only weakens the body but "makes
the contemplative faculty of the soul dejected and disinclined
to concentrate"[68].

St. John of the Ladder speaks characteristically of fasting:
"To fast is to do violence to nature. It is to do away with
whatever pleases the palate. Fasting ends lust, roots out bad
thoughts, frees one from evil dreams. Fasting makes for purity of prayer, an enlightened soul, a watchful mind, a deliverance from blindness. Fasting is the door of compunction,
humble sighing, joyful contrition, and end to chatter, an occasion for stillness, a custodian of obedience, a lightening of
sleep, health of the body, an agent of dispassion, a remission
of sins, the gate, indeed the delight of Paradise"[69].

All these things which he mentions, on the one hand show
the scope of fasting, and on the other hand indicate the fruits
which it brings to the striving soul. That is why all the saints
loved fasting. It is very important to mention that when a
person begins to repent, he also begins to fast of his own accord,
which shows that fasting goes with prayer and repentance.

To be sure, fasting is a means and not an end, it is "a tool
for training those who desire self-restraint"[70], but without it,
it is almost impossible to conquer the passions and attain
dispassion. St. John of the Ladder is clear about this. As the
Hebrews freed themselves from Pharaoh and experienced the
Passover after eating bitter herbs and unleavened bread, so
we too will be freed from the inner Pharaoh through fasting
and humility: "You must not fool yourself. You will not escape
from Pharaoh, and you will not see the heavenly Passover
unless you constantly eat bitter herbs and unleavened bread,

---

67. Sayings of the Desert Fathers, p. 68, 2
68. Diadochos of Photike. Philok.1, p. 266, 45
69. Ladder. Step 14. CWS p. 169
70. Diadochos. Philok.1, p. 267, 47

the bitter herbs of toil and hard fasting; and the unleavened bread of a mind made humble"[71].

It is essential that we keep the fasts which the Church has fixed, and strive not to give fullest satisfaction to the demands of the flesh.

Apart from fasting, another means of healing is the **vigil**. Through keeping vigils, which is also an ascetic method for therapy, a person is purified and healed of passions. The Lord taught us how to pray at night. He himself spent whole nights on the mountain. "And when he had sent the multitudes away, he went up on a mountain by himself to pray. And when evening had come, he was alone there" (Matt. 14, 23).

The holy Fathers experienced in their lives the beneficial effect of vigils. St. Isaac says in his ascetic writings: "A monk who perseveres in vigil with a discerning nous will not seem to be clad with flesh, for this is truly the work of the angelic estate." A soul which labours and excels in the practice of vigils "will have the eyes of Cherubim, that she may at all times gaze upon and espy celestial visions"[72].

St. John of the Ladder, with all his characteristic delicacy presents the model of a wakeful monk and the benefits of vigils: "Alertness keeps the mind clean. Somnolence binds the soul. The alert monk does battle with fornication, but the sleepy one goes to live with it. Alertness is a quenching of lust, deliverance from fantasies, a tearful eye, a heart made soft and gentle, thoughts restrained, food digested, passions tamed, spirits subdued, tongue controlled, idle imaginings banished. The vigilant monk is a fisher of thoughts, and in the quiet of the night he can easily observe and catch them"[73].

Prayer too goes with vigil. This is the method par excellence which heals the diseases of the soul. For much grace comes to the soul of man through prayer. But we shall deal

---

71. Ladder. Step 14. CWS p. 169
72. Isaac the Syrian. Ascetical Homilies, p. 101
73. Ladder. Step 20. CWS p. 196

with noetic prayer and the method we use in order to free the nous and see God when we come to the chapter entitled "Hesychia as a method of therapy". This is because we regard it as the most important means for the salvation of man.

There are also other therapeutic means for curing every passion of the soul. But we shall deal with them at length in a later chapter entitled "Orthodox Pathology".

Perhaps the reader is thinking that all these therapeutic means, which are salves for the eye of the heart (cf. Rev. 3, 18) can only be practised by monks. This certainly not true. Everyone, even we who live in the world, can live by the commandments of Christ. Prayer, repentance, mourning, compunction, fasting, vigil, and so on, are commandments of Christ, which means that everyone can live by them. Christ did not say things that are impossible for man. St. Gregory Palamas, speaking about purity of heart, emphasises that "it is possible even for those living a married life to pursue this purity, but with very great difficulty"[74]. Everyone can develop a life according to the Gospel by making the corresponding adjustment.

Moreover if there is a bishop and a divine Liturgy, it means that salvation is possible. Why does the Church exist and function? What is more, there is an appropriate application of Christ's commandments for each person. In patristic literature we have such cases. The Fathers, who have themselves been healed, have acquired the grace of discernment and they advise each person to find his path, which is essentially the path of the Orthodox tradition.

St. John of the Ladder is characteristic on this point. He tells of having seen a stupid physician dishonour and drive to despair a sick man who was contrite and humble in spirit. At the same time he had seen another "intelligent" spiritual physician operate on an "arrogant heart" with the knife of dishonour and thereby drain it of all the evil smell. He also says that he saw the same sick man sometimes treating his

---

74. To Xeni. Gk.Philok.4, p. 20-22

uncleanness with the medicine of obedience and sometimes healing "the sick eye of his soul" with stillness and silence[75]. Here it seems clear that the same sick man needed obedience at one time and stillness and silence at another. The appropriate medicines must be given at the appropriate time.

A discerning confessor, the same saint also says: "One man's medicine can be another man's poison." What is more, the same preparation for the same sick person can at one time be a medicine and at another time a poison. When given at a suitable time it serves as a medicine, but at the wrong time it is a poison[76].

Therefore we emphasise once more that a discriminating Orthodox therapist (physician-confessor) is essential for adjusting the medication and giving the appropriate therapeutic guidance.

In what follows I would like to quote some sayings of the desert fathers in which it is clearly apparent that there is variety in ascetic practice and great possibility for adjustment.

Someone asked St. Anthony: "What must one do in order to please God?" And he answered: "Wherever you go, have God before your eyes, whatever you do and say, have the Scriptures as your witness, and whatever place you are in, do not move away quickly. Keep these three and you will be saved"[77].

Another Father asked Abba Nistheroes: "What good work is there that I could do?" And he answered: "Are not all actions equal? Scripture says that Abraham was hospitable and God was with him. David was humble, and God was with him. Elias loved interi or peace and God was with him. So, do whatever your soul desires according to God and guard your heart"[78].

---

75. Ladder. Step 27. CWS p. 233
76. Ibid.
77. Sayings of the Desert Fathers p. 2, 3
78. Ibid. p. 130, 2

Joseph of Thebes says: "Three works are approved in the eyes of the Lord; the first, when a man is ill and temptations fall upon him, if he welcomes them with gratitude; secondly, when someone carries out all his works purely in the presence of God, having no regard for anything human; in the third place, when someone remains in submission to a spiritual father in complete renunciation of his own will. This last will gain a lofty crown indeed." And then he accentuates, "As for me, I have chosen illness"[79].

Likewise Abba Poemen said: If three men are in the same place and one of them fully preserves interior peace, and the second gives thanks to God in illness, and the third serves with a pure mind, these three are doing the same work"[80].

From all these examples it seems that men's struggle is a common one, but their ways of struggling vary. All have to keep the word of God, God's commandments, all must guard the purity of their hearts wherever they are working. Nevertheless there is a variety of applications which the spiritual father can make.

It may well be regarded as a shortcoming that we have not also listed Holy Communion within therapeutic treatment. But we must underline and lay great stress on the fact that we regard the Eucharist, the communion of the Body and Blood of Christ as indispensable for man. The Lord emphasised: "Unless you eat the flesh of the Son of Man and drink his blood, you have no life in you"(John 6, 53). But it is well known that holy Communion is preceded by purification and preparation. If the therapy about which we are speaking here does not come first, then the receiving of the Body and Blood of Christ is "unto judgement and condemnation". Ecclesiology and eschatology cannot be understood without therapeutic training. So we are not undervaluing the Holy Eucharist, but by emphasising the value of ascetic practice and therapy we

---

79. Ibid. p. 94, 1
80. Ibid. p. 144, 29

are exalting the great gift of the Eucharist. On the other hand, the aim of what we have written is mainly to make clear the precise path which ends at the altar, so that Holy Communion may become light and life.

I hope that these few words have shown clearly that Christianity is a therapeutic science. It heals sick man. This sickness is made evident in the nous. The Church with its teaching, worship, ascesis and sacraments frees the nous and makes it a temple of the Holy Spirit. This therapeutic way has been applied and confirmed by all the saints. It is the only path which leads to God. I think that the loss of the tradition is to be seen chiefly in the loss of the therapeutic method and of actual therapists. The way back to the Orthodox Tradition is essentially the way back to these two foundations.

2. The orthodox therapist

So far I hope we have established the truth that Christianity is mainly a therapeutic science. It is seeking the spiritual healing of man. Yet the right practice of medicine requires a good physician, a professional physician, and this applies to spiritual healing as well. There has to be a good doctor. He is the bishop and the priest.

As we have noted before, people today feel that the priest's function is to enable them to take part in the holy sacraments. They feel that he has been commanded by God, as His servant and deacon, so that they may confess their sins and have spiritual relief. They feel him to be the deacon of God, called to pray to Him that their labours may be blessed, and so forth. Certainly no one can deny that the priest will do such work as well. But usually people seem to regard the priest rather as a magician (if I may be forgiven this expression). For when we look at the life of worship apart from curing, then rather it is magic!

We repeat however, in order to make it clear, that the priest is properly a spiritual physician who cures people's sicknesses. Worship and sacraments must be placed within the therapeutic method and treatment.

Even as a confessor, the priest is mainly a therapist. The sacrament of confession is not simply a formal absolution, especially of the Western type, as if God were angry and demanded expiation. It is something more. It is a part of the therapeutic treatment. There are numerous Christians who make confession over a period of many years but are not healed of their spiritual ills. Ignorance on the part of both the people and the pastors contributes to this.

The task of the bishop, priest or confessor is to lead the people out of Egypt into the promised land, like another Moses. This guidance requires toil and labour, privation and anguish. It is mainly therapeutic supervision. The Fathers are very insistent upon this truth. Let us take St. John of the Ladder as an example. He advises that "those of us who wish to get away from Egypt and the Pharaoh need an intermediary with God, to stand between praxis and theoria and stretch out his arms to God, that those led by him may cross the sea of sin and put to flight the Amelek of the passions". The saint goes on to say that those who rely on their own powers and claim to have no need of a guide are deceiving themselves[1]. From the Old Testament story we know what Moses endured and how he guided that stiff-necked people.

This spiritual Moses is a physician. Furthermore, all of us are sick and have need of therapy and the physician.

St. Symeon the New Theologian, speaking to monks, makes this truth clear. As we know from the Orthodox Tradition, the monasteries are properly hospitals. It would be better to claim that they are medical schools. As sick people we are cured and after that we learn how to cure. That is why the early Church took priests from the monasteries, which are medical schools, to place them at the observation post of bishop.

So in speaking to monks, St. Symeon does not hesitate to say that we are all poor and needy. He then tells how all of us who are in the cells are injured and affected by different illnesses; therefore we can do nothing but cry out day and night for the doctor of souls and bodies to heal our wounded hearts and give us spiritual health. The saint writes: "And

---

1. Ladder. Step 1. CWS p. 75

that is not all: (apart from being poor and naked) we lie pitifully wounded, affected with various illnesses, or move with difficulty in our cells or monasteries as if in so many hospitals and homes for the aged. We cry out and groan and weep and call upon Him who is the physician of souls and bodies – at least in so far as we are aware of the pain of our wounds and ailments, for there are those who do not even know that they have a disease or an ailment – that He should come and cure our wounded hearts and give health to our souls that lie in the bed of sin and death. For all of us have sinned, as the holy Apostle said, and we have need of His mercy and grace"[2].

We have quoted this whole text because the mission of monasticism and the Church, as well as the work of the pastors, is shown clearly. It is chiefly a therapeutic task. We are sick in the bed of sin and death. Any who do not sense this truth are 'mad'. So the Christians who do not remain in the Church in order to be healed or who feel that they are well, are mad.

According to St. Symeon the New Theologian, the priest is a physician: a person comes to the "spiritual doctor ravaged with passion, his mind all distraught..."[3]. The "expert doctor", "who is human and compassionate, understands his brother's weakness, the inflammation caused by the ailment, the tumour; he sees the sick person wholly in the power of death". Then the saint describes the way in which the spiritual and expert physician approaches the sickness, and how it is to be cured[4].

We have previously mentioned two basic images which characterise the pastor's work: that he is a Moses who leads his spiritual children, and he is at the same time both a scientist and a sympathetic physician. Both these qualities

---

2. SC 129, 174
3. SC 129, 140
4. SC 129, 140-142

are contained in one of St. Symeon's poems describing his own healing by his spiritual father, his "personal" Moses. He applies to his life the journey of the Israelite people and the guidance by Moses. He writes:

"He came down and found me to be a slave and a
                                                    stranger
and he said: Come, my child, I will take you towards
                                                    God!".

He asked his Moses for "assurances" that he could do such a thing.

"He brought me close, he clasped me tight
and again he kissed me with a holy kiss
and there was a scent of immortality all about him.
I believed, I loved to go with him
and I longed to serve him alone...
He took me by the hand and walked before me
and in this way we began to travel the road".

And after a long journey in which, through the interventions of his spiritual father, he has succeeded in confronting the passions and being freed from slavery to them, St. Symeon begs his spiritual father:

"Come, I said, my lord, I will not part from you,
I will not disobey your commands but will keep them
                                                    all"[5].

However, in order for a person to be an Orthodox therapist and cure the spiritual ills of his spiritual children, he himself must previously have been healed as far as possible, he must stand "in the middle between praxis and theoria". How can one heal without having previously been healed or without having tasted the beginning of healing? Therefore St. Symeon accuses those who regard themselves as spiritual directors before being imbued with the Holy Spirit, rashly receiving

---

5. SC 174, 86-92. Hymn 18. pp. 82 and 84

others' confessions and daring to rule monasteries or occupy other positions of authority, "pushing themselves forward shamelessly by a thousand intrigues to be made metropolitans or bishops to guide the Lord's people..." before they have seen the bridegroom "in the bridal chamber" and become "sons of light and sons of the day"[6].

All this has been put matchlessly by St. Gregory the Theologian who writes: "It is necessary first to be purified, then to purify; to be made wise, then to make wise; to become light, then to enlighten; to approach God, then to bring others to him; to be sanctified, then to sanctify..."[7].

St. John Chrysostom, who has been hailed as an expert on the priesthood, writes in a famous passage in which he seeks to justify his refusal to be made a bishop, that he is aware of the weakness and smallness of his soul as well as the importance and difficulty of guiding the people: "I know how weak and puny my own soul is. I know the importance of that ministry and the great difficulty of it"[8].

In his discussion with St. Basil he asks him to have no doubt about what he has said, that while he loves Christ, he is afraid of provoking scandal by taking up the spiritual ministry "since the infirmity of my spirit makes me unfit for this ministry"[9]. The great purity of his thoughts and feelings caused him to feel that the weakness of his soul made him unfit for this great ministry. For indeed, as will be observed later, unhealed passions prevent a priest from helping to heal his spiritual children.

If the therapist has not previously been cured, he is "commonplace". "They simply take commonplace men and put them in charge of those things..."[10].

6. SC 129, 116-118
7. Or. 2, 71. NPNFns, vol. 7, p. 219
8. On the Priesthood III, 7, p. 77
9. Ibid. II, 4, p. 60
10. Ibid. III, 15, p. 91

All these things to which we have already referred point to the great truth that the priests who wish to cure the illnesses of the people must themselves have previously been cured of these illnesses, or at least have begun to be cured, and must feel the value and possibility of healing.

What is to follow will also be placed in this context. We should make it quite clear that we are not planning to look at the whole spectrum of the priesthood or the role of priests. It is not our purpose to explain the value and importance of the priesthood, but to look at this great and responsible office from the point of view that it is a therapeutic science whose main work is to cure men. If at some points we seem to be trying to underline the value of the priesthood, we do it solely in order to look at this side which we wish to emphasise here.

1. Prerequisites for the role of priest-therapist

It is the Holy Spirit and, in more general terms, the grace of the Holy Trinity which accomplishes the cure of sick Christians. The priest is a servant of this cure. The whole organisation of the Church is divine-human. Moreover the grace of God works secretly in the priest and he knows from experience this hidden action of the grace of God.

The value of the priesthood

The value of the priesthood is great. St. John Chrysostom writes: "The work of the priesthood is done on earth, but it is ranked among heavenly ordinances" since it was not ordained by man, angel, archangel or other created power, but by "the Paraclete himself"[11].

"As the sun excels the stars" so does the celebration by the

---

11. Ibid. III, 4, p. 70

priest "excel all psalmody and prayer" and differ from all the other services. This is because through the sacrament of the Eucharist we sacrifice the Only-begotten Himself who was slain for our sins[12]. If one celebrates properly "the divine, revered and awesome mysteries, the benefit derived from this will be greater than that which one derives from any work or from theoria"[13].

The value of the priesthood, which can sacrifice the fatted calf, is due to the fact that it helps man to go from the image of God to the likeness of God. It can guide him towards deification, which is in fact the healing of man, or rather manifests this healing.

The Fathers, comparing the priesthood with many other kinds of work, consider it greater, because other offices help man to solve worldly problems, while the priesthood leads him to deification. Therefore "the priesthood is higher even than a kingdom", since the one "governs divine things and the other governs earthly things"[14].

Indeed, as we have emphasised, in pastoral work the priesthood is the priesthood of Christ himself. The priests minister this grace upon the people and therefore are able to forgive and heal the sins of men.

We have said only these few things about the value of the priesthood, for it was not our purpose in this chapter to emphasise the great value of that work.

The calling and ordaining of the Apostles

The Lord calls those suitable for this work and grants them His priesthood. Thus the first bishops were the Apostles. The Lord called them to the apostolic rank, had them with Him

---

12. St. Theognostos. Philok. 2, p. 376, 72
13. Ibid. 71
14. Isidor of Pelusium, in Nikodemos, Commentary on the Epistles. vol. 1, p. 227, note 2. In Gk

for three whole years, then gave them the Holy Spirit to forgive sins, and sent them to preach to "all nations" and to guide people. He made them fishers of men and preachers of the Gospel. This choosing and sending them out is what made them Apostles. We have no evidence in Holy Scripture that the Lord used a special ceremony to confer the priestly service on the Apostles. We can say, however, that "the Lord, being Himself the one who instituted the sacraments, was not bound by them, but was able to make them effective through a simple expression of his will"[15]. At all events, the fact is that the calling of the twelve Apostles by Christ, his appearing to them after the Resurrection, the gift of grace to forgive sins and the coming of the Paraclete on the day of Pentecost established them as shepherds for the people of God.

We also have the case of the Apostle Paul, who was not a disciple of Christ in Christ's life-time, but he too was called to the apostolic rank. He himself considered himself to be Jesus Christ's apostle: "Paul, an apostle of Jesus Christ, by the commandment of God our Saviour and the Lord Jesus Christ..." (1 Tim. 1, 1). Indeed he writes elsewhere: "For I claim to have done no less than the very greatest of the apostles" (2 Cor. 11, 5). In another place the same apostle writes: "I thank Christ Jesus our Lord, who has given me strength. By calling me into his service he has judged me trustworthy" (1 Tim. 1, 12). He has the certainty that he was a genuine witness of the Resurrection, because while on the road to Damascus he saw the risen Christ. Therefore in recording the appearances of the risen Christ, he makes bold to claim: "Last of all, I too saw him, like the last child that comes to birth unexpectedly" (1 Cor. 15, 8). He counts himself among the witnesses of the Resurrection.

The appearance of Christ to Paul not only conferred on him the rank of apostle but represented his ordination into the priesthood of Christ.

---

15. Trempelas, Dogmatics vol. 3, p. 293. In Gk.

Prof. Romanides writes: "According to the Apostle Paul, the prophets in a parish (1 Cor. 14, 29) are those who, like the apostles (1 Cor. 15, 5-8), have attained deification, the vision of Christ in the glory of the Holy Trinity. Paul clearly emphasises this when he writes about the mystery of Christ 'which in other ages was not made known to the sons of men, as it has now been revealed by the Spirit to his holy apostles and prophets...' Eph. 3, 5). It is within this context that the saying introductory to the listing of the members of the body of Christ is to be understood: 'If one member is honoured, all the members rejoice with him' (1 Cor. 12, 26). That is to say, the honoured member is deified and made a prophet by God. This is why the Apostle, in enumerating the various members of Christ's body, begins with the apostles and prophets and ends with those speaking in tongues and interpreting them (1 Cor. 12, 28), which are the forms of noetic worship (Eph, 5, 19f). One who prophesies in Paul's terms is one who interprets the Old Testament - the New Testament did not yet exist - on the basis of the experience of the noetic prayer which is called 'different kinds of tongues'. By contrast, the Prophet is one who has attained deification. This is precisely the later patristic distinction between theologising and theology. All those from the Apostle down to the person prophesying and interpreting had 'varieties of tongues', that is to say, different kinds of worship of the Holy Spirit within their heart. They were therefore called by God to be members of the body of Christ and temples of the Holy Spirit. In being called by God they differed from the 'uninformed' (1 Cor. 14, 16) who had not yet received the anointing of the visitation of the Holy Spirit praying unceasingly in their hearts, and so had not yet become temples of the Holy Spirit. They had apparently been baptised with water for the remission of sins but not baptised by the Spirit, that is, chrismated. Probably the sacrament of anointing with chrism was done to confirm that the Holy Spirit had come to pray within them and therefore it came to be called 'confirmatio' in Latin.

"The deified apostles and prophets and illuminated teachers, together with those possessing gifts of miracles, healing, helps, administration, or varieties of tongues (1 Cor. 12, 28) apparently all constituted the anointed clergy and the royal priesthood, as the service of Holy Chrism indicates. The rest, as the Fathers testify, were the lay people. 'Those whom God has appointed in the Church' (1 Cor. 12, 28) clearly refers to those who have received the visitation of the Holy Spirit, with deification of the apostles and prophets and illumination of the rest, and not only through a liturgical act"[16].

Basic prerequisites for ordination

It is certain that the apostles transmitted this priesthood of Christ through a definite sacrament called the Sacrament of Holy Orders. The Church also fixed the canonical prerequisites for anyone to receive this great grace and to exercise this highest function.

One such ordination is that of the deacons in the first Church of Jerusalem. After they chose the seven deacons, writes the Book of Acts, "they set them before the apostles, and when they had prayed they laid hands on them" (Acts 6, 6). Here we have the laying on of hands and prayer. St. John Chrysostom, analysing this passage, writes: "He does not tell in what way it was done, but that they were ordained with prayer: for this is the meaning of the laying on of hands: the hand is laid upon the man, but the whole work is of God..."[17].

What must be noted in this case is that they were chosen by the whole body of Christians of the first Church. Several qualifications were set up. The basic qualification was that they had received the Holy Spirit. Concerning the choice of Stephen we read in the Acts of the Apostles: "They chose Stephen, a man full of faith and the Holy Spirit" (Acts 6, 5).

---

16. Romanides: RR, p. 27f. In Gk
17. Hom. 14 on Acts. LF vol. 33, p. 198

Thus they not only received the Holy Spirit at the time of ordination but they had the grace of the Holy Spirit.

Interpreting this, St. John Chrysostom says that he had the grace of the Holy Spirit "from the laver" of baptism. This grace alone was not enough, but ordination by the laying on of hands was also needed: "so that there was a further access of the Spirit"[18]. He also says that Stephen received more grace than the other deacons: "For though the ordination was common to him and them, yet he drew upon himself greater grace"[19]. This was due to his greater purity and the presence in him of the Holy Spirit.

This shows beyond doubt that the candidates for this great office of the priesthood do not simply wait for the day of their ordination in order to receive the Holy Spirit, but they must previously have opened themselves to the Holy Spirit.

The Church makes a great point of this. We also see this in the pastoral letters of the Apostle Paul. He writes to Timothy: "when I call to remembrance the genuine faith that is in you, which dwelt first in your grandmother Lois and your mother Eunice, and I am persuaded is in you also" (2 Tim. 1, 5). We know very well that the faith is not an abstract teaching, but it is an "understanding and vision of the heart", it is the life of the Holy Spirit in our soul.

The Apostle also writes to his disciple Timothy, whom he himself had ordained bishop: "Do not neglect the gift that is in you, which was given to you by prophecy with the laying on of the hands of the presbytery" (1 Tim. 4, 14). Elsewhere he writes: "This charge I commit to you, son Timothy, according to the prophecies previously made concerning you..." (1 Tim. 1, 18). St. Theophylactos offers this interpretation: "The rank of the priesthood, which concerns the instruction and protection of the people, being great and high, requires that the candidate be given approval from above by God. For this

---

18. Hom. 15 on Acts. Ibid. p. 207
19. Ibid.

reason also in olden times those who became priests and
bishops did so by divine prophecies, that is to say, by the Holy
Spirit"[20].

Much preparation and many prerequisites are involved in
the selection of priests and bishops for that great office. The
Apostle exhorts: "If a man is blameless" (Tit. 1, 6), let him be
appointed priest or bishop. He also recommends that such a
person should not be "a novice" (1 Tim. 3, 6), not a novice
because he must have previous spiritual experience and thus
have been baptised to that great office, he must have purified
himself, as we shall see later, and only then may he proceed
to ordination.

Indeed St. John Chrysostom writes that a priest has to
have more attentiveness and spiritual strength even than the
hermits themselves. For if the hermits, who are freed from
"the city, the market place and its people", are not secure in
the spirit, how much more strength and vigour needs to be
exercised by the priest in order to be able to "snatch his soul
away from all infection and keep its spiritual beauty inviolate". That is why he affirms that the clergy who live in the
world need even more purity than the monks[21].

This theme of safeguarding the purity of the priesthood
will engage us later. Here we wish rather to emphasise the
qualities which the Christian should have if he is to be ordained a priest. For if he himself has not been healed, how
will he be able to heal the spiritually weak and sick?

Preparation for the priesthood is one of the dominant themes in the works of St. Symeon the New Theologian. Anyone
who has not abandoned the world and been counted worthy to
receive the Holy Spirit as were the holy Apostles, who has not
undergone purification and illumination and been found worthy to "contemplate the unapproachable light", – "such a man

---

20. St. Nikodemos of the Holy Mountain. Commentary on the Epistles,
    vol. 3, p. 95. In Gk
21. Ibid. p. 118 note 1

would not dare to accept the priesthood and the authority over souls, or to push himself to accept such!"[22].

We find the same teaching in St. Theognostos. If the priest, he says, has "not been assured by the Holy Spirit" that he is an acceptable intermediary between God and man, he should not "presumptuously dare to celebrate the awesome and most holy mysteries"[23].

When ordination was imminent, the Fathers fled to the mountains, as we see in the life and teaching of St. Gregory the Theologian. In his "Defence of the Flight to Pontos" he seeks to defend this action, and says that no one can undertake to shepherd the spiritual flock unless he has previously become a temple of the living God, "a habitation of Christ in the Spirit", or unless he has traversed "by experience and contemplation" all the titles and powers of Christ, and learned the "hidden wisdom of God in a mystery", – that is to say if he is still a babe "fed with milk"[24].

Certainly the holy Fathers were not unaware of the fact that many were ordained without fulfilling these ideals and were neither purified nor healed. Therefore many of the ordinations originated "not from divine grace, but from human ambition"[25]. And indeed it is a well known saying of St. John Chrysostom that "God does not ordain all, but He works through all"[26].

The three degrees of priesthood

From a study of the sources, chiefly patristic literature, it seems clear that the degrees of priesthood (deacon, priest, bishop) are closely connected with the three basic degrees of

22. SC 196, 294-296
23. Philok. 2, p. 257, 14
24. Or. 2, 97-99. NPNFns, vol. 7, p. 224
25. Chrysostom, On the Priesthood ch. 4, 1, p. 108
26. Homily 2 on 2Tim. NPNF vol. 13, p. 481, 3

the spiritual life. This means that as a man progressed in healing he ascended the spiritual ladder of priestly grace and blessing. At least this is the teaching of the Fathers. We must develop further this fundamental point of patristic teaching by speaking about the healing grace of the priesthood.

In the preceding chapter we emphasised that the spiritual life is divided into three stages, purification, illumination and deification. We find this division in many of the Fathers, even though they give it different names. For example, St. Nicetas Stethatos writes that there are three stages of advancement towards perfection: the initial purifying stage, the interme- diate illuminating stage, and finally the mystical perfecting stage. As the Christian advances through these stages, he grows in Christ. The purifying work is to subdue the flesh and avoid any sin that excites passion; it gives rise to repentance, tears, and so on. The illuminating stage sees the beginning of dispassion, which is characterised by insight, "contemplation of the inner principles of creation" and "communion of the Holy Spirit". Its task is "purification of the intellect...uncover- ing the eyes of the heart...and revelation of the mysteries of the Kingdom of Heaven". And "the mystical and perfecting stage" enables the person to "search the hidden mysteries of God", fills him with "the fellowship of the Spirit", and shows him to be a "wise theologian in the midst of the great Church", and so on[27].

Thus a person living in the Church and aided by divine grace purifies the passible part of his soul, then his nous is illuminated and he ascends to mystical theology, blessed dei- fication.

In the theology of St. Maximus the Confessor these three stages are expressed as practical philosophy (negative and positive purification), natural theoria (illumination of the nous) and mystical theology (deification). The Fathers of the

---

27. Gnostic chapters, ch. 41-44. Gk. Philok. 3, p. 335-337

Church, having withdrawn from all creatures, ascend to the vision of God, and this vision reaches its highest degree in "theological science" or "theological mystagogy" or "mystical theology", which is also called "unforgettable spiritual knowledge"[28].

So the Fathers living in theoria (vision of God) are the real theologians or even the real theology, since theology fills their whole existence.

Moses, according to St. Maximus, was a theologian, because he pitched his tent outside the camp, "that is, when he established his will and mind outside the world of visible things he began to worship God". The three chosen disciples were also proven to be theologians on Mount Tabor when they were granted to see the light of the trisolar divinity. St. Paul too, who was caught up to the third heaven, was a theologian. St. Maximus explains that the three heavens correspond to the three degrees of man's mystical ascent, namely, practical philosophy, natural theoria and mystical theology[29].

We have presented this patristic teaching in order to go on to correlate it with the subject which concerns us in this chapter. St. Maximus links the three stages of the spiritual life with the three degrees of the priesthood. He writes: "He who anoints his nous for spiritual contest and drives all impassioned thoughts out of it has the quality of a deacon. He who illuminates his nous with the knowledge of created beings and utterly destroys false knowledge has the quality of a priest. And he who perfects his nous with the holy myrrh of the knowledge and worship of the Holy Trinity has the quality of a bishop"[30].

I would now like to compare with what we have just read another interpretation, namely that of St. Nicodemus of the

---

28. Rantosavlievits: The mystery of salvation according to Maximus the Confessor, p. 165. In Gk
29. Ibid. p. 171-172. cf. Philok. 2, p. 133, 84
30. Philok. 2, p. 68, 21

Holy Mountain, since it is basic to the practice of the Church that one saint interprets another saint, and thus through its saints the Church finds expression for its common experience. St. Nicodemus writes: "The god-inspired Maximus sees it as the deacon's task to cleanse others of their passions and evil thoughts through moral effort, that of the priest to illuminate others through natural theoria of the inner principles of things, and finally that of the bishop to perfect others in the light of the inner principles of theology... thus the chief priest does not have to be only a moral and natural or contemplative philosopher, but also a theologian, as those roles belong to the deacon and the priest"[31].

It should be noted that the connection of the three degrees of the priesthood with the three stages of the spiritual life is mentioned in the writings of St. Dionysios the Areopagite, which contain the tradition of the Church. And if these writings are taken to represent the norm of the Church in the first centuries, it seems clear that the three stages of the spiritual life must correspond to the three degrees of the priesthood. I should like to take this up in order to show this connection.

It is well known that in his work "The Ecclesiastical Hierarchy" St. Dionysios the Areopagite describes the three stages of the spiritual life - purification, illumination and perfection. Perfection is equivalent to deification. "The order of bishops is that which fully possesses the power of consecration... Its task is not only to consecrate but to perfect. The priestly order is illuminative, bringing light, while the task of the deacons is to purify and to discern the imperfect"[32]. The work of the clergy is liturgical, and sanctifying and perfecting, since it is through the sacraments that the spiritual life of man develops. In other words, the sacred rites of the Church are not forms, but they purify, illuminate and raise man to a state of perfection.

---

31. Handbook of Council (in Greek) p. 154, note 1
32. Ecclesiastical Hierarchy, ch. 5, parts 6-7. CWS p. 237f

Thus the work of the deacons, priests and bishops is connected with the spiritual growth of the Christians. According to the baptismal service as presented by St. Dionysios – and we believe that he is reflecting the usage in the first centuries of the Church – when a person is brought for baptism, the deacons divest him of his garments; this shows their role in the Church as purifying. The priests anoint the candidate's whole body; this shows their role in the Church as illuminators. The bishops bring the candidate to perfection by baptising him; this shows their perfecting role[33]. The order of bishops "performs every hierarchic consecration. It clearly teaches others to understand, explaining the sacred things, proportionate characteristics, and their holy powers". The priestly order "guides the initiates to the divine visions of the sacraments" but sends to the bishop "those longing for a full understanding of the divine rites which are being contemplated". Thus the priest illuminates Christians, under the authority of the bishop, but sends on to him those who desire perfection, since the divine order of bishops is the first to behold God. The order of deacons, before leading the candidates to the priest, "purifies all who approach by drawing them away from any dalliance with what is evil. It makes them receptive to the ritual vision and communion"[34].

It is very significant that, according to St. Dionysios, bishops are not solely occupied with perfection, but they illumine and purify as well. Similarly the priests have the understanding both to illuminate and to purify, while the deacons only know how to purify. "Inferiors may not trespass on the functions of their superiors"[35]. So the duties of each degree of the Church's ministry is strictly regulated in that each order possesses its own science and knowledge of the spiritual life. I think we must place here a characteristic

---

33. Ibid. ch. 2. CWS p. 202-203
34. Ibid. ch. 5. CWS p. 236-237
35. Ibid. p. 238

passage in which Dionysios sums up this whole teaching about
the work of the three orders: "The rank of the sacred ministers is divided in the following manner. Their first power
consists in purifying the uninitiated by way of the sacraments. Their middle power is to bring illumination to those
whom they have purified. Finally, they have the most mar-
vellous power of all, one which embraces all who commune in
God's light, the power to perfect these by way of the perfected
understanding they have of that to which they have been
initiated"[36].

As we study the teachings of St. Dionysios we come to see
that each of the three degrees of the priesthood corresponds
to a stage of the spiritual life. Since the task of the deacon is
to purify others of passions, he should himself, prior to ordination, have reached a stage of purification so that he is himself
a living exponent of the practical philosophy. Since according
to the patristic teachings it is the priest's task to illuminate
others, his ordination presupposes that he has an illuminated
nous, which, as we have seen, is a degree of theoria. Thus the
priest must remember God unceasingly in prayer, must know
spiritual work, be fluent in Holy Scripture and be able to
contemplate the inner principles of all created things. As for the
bishop, since his primary task is to perfect the people by the
inner principles of theology, he must experience the mystical
theology, live in communion with God. This close relationship
with God makes him a prophet, a divine initiate capable of
mystically imparting the word of truth to the people of God.

The form which the ordination of deacons, priests and
bishops takes is equally indicative of the spiritual condition
which they are assumed to have reached in order to fulfil
these essential tasks. For how can people be helped if the
helpers have no personal experience of the task which they
are to carry out?[37]

---

36. Ibid. p. 235
37. Ibid. p. 239-243

This applies more especially to the bishop, who is an instrument of grace par excellence and "in every act of episcopal consecration should be directly inspired by God Himself"[38]. Moses did not "confer a clerical consecration" on his brother Aaron until God commanded him to do so. He was submissive to God as chief consecrator, merely completing the divine consecration by a hieratic rite[39].

Therefore according to St. Dionysios, who expresses the tradition of the Church, the bishop is the supreme scientist of the spiritual life. He is the one who sees God and has personal experience of deification. "Therefore the divine order of the bishops is the first of those who behold God, yet it is the first and also the last"[40]. The bishop is a fruit of deification, and, having himself been deified, by grace he helps his fellow Christian along his own journey towards deification. "The being and proportion and order of the Church's hierarchy are in him (the bishop) divinely perfected and deified, and are then imparted to those below him according to their merit, whereas the sacred deification occurs in him directly from God"[41]. "Talk of 'bishop' and one is referring to a holy and inspired man, someone who understands all sacred knowledge, someone in whom an entire hierarchy is completely perfected and known"[42]. In all sustained effort to reach the One, by the complete death and dissolution of what is opposite to divine union the bishop is granted the immutable capacity to mould himself completely on the form of the divine"[43]. Thus the bishop, as the fruit of purification and illumination, is the God-inspired man who has reached perfection and so is directed by God personally. He is the

---

38. Ibid. p. 241
39. Ibid.
40. Ibid. p. 236
41. Ibid. ch. 1. CWS p. 196
42. Ibid. p. 197-198
43. Ibid. ch. 2. CWS p. 207

"mouthpiece of truth" and the one who sits "in the form and place" of Christ.

We cannot resist referring to a characteristic passage in St. Dionysios which says that divine rays are granted to those who are most godlike, most suitable for spreading and sharing the Light. It is the task of those who see God to reveal to the priests "in proportion to their capacity" the divine visions which they have beheld. Likewise it is their task "to reveal all that has to do with their hierarchy, since they have received power to give this instruction"[44]. This means that it is only after personal perfecting that one can rise to a higher position; and the higher position is occupied by a God-inspired person, one who knows God through experience.

These were the actual qualifications for Christians to enter the priesthood. They had to go through these three stages for it to be confirmed and certified that they had been cured and were able to cure the Lord's people. These things show precisely that the bishop, priest and deacon are not only liturgical persons ordained to perform the sacraments, but they are spiritual physicians who help the people to be purified, to be sanctified and to advance to communion with God. St. Symeon the New Theologian wrote that a man can proceed to celebrate the Liturgy when he celebrates "with the conscience of a pure heart, in honour of the pure, holy and immaculate Trinity", if he has seen Christ, if he has received the Spirit and has "been brought to the Father through these two"[45].

Entry into the priesthood is thus a pure calling of God. And this calling is not simply an abstract feeling of being called by God to serve the Lord's people but is the certitude through one's own transformation that one is able to shepherd the people. And shepherding the people is primarily healing the people. Therefore without healing, a man cannot reach God, cannot see God, and this vision cannot become a light which

---

44. Ibid. ch. 5. CWS p. 236
45. Hymn 19. SC 174, 98-100

will illuminate him, rather than a fire that will consume him. St. Theognostos refers to the "supramundane grace of the priesthood"[46]. If one does not sense this calling from above, that is if one has not been healed, then "the burden is heavy indeed; for it is borne by someone unworthy, whose power it exceeds"[47].

People often speak of the apostolic tradition and the apostolic succession, implying that this was a succession of laying on of hands. Indeed no one can deny this reality, but at the same time it is an incontestable fact that the apostolic succession was not simply a series of layings on of hands but a tradition of the entire life of the Church. The Apostles and then the Fathers did not simply transmit the grace of the priesthood, but they transmitted Christ and the whole life of Christ. They engendered. For this reason the bishop bore and bears the grace of truth. Prof. John Romanides observes: "The basis of the apostolic tradition and succession was not this laying on of hands, but what accompanied it from generation to generation, the transmission of the tradition of healing, illumination and deification. The parish Council and the provincial Council were organised to unite the true therapists, to exclude from the clergy the false prophets who pretended to have charismatic gifts, and to protect the flock from the heretics. The most important part of ordination was the selection and examination of the candidate"[48].

This was the basis of the Church. Especially for selecting a bishop it was a fundamental principle that he should be chosen from the monks, because monasticism is the medical school from which the skilful physicians capable of healing men's sicknesses could come.

Kallistos Ware, Bishop of Diocleia, writes: "One of the twenty 'principle' monasteries (probably referring to the Great Lavra

---

46. St. Theognostos. Philok. 2, p. 370, 51
47. Ibid. p. 371 52
48. Romanides: RR vol. 1, p. 28-29. In Gk

of the Holy Mountain) alone has nurtured twenty-six patri-
archs and 144 bishops. This gives some idea of the importance of Athos to the Orthodox Church"[49].

St. Nicodemus of the Holy Mountain, explaining this holy
custom of the Church, writes in the introduction to his
"Handbook of Council": "Oh what happy and golden times
were those when the excellent custom prevailed of selecting
from the modest order of monks all (excepting a few laymen
chosen because of their surpassing virtue) who were to ascend to an episcopal throne, and entrusting the guardianship
of souls to them". The minutes of a council in St. Sophia
reflect just such a custom: representatives of the Church in
Caesarea and Chalcedonia told Pope John's deputy: "In the
East if no monk has been produced, there is no bishop, nor
patriarch"[50].

To be sure, in all the history of the Church things have not
been so "rosy". There have been situations when this truth
was lost, and then the people were in the darkness of ignorance. They did not know that there was such a thing as
spiritual healing or how healing took place, because there
were not men to teach the way of healing. As early as the
fourth century Isidor of Pelusium was showing how the early
pastors differed from those of his time. At that time, he said,
pastors died for their sheep, while today they themselves slay
the sheep. He goes on to write characteristically: "In the old
days lovers of virtue entered the priesthood; now it is lovers
of money. Once they fled from the office because of its magni-
tude; now they run after it with pleasure. Then they were
willing to take pride in their poverty; now they gladly and
greedily hoard up money. Once the divine court of justice was
before their eyes, but now it is a thing of indifference. Once
men were subject to blows; now they inflict them. Need I
continue? The priestly office seems to have changed into a

---

49. "Orthodox Witness" Sept. -Dec. l985. p. 12. In Gk
50. Handbook of Council (in Gk.) p. 15

mode of tyranny: humility has been transformed into arrogance, fasting into luxury, economy into despotism; for as economists they are not fit to administrate, but as despots they embezzle..."[51].

Prof. John Romanides, who has dwelt particularly on this subject, writes about the loss of this Orthodox tradition: "With the passage of time, however, there could not always and everywhere be found deified or even illuminated men for selection and ordination as bishops and priests. And even if there were such men, the electors would not want them. Many times men who were simply moral and good but without having the traditional therapeutic education of illumination and deification have been preferred. Bishops are emerging who in a former period would have been simply laymen, since they do not have the Holy Spirit praying unceasingly in their hearts. This is the way St. Symeon the New Theologian explains matters.

"St. Symeon instigated a rebellion against the situation which he described, with the result that the healing mission of the Church was restored to a central position in Orthodoxy and the hesychasm of the Fathers took hold of the hierarchy once more, as St. Dionysios the Areopagite anticipated. Under the leadership of the hesychasm of the Fathers, the Church and the nation survived after the dissolution of the empire, because the patristic therapeutic training which we have described gave the Church the power to blossom in the hard times of Arab, Frankish and Turkish rule...

"That is to say, the prophets as deified persons and therapists, were like a team of hospital doctors, one of whom, without implying any inequality, was chosen as chairman. The same thing happened among the apostles: Peter had first place, although it was James, as Bishop of the local Church, who presided at the gathering of apostles in Jerusalem.

"When parishes began to multiply and no prophet or proph-

---

51. Ibid. p. 112-113 note 1

ets in the apostle Paul's sense were to be found, the Church had to resolve the problem of whether it was right to ordain as bishops men who were undeified but were illuminated. In the face of this dilemma the Church chose to ordain priests to preside at the parochial meetings. Thus the bishops gradually acquired supervisory responsibility over the presiding parish priests, like doctors at medical centres with attendants at the head. Because the Synod did not find enough doctors to supervise all the hospital centres, it appointed attendants as priests. To call the attendant a doctor, that is to call a person who is not deified a bishop is unrealistic and leads to the dissolution of the therapeutic work of the Church.

"With the passage of time, however, there appeared bishops and priests neither of whom had even reached the stage of illumination. It was this state of affairs which provoked the revolution brought about by St. Symeon the New Theologian and the taking over of the hierarchy by the hesychasts, which was not fully achieved until the time of St. Gregory Palamas.

"Apostolic therapeutic treatment was preserved in the post-apostolic period up to the appearance of Frankish and imperial and Neo-Hellenic Orthodoxy, by the concentration of this apostolic tradition in monasticism. That is, therapeutic training for illumination and deification was transferred from the secular parish, which had become weak, to the monastic parish. At the same time the metropolitan sees and the bishoprics became monasteries. That is why St. Sophia was called the Great Monastery even in the lay tradition. Monasticism became a kind of medical school where the candidates for bishop studied apostolic therapeutics. Parallel with this it was the task of every secular parish to imitate the monastic parish as best it could - because illumination and deification are indispensable for the healing of all people, since all have a darkened nous. From the doctrinal point of view there is no difference between secular and monastic parishes with regard to the sacraments offered and the need for healing. The difference lies in the quantity and quality of success in healing"[52].

2. Rekindling the Spiritual Gift

Thus far it has been shown that the priesthood is a great gift given to those who have been healed of passions and are placed in the position of physicians to cure the passions of the people.

But the physician needs continual renewal. Otherwise he cannot cure men's diseases with new methods. The same applies to some degree in the case of priests. It requires vigilant attention and a great struggle to maintain this gift of the priesthood at all times. The priest bears within him the priesthood of Christ and must keep it undefiled. This has a deep meaning.

There are priests who have not been dethroned and consequently can celebrate the Liturgy and perform the sacraments by the grace of God. Outwardly their priesthood is unhindered, because they have not been condemned by the Church. But their priesthood has no power because they defile it by their lives. They can consecrate the gifts, but they themselves cannot be sanctified by them, as Nicholas Cabasilas says.

Where does this spiritual powerlessness appear? It appears mainly in the fact that they cannot heal and do not know how to heal. To perform the sacraments is of God's grace which is given in the sacrament of the priesthood. But to cure people's sicknesses is of God's grace which is given to that person who makes productive the gift of baptism, who puts to use the kingly gift of grace. This explains why many priests do not know how to heal men's passions and are unable to do it. They do not know what method to apply. They

---

52. Romanides. RR, p. 29-31. In Gk

have no idea of what the heart and nous are, how the nous is taken captive or how the heart dies. They often regard these teachings as referring only to monks. Thus they divide the teachings of Christ and the Fathers into monastic and secular. But no such distinction exists in the teaching of our Orthodox Church.

In what follows we would like to set forth the teaching of the Church, through the Apostles and Fathers, on the necessity for the priest to nurture the gift of priesthood, to rekindle the grace received at the sacrament of ordination, for otherwise he cannot heal men's spiritual illnesses.

Basic qualities of priest therapists

The Apostle Paul advised his disciple Timothy: "Do not neglect the gift that is in you" (1 Tim. 4, 14). This exhortation is analogous to the exhortation to the Christians: "As a fellow-worker we urge you not to let the grace you received come to nothing" (2 Cor. 6, 1) and the same apostle's words: "The grace he has shown me has not been without fruit" (1 Cor. 15, 10). He also instructs the Apostle Timothy: "That is why I would remind you to fan the flame of that special grace which God kindled in you when my hands were laid upon you" (2 Tim. 1, 6).

In the pastoral epistles the Apostle Paul often refers to this subject. The bishop and the clergy in general must, through their struggle to preserve the gift of the priesthood, serve God and men in a worthy manner and guard the sacred heritage.

We would like to cite a few of the many characteristic passages: "Train yourself for godliness" (1 Tim. 4, 7). "You will be a good minister of Jesus Christ nourished in the words of the faith and of the good doctrine which you have carefully followed" (1 Tim. 4, 6). "Be an example to the believers in word, in conduct, in love, in faith, in purity" (1 Tim. 4, 12). He requests Timothy to fulfil his charge "without spot, blameless until our Lord Jesus Christ's appearing" (1 Tim. 6, 14). He exhorts him to keep the tradition: "That good thing which was committed to you, keep by the Holy Spirit who dwells in us" (2 Tim. 1, 14). This keeping of the tradition must be done through the Holy Spirit who dwells within Timothy. He exhorts him to have watchfulness, attentiveness, vigilant care to live up to the great calling of God: "Be watchful in all things, endure afflictions, do the work of an evangelist, fulfil your ministry" (2 Tim. 4:5).

The patristic teachings refer to all the essential qualities which should adorn the priest in order for him to be able to live up to his great task and high calling. In what follows we shall try to make a selection from those teachings, mainly from St. John Chrysostom and St. Theognostos. The teaching of these two Fathers expresses that of the holy Orthodox Church.

According to St. Theognostos, the priest must not only be filled with the human traditions but have the grace of God mystically hidden in him. "Make sure that you do not rely only on human traditions in celebrating the divine mysteries, but let God's grace inwardly and invisibly fill you with the knowledge of higher things"[53]. "The priestly dignity, like the priestly vestments, is full of splendour, but only so long as it is illumined from within by purity of soul"[54]. Therefore the priest must guard this divine gift "as he would the pupil of his eye" and keep its honour unsullied[55].

These things show that great watchfulness is required on the part of the priest. And this requires much suffering. The priest should celebrate the Divine Liturgy first of all on his own behalf "watchfully and sedulously"[56].

St. John Chrysostom insists on this constant attention to guarding the priestly grace. He says that a priest must be sober and clear-sighted and "possess a thousand eyes looking

---

53. Philok. 2. p. 362, 18
54. Ibid. p. 372, 56
55. Ibid. p. 370, 50
56. Ibid. p. 373, 60

in every direction"[57]. He should resemble the many-eyed
Cherubim in order to worship the Lord of hosts in purity. He
should be encircled with walls all round, and "have intense
zeal and constant sobriety of life" in order not to be harmed[58].
According to St. John Chrysostom, just as fire requires fuel,
"so grace requires our alacrity that it may be ever fervent".
This grace is in our power to quench or kindle. The grace "for
presiding over the Church" is quenched "by sloth and carelessness" but is kept alive "by watchfulness and diligence"[59].

Watchfulness is indispensable for keeping oneself pure and
thus for the priestly grace and blessing to remain. According
to St. Theognostos, the priesthood "requires of us an angelic
purification, and a degree of discretion and self-restraint
greater than in our previous life"[60]. According to St. John
Chrysostom, the priest must be as pure as if he were standing
in heaven itself, in the midst of the angelic powers[61]. The
priest's soul must be purer than the rays of the sun, "in order
that the Holy Spirit may never leave him desolate"[62].

Repentance is another spiritual quality indispensable for a
priest. "With streams of tears" let him become whiter than
snow, and then, with a clear conscience, let him "in holiness
touch holy things"[63].

The purity of a priest should shine and beam on the Christians. A priest should be pure from passions, "especially unchastity and rancour, and should keep his imagination passion-free"[64]. Many Fathers emphasise that these two passions
(unchastity and rancour) should not come near priests, because otherwise the grace of God does not work for the heal-

57. On the Priesthood. III, 12, p. 82
58. Ibid. 14, p. 86
59. Hom. 1 on 2 Tim, 1. NPNF vol. 13, p. 477, 2
60. Philok. 2, p. 370, 49
61. On the Priesthood. III, 4, p. 70
62. Ibid. VI, 1, p. 137
63. Theognostos. Philok. 2, p. 362-3, 18
64. Ibid. p. 362, 17

ing of his spiritual children. Then the priest is sick, as we have indicated. He must have committed himself "sacrificially to die to the passions and to sensual pleasure"[65]. Besides, according to Abba Dorotheos, "Everything which is offered as a sacrifice to God, whether it be a sheep or a cow or something of the sort is a 'victim'"[66]. He must be wholly consecrated to God.

The Gospel, which describes the journey of the Christian struggling to reach communion with God should be applied first of all by his servant, the priest. The ascetic life of the Church which we describe in this book should be known to the pastors of the Church. And when we say 'known', we do not mean that it should be known in the head through lectures or reading, but it should be their living experience. For what passes through the heart helps faithful Christians. One person offers his blood for another to be nourished. It is shared out and the people are filled.

However, in addition to his purification and repentance, sobriety and watchfulness, the priest must be filled with all the graces of the Spirit, all the virtues. The basic virtue is holy humility which, according to St. Isaac the Syrian, is the raiment of divinity, since Christ, in order to save man, "humbled himself", as the Apostle says. Besides, the Eucharist which the priest celebrates shows us this humility of Christ. Through the Eucharist we may enter into holy humility and acquire that sacrificial way of life. Therefore in celebrating the Divine Liturgy we are not simply looking for the bread and wine to be transformed into the Body and Blood of Christ but seeking to acquire Christ's way of life. And this is humility. We seek to clothe ourselves in the spirit of the Eucharist, which is self-emptying.

Within this perspective St. Theognostos advises: "Humble yourself like a sheep for the slaughter, truly regarding all

---

65. Ibid. p. 361, 13
66. SC 92, p. 476, 175

men as your superiors"[67]. Indeed the same Father exhorts characteristically: "Regard yourself as dust and ashes, or as refuse, or as some cur-like creature..."[68]. One should perform the priestly service "with fear and trembling", and in this way rightly divide the word of truth and work out one's salvation[69]. However, the Fathers recognise the actual reality. They are not unaware of the existence of many unworthy priests who, without having these essential qualities, dare to minister the Holy Sacrament. According to St. John Chrysostom, the priesthood, far from covering over man's passions, exposes them, makes them manifest. As fire tests metals, "so the touchstone of the ministry distinguishes men's souls. If a man is hot-tempered or conceited or boastful or anything like that, it soon uncovers all his shortcomings and lays them bare. Not only does it lay them bare, but it also makes them more tough and intractable"[70].

St. John of the Ladder says that he has seen aged priests "mocked by demons"[71].

The Fathers do not hesitate to expose the punishment of unworthy priests, those who practise this great office without the proper testing, preparation and life. This is because instead of healing the souls of the flock, they tempt them.

Isidor of Pelusium writes: "Let us not trifle with divine things"[72].

St. John Chrysostom says: "The priestly office might well accuse us of not handling it rightly"[73].

St. Theognostos addresses the incorrigible priest who does not renounce the sacred ministry: "Expect to fall into the

---

67. Philok. 2, p. 376, 70
68. Ibid. p. 362, 16
69. Ibid. p. 371, 53
70. On the Priesthood VI, 8 p. 147
71. Ladder. Step 14. CWS p. 166
72. Nicodemos of the Holy Mountain. Commentary on the Epistles. Vol. 3, p. 112, note 1. In Gk
73. On the Priesthood. III, 9 p. 78

hands of the living God and experience his wrath. God will not spare you out of compassion"[74]. He informs us that "many unworthy priests have been snatched away by sudden death and sent to the halls of judgement"[75].

He has in mind two examples of unworthy priests with different consequences. There was one who seemed outwardly honourable among men but nevertheless "within he was licentious and defiled", and so at the time of the cherubic hymn when he was reading "No one is worthy...", "he suddenly died"[76]. The other priest had fallen into the passion of unchastity. Therefore he became incurably sick and was near death. When he came to realise his unworthiness and took a vow that he would desist from celebrating the mysteries, "he recovered at once so that not even a trace of his illness remained"[77].

We have lingered on this topic though it seemed to be outside the subject of our study because we wanted particularly to emphasise that the priesthood is a pastoral service to the people. The priest and bishop have this great honour of serving the people. Serving the people is healing first and foremost. The Church does not exist simply to do social work and to serve the social needs of the people, but to guide them to salvation, that is, to the healing of their souls. This work demands many qualities. The priest must be indwelt by the uncreated grace of God. He is not there simply to perform the sacraments, but also in order to be sanctified by them so that, being sanctified, he can sanctify men by his being. This work is very high, and therefore St. John Chrysostom declares: "I do not think that there are many of the priests who are saved but many more that perish; this is because the matter requires a great soul"[78].

---

74. Philok. 2 p. 371, 54
75. Ibid. p. 363, 20
76. Ibid. p. 363, 21
77. Ibid. p. 372, 55
78. Hom. 3 on Acts. LF vol. 33 p. 48, 4

3. Spiritual Priesthood

We have already said that the priest has a double task. One is to perform the sacraments and the other is to heal people so that they can worthily approach and receive Holy Communion. We have further pointed out that there are many priests who are priests outwardly and perform their function unhindred but in essence have defiled the priesthood, and that this is apparent from the fact that they are not able to heal. They perform the sacraments, and the gifts are sanctified through them, but they cannot cure others or save their own souls.

On the other hand, there are laymen and monks who do not have the sacramental priesthood but can heal people because they have spiritual priesthood. We should like to dwell briefly on this point.

Through baptism and the effort to keep Christ's commandments all Christians have put on Christ, and in this way we share the royal, prophetic and high priestly office of Christ.

This teaching is recorded in the texts of the New Testament. In the Book of Revelation John the Evangelist writes: "To him who loved us and washed us from our sins in his own blood and has made us kings and priests to his God and Father..." (Rev. 1, 5f). The Apostle Peter says: "You are a chosen generation, a royal priesthood, a holy nation, his own special people" (1 Pet. 2, 9). And the Apostle Paul writes to the Christians of Rome: "I appeal to you therefore, brethren, by the mercies of God, to present your bodies as a living sacrifice, holy and acceptable to God, which is your spiritual worship" (Rom. 12, 1).

In many Fathers too we find this teaching that every person is a priest of Christ in the sense which we defined and will develop further later on. St. John Chrysostom presents Abraham too as a priest because "where there is fire, an altar and a knife, why do you doubt his priesthood?" Abraham's sacrifice was twofold. He offered both his only-begotten son

and the ram, "and above all, his own will". With the blood of
the ram he sanctified his right hand, with the slaying of the
child (which he had decided to do) he sanctified his soul.
"Thus he was ordained a priest, by the blood of his only-begotten, by the sacrifice of the lamb." Just after this, St. John
Chrysostom exhorts his listeners: "So you too are made king
and priest and prophet in the laver: a king, having dashed to
earth all the deeds of wickedness and slain your sins, a priest
in that you offer yourself to God and sacrifice your body, and
are yourself being slain also"[79].

All the faithful baptised in the name of the Holy Trinity
and living according to the will of the Holy Trinitarian God
are priests, they have spiritual priesthood. We prefer the
expression 'spiritual priesthood' to other terms like 'general'
or 'lay' priesthood, because clergy and lay people alike can
have this priesthood, and because not all the baptised have it,
but only those who have become the dwelling place of the
Holy Trinity. The faithful who have noetic prayer have spiritual priesthood, especially those who have reached such a
degree of grace as to pray for the whole world. This is the
spiritual service on behalf of the world. The prayers of these
people who sacrifice themselves, praying on behalf of all,
sustain the world and heal men. Therefore by prayer they
become exorcists, driving out the demons which rule in
human societies. This is the great work of those who pray
unceasingly for the whole world.

St. Gregory of Sinai wrote about this spiritual priesthood,
which is also the essential foundation of the sacramental
priesthood. For as we have said, those of the faithful who
were healed and had noetic prayer were chosen to receive the
special grace of the priesthood as well. According to St. Gregory, noetic prayer is "the mystical liturgy of the mind"[80]. A
person who possesses the gift of noetic prayer senses the

---

79. Hom. on 2Cor. LF vol 27 50-51
80. Acrostics, 111. Writings from the Philokalia. p. 61

operation of grace within him, which is purifying, illuminating and mystical.

All who reach this state are priests. "A true sanctuary is a heart that has been freed from evil thoughts and receives the operation of the Spirit, for everything in that heart is said and done spiritually"[81].

This passage from the holy Father prompts me to say that the spiritual priesthood is that which is to be consummated in another age, in the kingdom of heaven. Without wishing to dwell on the subject of the ineffaceable or non-sacramental priesthood, we stress the truth that the sacramental priesthood is for the benefit of the laity, to serve its needs, while the spiritual priesthood is that which will continue to be celebrated at the heavenly altar in the life to come. All who have spiritual priesthood are "true clergy" "now and for ever". This priesthood can include all categories of men, and naturally also of women. Therefore it is not very important that in the Orthodox tradition women cannot receive sacramental priesthood. They have the possibility of being the "true clergy".

Elsewhere St. Gregory of Sinai is explicit: "All devout kings and priests are truly anointed in baptismal renewal just as those of old were anointed symbolically." The priests of the Old Testament were "truly symbols of our truth", but "our kingdom and priesthood" are not "the same in character and form"[82].

When a man's nous has been discovered, when he has been freed from his captivity and received the Holy Spirit, it is "spiritual priesthood" and then he celebrates a mystical liturgy in the sanctuary of his soul and partakes of the lamb in betrothal with God. In this spiritual priesthood he eats the lamb of God in the spiritual altar of his soul, but at the same time he becomes like the lamb. Thus we understand well that when noetic prayer is working in us, there is an unceasing

---

81. Ibid. p. 38, 7
82. Ibid. p. 72, 133

divine liturgy which nourishes our whole existence. St. Gregory of Sinai writes: "The noetic work of the nous is a spiritual liturgy. Like a betrothal before the coming delight which surpasses all understanding, this liturgy is performed by the nous, which mystically sacrifices the Lamb of God on the altar of the soul and partakes of it. To eat the Lamb of God on the inner altar of the soul means not only to apprehend it, or partake of it, but also to become like it in the future life. Here we enjoy the words of the mysteries, but there we hope to receive their very substance"[83].

The same saint also writes that the kingdom of heaven is like the tabernacle fashioned by God for Moses, "for in the world to come it too will have two veils". And all the "priests of grace" will enter the first tabernacle, but only those will enter the second tabernacle who are henceforth to celebrate "in the darkness of theology hierarchically in perfection" having Jesus as the first celebrant and bishop before the face of the Trinity[84].

Therefore all who have acquired the gift of theology as we explained it above, that is, all who after natural theoria have entered the divine darkness, are themselves priests of God; they constitute this true and spiritual priesthood. And since they are the spiritual priesthood, they can heal the sick.

Nicetas Stethatos teaches that if any priest, deacon, or even monk participates in divine grace with all the presuppositions set down by the Fathers, "he is a true bishop" even if he has not been ordained a bishop by men. On the contrary, anyone who is unitiated in the spiritual life is "falsely named even if by ordination he is set over all the others in rank and mocks them and behaves arrogantly"[85].

Probably what we quoted earlier, that "all who constitute the spiritual priesthood can heal the sick", was not well re-

---

83. Ibid. p. 60-61, 112
84. Acrostics, 43
85. Mantzarides. Palamika. p. 279-280. In Gk

ceived. However, the teaching of St. Symeon the New Theologian on this point is very revealing.

The saint writes that the power of binding and loosing sins belonged only to the bishops, who had received it by succession from the Apostles. But when "the bishops became good for nothing, this awesome function passed to priests who led a blameless life worthy of the grace of God". When the priests too, along with the bishops, fell into spiritual error, "this function was transmitted to the chosen people of God, namely the monks, not that it was taken away from the priests and bishops, but they estranged themselves from it"[86].

According to St. Symeon, the power of binding and loosing sins was not given "simply because of their ordination". The laying on of hands only gave the metropolitans and bishops permission to celebrate the Eucharist. The power to remit sins was given "only to those of the priests and bishops and monks who could be numbered among the disciples of Christ on account of their purity"[87].

We believe that St. Symeon developed this teaching in the first place in order to emphasise that the sacrament of priesthood did not magically transmit the authority to forgive men their sins if one did not have inner spiritual priesthood, secondly, to show the wretched state of the clergy of that time, thirdly to underline the value of the spiritual priesthood, which lies in noetic prayer and vision of God – and these unfortunately, then as now, were neglected – and fourthly because he himself had personal experience of this: his spiritual father, who had not been ordained by a bishop, had the grace of the Holy Spirit and was able to forgive sins.

Nevertheless his spiritual father, Symeon the Pious, did not overlook the sacrament of ordination. St. Symeon the New Theologian writes: "I know that the grace of binding and loosing sins is given by God to those who are sons by adoption

---

86. Krivocheine: In the Light of Christ. p. 134f
87. Ibid. p. 136

and his holy servants. I too was a disciple of such a father who had not received the laying on of hands on the part of men but who through the hand of God, that is, the Spirit, enrolled me among the disciples and ordered me to receive the laying on of hands by men according to the prescribed form – I who for a long time had been impelled by the Spirit toward such a reality". "Having heard the commandments of Christ, he became a partaker of His grace and of His gifts and received from Him the power to bind and loose, kindled by the Holy Spirit"[88].

When we speak of remission of sins we should understand it mainly as the curing of passions. Thus we see clearly today that "gifted" monks heal us without having sacramental priesthood. Being clear-sighted, they perceive the problem which is troubling us, they give us a remedy and a method of healing, and so we are cured of what was inwardly disturbing us. The existence of such holy men is a comfort for the people.

4. The Search for Therapists

We come now to the fourth section of this chapter, which is the search for therapists. Since we have been made aware of spiritual illness and of the great value of priest-therapists, we must search for them in order to be freed from the ulcers in our souls. A really great effort is needed in order to find these true leaders of the people, the doctors of our souls and bodies, since certainly many bodily illnesses are of spiritual origin.

In his homily on the New Sunday Gospel, St. Gregory Palamas advises: let every Christian after attending church on Sunday "diligently seek" someone who, imitating the Apostles who were in the upper room after the Crucifixion, remains "completely enclosed most of the time, desiring to be with the Lord in silent prayer and psalmody as well as in other ways". Let him approach him then, let him enter his house with faith

---

88. Ibid. p. 137

"as a heavenly place having within it the sanctifying power of the Holy Spirit". Let him sit with the man who lives there, let him remain with him as long as he can, asking "about God and the things of God", learning with humility and appealing for his prayer. Then, says the saint, "I know that Christ will come to him invisibly and grant inner peace to the pondering of his soul and increase his faith and give him support, and in time to come will enrol him in the kingdom of heaven"[89].

It is necessary to seek out such a spiritual father. On this point it is worth while to listen to what St. Symeon the New Theologian has to say. Ask God, he says, to show you a man "who is able to direct you well, one whom you ought to obey". We should show obedience to the man whom God shows us "mystically in person or outwardly through His servant", and revere him "as if he were Christ himself"[90].

We should show our dispassionate spiritual father the kind of confidence and love that a sick person shows to his doctor, expecting treatment and healing from him. Rather we should have even more confidence and love, in view of the difference between the soul and the body. Christ himself is present in the spiritual father. He is "the mouth of God".

Further on, St. Symeon matches the Apostles' attitude towards Christ to the attitude which we should have towards our spiritual father, because it is in that way that our soul can be healed. As the Apostles followed Christ, let us do so also. When people dishonour and pour scorn on our spiritual father, we must not abandon him. And as Peter took his sword and cut off the ear, "take the sword and stretch forth your hand and cut off not only the ear but the hand and the tongue of him who attempts to speak against your father or to touch him". If you deny him, weep like Peter. If you see him crucified, die with him if you can. If that is not possible, do not join with the traitors and evil men. "If he is released from

---

89. Palamas. Hom. 17, 22. EPE vol. 9, p. 512-514. In Gk
90. SC 104, p. 334. CWS p. 232

imprisonment, return to him again and venerate him the more, like a martyr. If he dies from ill treatment, then boldly seek his body and pay him more honour than when you attended on him while he was alive, and so anoint it with perfumes and give it a costly burial"[91].

It is very characteristic that the spiritual father, the therapist, is put in the place of Christ.

St. Symeon also uses a type of prayer in which one asks to find a suitable spiritual guide who will offer us spiritual healing.

"O Lord, who desirest not the death of a sinner but that he should turn and live, Thou who didst come down to earth in order to restore life to those lying dead through sin and in order to make them worthy of seeing Thee the true light as far as that is possible to man, send me a man who knows Thee, so that in serving him and subjecting myself to him with all my strength, as to Thee, and in doing Thy will in his, I may please Thee the only true God, and so that even I, a sinner, may be worthy of Thy Kingdom"[92].

If a Christian prays in this way, God will show him the spiritual father suitable for him, to tend the illnesses and wounds of his soul.

Certainly one should not overlook the fact that such therapists, both in St. Symeon's time and today, are rare. He says: "In truth those who have the skill properly to direct and heal rational souls are rare, and especially so at the present time"[93].

In conclusion it should be said that it is necessary to seek out and find such scientific doctors, therapists, or even nurses, in order to be spiritually healed. There is no other way of healing. God is our true Healer, but so are the friends of Christ, the saints in whom dwells the Trinitarian God Himself.

---

91. Ibid. p. 340-342. CWS p. 235
92. SC 129, p. 186-188
93. SC 104, 346. CWS p. 236

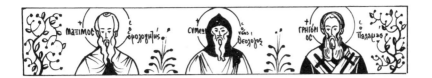

3. Orthodox psychotherapy

In developing the subject of Orthodox psychotherapy, in this chapter we must see what the soul is and how it is healed, secondly, what is the nature of the interrelationships of image, soul, nous, heart and mind, and thirdly, how nous, heart and mind (thoughts) are healed. I believe that these are the most important and essential topics for a knowledge of the inner purification and therapy of the soul, as well as for their attainment.

1. The Soul ('Psyche')

What the soul is

"The word 'soul' is one of the most difficult words in the Bible and in Christian literature"[1]. 'Soul' has many meanings in Holy Scripture and in patristic literature. Professor Christos Yannaras says: "The Septuagint translators of the Old Testament carried over into Greek with the word 'psyche' ('soul') the Hebrew 'nephesh', a term with many meanings. Anything which has life is called a soul, every animal, but more commonly within the Scripture it pertains to man. It signifies the way in which life is manifested in man. It does not refer just to one department of human existence – the

---

1. Christos Yannaras: Elements of Faith p. 55

spiritual in opposition to the material – but signifies the whole man, as a single living hypostasis. The soul does not merely dwell in the body, but is expressed by the body, which itself, like the flesh or heart, corresponds to our ego, to the way in which we realise life. A man is a soul, he is a human being, he is someone..."[2]. The soul is not the cause of life. It is, rather, the bearer of life[3].

Soul is the life which exists in every creature, as in plants and animals. Soul is the life that exists in man, and it is also every man who has life. Soul is also the life which is expressed within the spiritual element in our existence, it is that spiritual element in our existence. Since the term 'soul' has many meanings, there are many places where things have not been clarified.

In what follows we shall try to look at some uses of the term 'psyche' in texts from the New Testament and the texts from the Fathers of the Church.

The term is used by the Lord and the Apostles to mean life. The angel of the Lord said to Joseph, who was betrothed to the Mother of God: "Arise, take the young child and his mother, and go to the land of Israel, for those who sought the young child's life are dead" (Matt. 2, 20). The Lord, describing Himself, said: "I am the good shepherd. The good shepherd gives his life for the sheep" (Jn. 10, 11). Likewise the Apostle Paul, writing about Priscilla and Aquila, says they "risked their own necks for my life" (Rom. 16, 4). In these three cases the term used for 'life' is 'psyche'.

'Psyche' is used further, as we said, to indicate the spiritual element in our existence. We shall cite a few scriptural passages to confirm this. The Lord said to his disciples: "Do not fear those who kill the body but cannot kill the soul. But rather fear him who is able to destroy both soul and body in hell" (Matt. 10, 28). Men cannot murder the soul, whereas the

---

2. Ibid.
3. Ibid.

devil can, which means that if the soul is without the Holy Spirit, it is dead. The devil is a dead spirit, for he has no part in God and he transmits death to those who join with him. He is a living entity, but he does not exist in relation to God. In the parable of the rich young man the Lord says to him: "You fool! This night your soul will be required of you; then whose will those things be which you have provided" (Luk. 12, 20)?

The difference between soul (psyche) on the one hand, as the spiritual element in human existence, which is mortal by nature but immortal by grace, and life (psyche) on the other hand appears also in another of Christ's teachings: "Whoever cares for his own safety (psyche) is lost; but if a man will let himself (psyche) be lost for my sake, he will find his true self (psyche)" (Matt. 16, 25, NEB). In one case the Lord uses the term 'psyche' to mean the spiritual element in our existence and in the other case it means life. In a letter to the Thessalonians the Apostle Paul prays: "May the God of peace himself sanctify you completely; and may your whole spirit and soul and body be preserved blameless at the coming of our Lord Jesus Christ" (1 Thess. 5, 23). Here it is not a question of the so-called tripartite composition of man, but the term 'spirit' is used to mean the grace of God, the charisma, which the soul receives. What we wish to point out here is that there is a distinction between soul and body. John the Evangelist writes in his Revelation: "I saw under the altar the souls of those who had been slain for the word of God and for the testimony which they held" (Rev. 6, 9). The body was slain, but the soul is close to God and is certainly in converse with God, as the Evangelist says in what follows.

The word 'soul' is also used to refer to the whole man. The Apostle Paul recommends: "Let every soul be subject to the governing authorities" (Rom. 13, 1).

I believe that this little analysis demonstrates that the term 'psyche' has many meanings in Scripture. The term is used to mean the whole man and the spiritual element in his existence, as well as the life which exists in man, plants and animals, in all things that participate in the life-giving energy of God. St. Gregory Palamas, speaking of the uncreated light which comes to be in the God-bearing soul "through the indwelling God", says that this is God's energy and not His essence, and as the essence is called light, so also the energy is called light. The same is true of the soul. The spiritual life and the biological life are both called 'soul', but we are well aware that the spiritual and the biological are different: "Just as the soul communicates life to the animated body û and we call this life 'soul', while realising that the soul which is in us and which communicates life to the body is distinct from that life û so God, Who dwells in the God-bearing soul, communicates the light to it"[4].

We have cited this passage in order to show that the Fathers are well aware that the term 'soul' refers both to the spiritual element in our existence and to life itself, and that there is a great difference between the two meanings. We shall see this better later on, when we examine the difference between the souls of animals and of men.

To attempt a definition of 'soul' in the sense of the spiritual element in our existence we turn to St. John of Damascus, who says: "Now a soul is a living substance, simple and incorporeal, of its own nature invisible to bodily eyes, using the body as an organ and giving it life endowed with will and he body, so is the mind to the soul. It is free, endowed with will and the power to act, and subject to change, that is, subject to change of will because it is also created. "And this it has received according to nature, through that grace of the Creator by which it has also received both its existence and its being naturally as it is"[5].

The soul is simple and good "because created thus by its Master"[6].

---

4. Triads, 1, 3, 23. CWS p. 39
5. The Orthodox Faith. FC vol. 37. p. 236
6. Hesychios the Priest. Philok. 1, p. 170, 43

Almost the same definition as that of John of Damascus had in fact been given before him by St. Gregory of Nyssa: "The soul is an essence created, living, and noetic, transmitting from itself to an organised and sentient body the power of living and of grasping objects of sense, as long as a natural constitution capable of this holds together"[7].

St. Gregory Palamas, interpreting the Apostle Paul's: "The first man Adam became a living soul" (1 Cor. 15, 45), says that 'living soul' means "ever-living, immortal, which is to say intelligent, for the immortal is intelligent; and not only that, but also divinely blessed with grace. Such is the living soul"[8].

He says that the soul is immortal. We are well aware that this idea of the immortality of the soul is not of Christian origin, but the Christians accepted it with several conditions and several necessary presuppositions. Prof. John Zizioulas writes: "The idea of the immortality of the soul, even though it is not of Christian origin, passed into the tradition of our Church, permeating even this hymnography of ours. No one can deny it without finding himself outside the climate of the very worship of the Church... The Church did not accept this Platonic idea without conditions and presuppositions. These presuppositions include, among other things, three basic points. One is that souls are not eternal but created. Another is that the soul should by no means be identified with man. (Man's soul is not man. The soul is one thing and man, who is a psychosomatic being, is another.) And the third and most important is that the immortality of man is not based on the immortality of the soul, but on the Resurrection of Christ and on the coming resurrection of bodies"[9].

We have emphasised that man's soul is immortal by grace and not by nature, and yet it must be stressed that in the Orthodox patristic tradition man's immortality is not the

---

7. On the Soul and Resurrection. FC vol. 58 p. 205-206. PG 46, 29
8. Palamas: On the Holy Spirit ch. 2, 8
9. Synaxi No. 6. p. 81-82. (in Gk.)

soul's life after death, but a passing over death by the grace of Christ. Life in Christ is what makes man immortal, for without life in Christ there is dying, since it is the grace of God that gives life to the soul.

Having presented several elements that make up the definition of the soul, we must proceed a little further to the topic of the **creation** of the soul. The soul is created, since it was made by God. Our basic source is the revelation which was given to Moses: "The Lord God formed man of the dust of the ground, and breathed into his nostrils the breath of life; and man became a living being" (Gen. 2, 7). This passage describes the creation of man's soul. In his interpretation of it, St. John Chrysostom says that it is essential to look at what is said with the eyes of faith and that these things are said "with much condescension and because of our weakness". The phrase "God made man and breathed into him" is "unworthy of God, but Holy Scripture explains it in this way for our sake because of our weakness, condescending to us so that, being made worthy of this condescension, we may have strength to rise to that height"[10]. The way in which God formed man's body and made him a living soul as described in Holy Scripture is condescending. It is described thus because of our own weakness.

St. John of Damascus writes that whatever is said about God in human terms is "said symbolically" but has a higher sense, since "the divine is simple and formless". And since Scripture says that God breathed into man's face, we may look at the interpretation by St. John of Damascus concerning the mouth of God: "By His mouth and speech let us understand the expression of His will, by analogy with our own expression of our innermost thoughts by mouth and speech"[11]. Certainly mouth and breath are two different things, but I mention this as indicative, since there is a relationship and a

---

10. Homily 12 on Gen. 2. FC vol. 74, p. 164. PG 53, 102-105
11. The Orthodox Faith. FC vol. 37, p. 192

connection. Generally, as St. John of Damascus says, everything that has been affirmed of God in bodily terms, apart
from what was said about the presence of the Word of God in
the flesh, "contains some hidden meaning which teaches us
things that exceed our nature"[12].

Therefore the soul, like the body, is created by God[13] . St.
John Chrysostom interprets this breath of God by saying that
it is "not only senseless but also out of place" to say that what
was breathed into Adam was the soul and that the soul was
transmitted to the body from the substance of God. If this
were true, then the soul would not be wise in one place and
foolish and senseless in another, or just in one place and
unjust in another. The "substance of God is not divided or
changed but is unchangeable." So the divine breath was the
"energy of the Holy Spirit". As Christ said "Receive the Holy
Spirit", so also the divine breath "humanly heard is the
venerated and holy Spirit". According to the saint, the soul is
not a piece of God, but the energy of the Holy Spirit, which
created the soul without becoming soul itself. "This Spirit
proceeded, it did not become soul, but created a soul; it did not
change into a soul, but it created a soul; for the Holy Spirit is
a creator, it has a share in the creation of the body and in the
creation of the soul. For Father and Son and Holy Spirit by
divine power create the creature"[14].

Another important point emphasised by the holy Fathers is
that we have no existence of the body without a soul nor
existence of a soul without the body. The moment God creates
the body He creates the soul too. St. Anastasios of Sinai
writes: "Neither does the body exist before the soul nor the
soul exist before the body"[15]. St. John of Damascus emphasises in opposition to Origen's view: "Body and soul were

---

12. Ibid. p. 192-193
13. Hesychios. Philok. 1, p. 196, 192
14. Festal Menaion (in Greek) p. 73, note 1
15. Q 91. PG 89, 724

formed at the same time, not one before and the other afterwards"[16]. St. John of the Ladder says this as well[17].

Man is made in the image of God. This image certainly does
not refer to the body, but mainly and primarily to the soul.
The image in man is stronger than that in the angels, for as
we shall see, man's soul gives life to the attached body. In
general we can say that the soul is in the image of God. And
as God is threefold – Nous, Word and Spirit – so also man's
soul has three powers: nous, soul and spirit[18]. In all nature
there are "iconic examples" of the Holy Trinity[19], but this
appears mainly in man. The image in man is stronger than
the image in the angels. St. Gregory Palamas, speaking of the
baptism of Christ in the Jordan River and explaining why
"the mystery of the created and recreated (man) reveals the
mystery of the Holy Trinity", writes that this came about not
only because man alone is an initiate and earthly worshipper
of the Holy Trinity, but also because "he alone is in its image".
The sentient and irrational animals have only a vital spirit
and this cannot exist of itself; they have no nous and word.
The angels and archangels have nous and word, since they
are noetic and intelligent, but they have no life-giving spirit,
since they have no body which receives life from the spirit. So
since man has nous, word and life-giving spirit that gives life
to the body joined to it, "he alone is in the image of the three-
personal nature"[20].

St. Gregory Palamas develops the same teaching in his
natural and theological chapters. As the Trinitarian God is
Nous, Word and Spirit, so is man. Man's spirit, the life-giving
power in his body, is "man's noetic love", "it is from the nous

---

16. FC vol. 37, p. 235
17. Ladder, Step 26, note 2, p. 136, Gk. edition
18. 150 Chapters, ch. 36-37
19. Monk Amphilochios Rantovits: The Mystery of the Holy Trinity ac-
    cording to St. Gregory Palamas, p. 38 (in Greek)
20. St. Gregory Palamas: Homily 60. EPE 11, p. 512 (Gk.)

and the word, and it exists in the word and the nous and possesses both the word and the nous within itself"[21]. While the noetic and rational nature of the angels has nous, word and spirit, yet "it does not have this spirit as life-giving"[22]. As we have indicated, the image refers primarily to the soul, but since the body is given life by the spirit, therefore the image in man is stronger than that in the angels.

St. Gregory also sees the difference between the image of man and the image of the angels from another point of view. His teaching is well known that in God there is essence and energy, and these are connected separately and separated connectedly. This is the mystery of the indivisible joining of essence and energy. The essence of God is not shared by man, while the energies are shared. And since man is in the image of God, this teaching about essence and energy applies to the soul as well. So the soul is inseparably divided into essence and energy.

In comparing the soul of man with that of animals, St. Gregory says that animals possess a soul not as essence, but as an energy. "The soul of each of the irrational animals is the life for the body it animates, and so animals possess life not essentially but as an energy, since this life is dependent on something else and is not self-subsistent." Therefore since the soul of animals has only energy, it dies with the body. By contrast, the soul of man has not only energy but also essence: "The soul possesses life not only as an activity but also essentially, since it lives in its own right... For that reason, when the body passes away, the soul does not perish with it." It remains immortal. The intelligent and noetic soul is composite, but "since its activity is directed towards something else it does not naturally produce synthesis"[23].

---

21. 150 Chapters, ch. 38
22. Ibid.
23. Ibid. ch. 30-33

In his teaching St. Maximus the Confessor states that the soul has three powers: a) that of nourishment and growth, b) that of imagination and instinct, and c) that of intelligence and intellection. Plants share only in the first of these powers. Animals share in that of imagination and instinct as well, while men share all three powers[24]. This shows the great value of man relative to irrational animals. Likewise what was said previously shows clearly also how angels differ from men. Therefore when Christ became man he received a human body and not the form of an angel, he became God-man, and not God-angel.

What has been said makes it possible for us to see the **dividedness** of the soul. We do not intend to enlarge on this topic but we shall present those things which have an essential bearing on the general topic of this study.

St. John of Damascus says that the soul is intelligent and noetic. God gave man "an intelligent and noetic soul for proper breathing"[25]. It is a basic teaching of the Fathers that nous and intelligence are two parallel energies of the soul. St. Gregory Palamas, referring to the fact that the soul is in the image of the Holy Trinity, and writing that the Holy Trinity is Nous, Word and Spirit, says that the soul, created by God in His image "is endowed with nous, word and spirit." Therefore she must guard her order, relate entirely to God. She must look at God alone, adorn herself with constant memory and contemplation and with the warmest and ardent love for Him[26].

The soul is broken up by passions and sins. Therefore it must be unified, offered to God. Unification takes place in many ways, mainly by putting Christ's word into practice. Theoleptos, Metropolitan of Philadelphia, emphasises particularly the value of prayer. "Pure prayer, after uniting in itself

---

24. Philok. 2, p. 88, 32
25. FC vol. 37, p. 235
26. 150 Chapters, ch. 40

nous, word and spirit, invokes the name of God in words, looks up at God Whom it is invoking, with a nous free from wandering, and shows contrition, humility and love. Thus it inclines towards itself the eternal Trinity, the Father, the Son and the Holy Spirit-One God"[27]. With the word we constantly remember the name of Christ, with a nous free from wandering we gaze at God, and with the spirit we are possessed of contrition, humility and love.

In this way the three powers of the soul are united and offered to the Holy Trinity. This is how the healing of the soul takes place, and we shall deal with it at greater length elsewhere. The scattering of the powers of the soul is sickness and their unification is healing.

Nicetas Stethatos divides the soul into three parts but speaks mainly of two, the intelligent and passible parts. The intelligent part is invisible and unrelated to the senses, "as if existing both within and outside them". I think that he is referring to the nous here. Later we shall distinguish between intelligence and nous, but now we must emphasise that the nous has a relationship with God, it receives the energies of God; God reveals Himself to the nous, while intelligence, as an energy, is that which formulates and expresses the experiences of the nous. The passible part of the soul is divided into the sensations and the passions. The passible part is so called because it is "subject to the passions"[28].

St. Gregory of Sinai, analysing the powers of the soul and describing precisely what takes hold in each power, says that evil thoughts work in the intelligent power; bestial passions in the excitable part; recollection of animal lusts in the appetitive part; fantasies in the noetic part; and notions in the reasoning part[29].

The same saint says that when by His life-giving breath

---

27. Writings, p. 391, 20
28. Gnostic Chapters, ch. 9. Philok. 3, p. 328 (in Gk.)
29. Acrostics, 63. Writings, p. 48

God created the intelligent and noetic soul, "He did not make it have rage and animal lust; He endowed the soul only with the appetitive power and with the courage to be lovingly attracted"[30]. With the creation of the soul "neither lust nor anger was included in its being"[31]. These came as a result of sin.

Here we shall not develop further the subject of the divided soul because the relevant material is described in the fourth chapter, which deals with the passions. We had to include a little about the soul's dividedness at this point because we are on the particular subject of the soul.

Yet there does exist a relationship and a connection between the soul and the body. But what is this relationship and to what extent does it exist? It is a topic which we shall look at here.

Man is made up of body and soul. Each element alone does not constitute a man. St. Justin, the philosopher and martyr, says that the soul by itself is not a man, but is called 'a man's soul'. In the same way the body is not called a man but is called 'a man's body'. "Though in himself man is neither of these, the combination of the two is called man; God called man into life and resurrection, and he did not call a part, but the whole, which is the soul and the body"[32].

The soul, as we have pointed out, was created with the body at conception. "The embryo is endowed with a soul at conception." The soul is created at conception and "the soul at that time is just as active as the flesh. As the body grows so the soul increasingly manifests its energies"[33].

There is a clear distinction between soul and body, since "the soul is not body but bodiless"[34]. Besides, it is altogether impossible for the body and soul to exist or be called body or

---

30. Ibid. p. 52, 82
31. Ibid. p. 52, 81
32. Justin Martyr. On Resurrection. BEPES vol. 4, p. 229 (in Gk.)
33. Ladder, Step 26, note 2, p. 136, Gk. edition
34. See St. Gregory The Theologian, P.G. 10, 1141

soul unrelated to and independent of each other. "For the relationship is fixed"[35].

The ancient philosophers believed that the soul is at a specific place in the body, that the body is the prison of the soul and that the salvation of the soul is its release from the body. The Fathers teach that the soul is everywhere in the body. St. Gregory Palamas says that the angels and the soul, as incorporeal beings, "are not located in place, but neither are they everywhere". The soul, as it sustains the body together with which it was created "is everywhere in the body, not as in a place, nor as if it were encompassed, but as sustaining, encompassing and giving life to it because it possesses this too in the image of God"[36].

The same saint, seeing that there are some people (the Hellenisers) who locate the soul in the brain as in an acropolis and that others place it at the very centre of the heart "and in that element therein which is purified of the breath of animal soul" as the most genuine vehicle (Judaisers), says that we know precisely that the intelligent part is in the heart, not as in a container, for it is incorporeal, nor is it outside the heart, since it is conjoined. The heart of man is the controlling organ, the throne of grace, according to St. Gregory Palamas. The nous and all the thoughts of the soul are to be found there. The saint affirms that we received this teaching from Christ Himself, Who is man's Maker. He reminds us of Christ's sayings: "It is not what goes into a man's mouth that defiles him, but what comes out of it" (Matt. 15, 11), and: "For out of the heart proceed evil thoughts" (Matt. 15, 19). The saint adds further that St. Makarios said: "The heart directs the entire organism, and when grace gains possession of the heart, it reigns over all the thoughts and all the members, for it is there in the heart that the nous and the soul have their

---

35. St. Maximus: Philosophical and theological studies, Vol. 1, p. 222. (in Gk.)
36. 150 Chapters. Ch. 61

seat." Therefore the basic aim of therapy, he says, is to bring back the nous, "which has been dissipated abroad by the senses from outside the heart", which is "the seat of thoughts" and "the first intelligent organ of the body"[37].

We shall return to this subject, but what we mainly wish to underline is that according to the teaching of the Fathers, the soul uses the heart as its organ and directs the body. The soul is in union with the body; it is no stranger to it. Nemesius of Emesa teaches that "the soul is incorporeal, and not circumscribed to a particular portion of space, but spreading entire throughout: like a sun that spreads wherever its light reaches as well as throughout the body of the sun, not being just a part of the whole that it illuminates, as would be the case if it were not omnipresent in it." Furthermore, "the soul is united to the body and yet remains distinct from it"[38].

The soul activates and directs the whole body and all the members of the body. It is a teaching of the Orthodox Church that God directs the world personally without created intermediaries, by His uncreated energy. Thus, just as God activates the whole of nature, in the same way "the soul too activates the members of the body and moves each member in conformance with the operation of that member"[39]. Therefore just as it is God's task to administer the world, so also it is "the soul's task to guide the body"[40].

St. Gregory Palamas, who dwelt much upon the theme of the relationship between soul and body, says that what takes place through God takes place through the soul. The soul has within it in simple form "all the providential powers of the body". And even if some members of the body are injured, if the eyes are removed and the ears deafened, the soul is no less possessed of the providential powers of the body. The soul

37. Triads, 1, 2, 3. CWS p. 42-43
38. The Nature of Man, Ch. 3. LCC Vol. 4, p. 298. PG 40, 597 and 600
39. Acrostics. Gk. Philok. 4, p. 42, 81. Writings, p. 52, 81
40. Thalassios. Philok. 2, p. 308 31

is not the providential powers but it has providential powers. In spite of the presence in it of the providential powers, it is "single and simple and not composite", not "compound or synthetic"[41].

It is very characteristic that in this passage St. Gregory links what takes place through the soul in relation to the body, with God's relation to the whole of creation. God directs the world with His providential powers. God had the providential powers even before the world was created. Yet God, who not only possesses many powers but is all-powerful, is not deprived of His unicity and simplicity because of the powers that are in Him[42]. This shows clearly that the soul is "in the image of God". What takes place in God takes place analogously in the soul of man.

St. Gregory of Nyssa says that the soul is immaterial and bodiless "working and moving in a way corresponding to its peculiar nature, and evincing these peculiar emotions through the organs of the body"[43]. The same saint epigrammatically teaches that the soul is not held by the body but holds the body. It is not within the body as in a vessel or bag, but rather the body is within the soul. The soul is throughout the body, "and there is no part illuminated by it in which it is not wholly present"[44].

The general conclusion with reference to the relationship between soul and body is that the soul is in the whole body, there is no sector of a man's body in which the soul is not present, that the heart is the first intelligent seat of the soul, that the centre of the soul is there, not as in a vessel but as in an organ which guides the whole body and that the soul, while distinct from the body, is nevertheless most intimately linked with it.

---

41. Triads, 3, 2, 22
42. Ibid.
43. On the Soul and Resurrection. FC. vol. 58, p. 206. PG 46, 29
44. On the Soul. PG 45, 217B

All these things have been said because they are very closely connected with the subject of this study. For we cannot understand the fall and sickness of the soul if we do not know just what the soul is and how it is linked with the body.

Sickness and dying of the soul

In church we often speak of the fall of man and the death which came as a result of the fall. Spiritual death came first, and bodily death followed. The soul lost the uncreated grace of God, the nous ceased to have a relationship with God and was darkened. It transmitted this darkening and dying to the body. According to St. Gregory of Sinai, man's body was created incorruptible and "such it will be resurrected", and the soul was created dispassionate. Since there was a very tenacious link between soul and body because of their interpenetration and communication, both were corrupted. "The soul acquired the qualities of the passions, or rather of the demons, and the body became like irrational beasts due to the condition into which it fell and the prevalence of corruption." Since the soul and body were corrupted, they formed "one animal being, unreasoning and senseless, subject to anger and lust". This is how, according to the Scriptures, man became "joined to the beasts and like them"[45]. Through the fall, man's soul filled with passions, his body became like the beasts. Man wore the skin garments of decay and mortality and became like irrational animals.

This sickness, bondage, impurity and dying of the soul is admirably described in the patristic works. Every sin is a repetition of Adam's sin, and with every sin we undergo the darkening and dying of the fallen soul. Let us take a closer look at these fallen states of the soul.

When man leaves his senses free and through the senses

---

45. Acrostics, 82. Writings, p. 52

his nous pours out of his heart, then his soul is taken captive. "The unloosing of the senses lays fetters on the soul." This bondage is equivalent to darkening. The setting of the sun creates night. And when Christ withdraws from the soul and the darkness of passions lays hold of it, then "the immaterial beasts tear it to pieces"[46]. Man's soul falls into impenetrable darkness and the demons work on him. He finds himself in a moonless night.

This also constitutes the soul's disease. St. Thalassios says: "The soul's disease is an evil disposition, while its death is sin put into action"[47]. The ailing soul is led step by step to death.

Actually the soul's disease is its impurity. "Impurity of soul lies in its not functioning in accordance with nature. It is because of this that impassioned thoughts are produced in the intellect"[48]. According to St. Maximus, "A soul filled with thoughts of sensual desire and hatred is unpurified"[49].

Hesychios the Priest describes the way in which the soul sickens and is finally killed. God created the soul simple and good, but it delights in the provocations of the devil, and "once deceived, it pursues something sinister as though it were good". In this way "its thoughts become entwined in the fantasy provoked by the devil". Then "the soul assents to the provocation and, to its own condemnation, tries to turn this unlawful mental fantasy into a concrete action by means of the body"[50].

St. Gregory Palamas, citing passages from Scripture, such as the Apostle Paul's words: "...even when we were dead in trespasses He made us alive together with Christ" (Eph. 2, 5), the words of John the Evangelist: "There is sin leading to death" (1 Jn. 5, 16), and Christ's words to his disciple: "Let

---

46. Theoleptos. Philok. 4, p. 6. (In Gk.). Writings p. 386, 9
47. Philok. 2, p. 318, 89
48. Ibid. p. 89, 35
49. Ibid. p. 54, 14
50. Philok. 1, p. 169f, 43

the dead bury their own dead" (Matt. 8, 22), says that although the soul is immortal by grace, nevertheless when
"dissipated, abandoned to pleasures and self-indulgent, it is
dead even while it lives". This is the way he interprets the
Apostle Paul's words: "She (the widow) who lives in pleasure
is dead while she lives" (1 Tim. 5, 6). Although the soul is
alive, it is dead, since it has not the true life which is the
grace of God[51]. When our ancestors withdrew from the remembrance and theoria of God and disregarded His com-
mand and took the side of the deathly spirit of Satan, they
were stripped of "the luminous and living raiment of the
supernal radiance and they too, alas, became dead in spirit
like Satan"[52]. This is how it always goes. When someone joins
with Satan and does his own will, his soul dies, because Satan
is not only a deathly spirit but he also brings death upon
those who draw near to him[53].

When the soul is not working according to nature it is dead.
"...when it is not healthy, though it retains a semblance of
life, it is dead...When, for instance, it has no care for virtue,
but is rapacious and transgresses the law, whence can I tell
you that you have a soul? Because you walk? But this belongs
to the irrational creatures as well. Because you eat and
drink? But this too belongs to wild beasts. Well then, because
you stand upright on two feet? This convinces me rather that
you are a beast in human form"[54].

In the teaching of the Apostle Paul the 'dead' man is called
'carnal' or 'unspiritual'. In his letter to the Corinthians he
writes: "The unspiritual man does not receive the gifts of the
Spirit of God" (1 Cor. 2, 14). He also writes: "While there is
jealousy and strife among you, are you not carnal, and behaving like mere men?" (1 Cor. 3, 3) According to Prof. John

---

51. 150 chapters, ch. 45
52. Ibid. ch. 46
53. Ibid.
54. Homily 6 on 2 Corinthians. NPNF vol. 12 p. 307f

Romanides the words used for 'unspiritual' (psychikos) and 'carnal' (sarkikos) and 'behaving like mere men' have the same meaning[55]. In another place in his book he writes: "The carnal and unspiritual man is the whole man, soul and body, who lacks that energy of the Holy Spirit which renders one incorruptible"[56]. "When a man does not follow the Spirit, he is deprived of God's life-giving energy and is rendered unspiritual"[57].

Therapy of the soul

The whole tradition of the Orthodox Church consists in healing and bringing to life the soul which is dead from sin. All the sacraments and the whole ascetic life of the Church contribute **to this healing**. Anyone who is not aware of this fact is unable to sense the atmosphere of the Orthodox Tradition. We shall see in what follows what this health and vitalising of the soul is, and several ways of attaining it, and how a healthy and living soul functions.

Health of the soul consists in dispassion and spiritual knowledge[58]. "The soul is perfect when permeated by the virtues"[59]. A soul is perfect "if its passible aspect is totally oriented towards God"[60]. A pure soul is "one that loves God"[61]. A pure soul is "one freed from passions and constantly delighted by divine love"[62].

The holy Fathers also describe several ways in which the soul is revived, vitalised and healed. Godly sorrow, or repentance, puts an end to sensual pleasure, but "the destruction of sensual pleasure is the soul's resurrection"[63]. Anthony, the

---

55. John Romanides: The Ancestral Sin (in Greek) p. 131
56. Ibid. p. 130
57. Ibid. p. 131
58. St. Thalassios. Philok. 2, p. 313, 2
59. Ibid. p. 316, 54
60. St. Maximos. Philok. 2, p. 99, 98
61. St. Thalassios. Philok. 2 p. 317 79
62. St. Maximus. Philok. 2 p. 56, 34
63. St. Thalassios. Philok. 2 p. 309, 39

great servant of God, said that we must purify our minds. "For I believe that when the mind is completely pure and is in its natural state, it gains penetrating insight, and it sees more clearly and further than the demons, since the Lord reveals things to it"[64]. That is to say, this holy servant of the soul enjoins us to purify our minds. It has been observed that if anyone keeps his nous pure from evil thoughts and various images, then he can keep his soul pure.

Theoleptos, Metropolitan of Philadelphia, teaches: "When, having put an end to external distractions, you also master inner thoughts, then your nous is stirred to spiritual acts and words." The effort to keep one's mind pure and to free oneself from the many distractions results in the appearance within us of the nous, which had been dead and unseen. Therefore again Theoleptos advises: "Put an end to mixing with the outer world and fight with the inner thoughts until you find the place of pure prayer and the home where Christ dwells"[65]. The heart, as we shall point out in another place, is the home where God dwells. We shall discover it only when we strive to live quietly and when we struggle against the thoughts which hold sway in us. Purity of the nous is very important. This method is simple but comprehensive and brings great benefit to man's soul, since it makes it a temple of the Holy Spirit.

The soul is healed when it rejects relations with inferior things and cleaves in love to one who is superior[66].

St. Gregory Palamas, interpreting the whole tradition of the Orthodox Church, says that through transgression and sin we lost the likeness of God, but "we did not lose the image". Precisely because we did not lose the image we can restore the soul. The soul, freed from relations with inferior things and cleaving in love to one who is superior and submitting to him through the works and ways of virtue, "receives from

---

64. Hesychios the Priest. Philok. 1 p. 194, 179
65. Philok. 4, p. 6 (in Gk.). Writings, p. 385f
66. Gregory Palamas. 150 chapters, ch. 39

him illumination, adornment and betterment and it obeys his counsels and exhortations, from which it receives true and eternal life"[67]. When the soul obeys God's law, it gradually becomes healthy, is illuminated and receives eternal life.

Beside the practical method for healing the soul, Nicetas Stethatos also offers another method, through theoria. Where there is love for God, an active nous, and participation in the unapproachable light, "there is also peace in the powers of the soul, purification of the nous and indwelling of the Holy Trinity"[68]. Therefore, beside the effort to keep our nous pure, it is necessary to accustom the nous to inner action and inner prayer, to acquire charity and love for God – because where this love dwells, peace comes to the powers of the soul – and purity of the nous.

In another section of this book we speak more analytically about how the soul is healed when it moves according to nature, and there we describe the natural movement of each part of the soul. Here, since we are speaking of the healing of the soul we shall just briefly emphasise a few facts.

St. Gregory Palamas writes that we struggle to drive the law of sin out of our body and to install in its place the oversight of the nous, in this way establishing a law appropriate for each power of the soul and for every member of the body. For the senses we ordain self-control. For the passible part of the soul, love. We improve the intelligence by rejecting everything which impedes the mind's ascent towards God, and this we call nepsis. If a person has purified his body through self-control, has made his emotions and desires an occasion of virtue, and presented to God a mind purified by prayer, then he "acquires and sees in himself the grace promised to those whose hearts have been purified"[69].

---

67. Ibid.
68. Natural chapters, ch. 2. Gk. Philok. 3, p. 298
69. Triads, 1, 2, 2. CWS p. 42

St. Maximus, in the Orthodox tradition, exhorts: "Bridle your soul's incensive power with love, quench its desire with self-control, give wings to its intelligence with prayer, and the light of your nous will never be darkened"[70].

It is not advice or medicines that heal the sick soul, that give life to the dead nous, that purify the impure heart, but the ascetic method of the Church, self-control, love, prayer and guarding of the nous from Satan's provocations through evil thoughts. Therefore we believe that the Orthodox tradition is very important for our time, for it is the only thing that can free a man and heal him from the anxiety and insecurity brought on by the death of his soul.

2. Interrelations of soul, nous, heart and mind

In the texts of Holy Scripture and the holy Fathers there is confusion, but also distinction, among the terms soul, nous, heart, and mind (dianoia). Anyone delighting in the writings of the Fathers and the New Testament, first faces the problem of the confusion among these concepts and terms. These terms are interchanging. I was occupied with this topic for many years and tried to find a solution. In reading the bibliographies on the subject I found that the interpreters, with very few exceptions, were unable to determine the relations and distinction of these terms. Therefore in this section we shall attempt to distinguish them and to describe the framework within which each term moves.

We have so far explained that man's soul is in the image of God, and since the soul gives life to the attached body, the image in man is stronger than the image in the angels. Since the soul is all through the body, both the whole man and the body itself can be regarded as in the image of God. The hymn

---

70. Philok. 2, p. 110, 80

by St. John of Damascus sung in the funeral service is characteristic. "I weep and I wail when I think upon death, and
behold our beauty, fashioned after the image of God, lying in the
tomb disfigured, dishonoured, bereft of form." It is plain that in
this hymn the image refers to the body which is in the tomb.

Nous and soul

In the texts of the New Testament and the Fathers the soul
is identified with the nous. The terms 'nous' and soul interchange. St. John of Damascus writes that the nous is the
purest part of the soul, it is the eye of the soul: "The soul does
not have the nous as something distinct from itself, but as its
purest part, for as the eye is to the body, so is the nous to the
soul". Thus he is saying that the soul has the nous as its eye[71].
St. Gregory Palamas uses the term 'nous' in two senses. It
is the whole soul, the image, and it is also a power of the soul,
as we explained in another section, because, as the Trinitarian God is Nous, Word and Spirit, so the soul too has nous,
word and spirit. According to this Athonite saint, the nous is
identified with the soul, but it is also a power of the soul. I
shall cite a characteristic passage containing these concepts.
After the creation of man, writes the saint, the angels saw
with their eyes "the soul of man joined to sense and flesh, and
they were seeing another god not only come into being on
earth through divine goodness, intellect and flesh the same
man, but transformed by this extravagance and by the grace
of God so as to be the same flesh and nous and spirit, and so
that the soul had the image and likeness of God, as completely unified in nous and word and spirit"[72].
The following things appear in this text. In the beginning it
speaks of the soul which is joined with flesh and the senses. A
little further on the terms 'soul' and 'nous' are interchanged.

---

71. The Orthodox Faith. FC vol. 37, p. 236
72. St. Gregory Palamas. On the Holy Spirit 2, 9

Instead of 'soul' he uses 'nous', "nous and flesh the same man". In what follows he uses the division: flesh, nous and spirit, the spirit being the grace of the Holy Spirit, since God did not form man only of soul and body, "but also divinely favoured with grace. For such is the truly living soul"[73]. After this he writes that the soul is in the image and likeness of God, "completely unified in nous and word and spirit." So it seems clear in this text that the soul is in the image of God, that the nous is sometimes identified with soul and at other times regarded as a power of the soul, the eye of the soul, as St. John of Damascus says.

The identification of nous with soul is clear also in another passage of St. Gregory Palamas. He writes in one of his chapters: "For it is not the bodily constitution but the very nature of the nous which possesses this image and nothing in our nature is superior to the nous"[74].

Man's soul, being in the image of God, is triadic. It is nous, word and spirit. Since in the general meaning the nous is identified with the soul, it means that the nous too has three powers. While the nous is one of the powers of the soul, at the same time it is also the whole soul. We shall cite one characteristic passage in St. Gregory. "When the oneness of the nous becomes threefold while yet remaining single, it is united with the Divine Threefold Oneness... The oneness of the nous becomes threefold while remaining single, when it returns to itself and rises through itself to God"[75]. Thus the soul "is one, although it has many powers"[76], one of which is the nous, but in addition the soul as a whole with its three powers is also called the nous.

We have already seen that the Fathers refer the image of God to the soul. But at the same time it is also said that the

---

73. Ibid. 8
74. 150 chapters, ch. 27
75. On the Hesychasts. cf. EF p. 409f. Gk. Philok. 4, p. 133
76. Ibid. EF p. 410, 3

image refers to the nous: "It is not the bodily constitution but the very nature of the nous which possesses this image"[77].

Inasmuch as God has essence and energy, so too the soul, which is in the image of God, has essence and energy. But since, as we have seen, the nous is also identified with the soul, the nous too has essence and energy.

St. Gregory Palamas, with all his wisdom and discrimination, analyses this fact. The heart is the essence of the soul, and the activity of the nous consisting of thoughts and conceptual images is the energy of the soul. Therefore the nous too has essence and energy. So the term 'nous' is used sometimes to mean essence and sometimes to mean energy or action. The saint writes characteristically: "What is called nous is also the activity of the nous, consisting of thoughts and conceptual images. Nous is also the power which produces this and which in Scripture is called the heart"[78]. Since St. Gregory's contemporaries reproached him when he spoke of the return of the nous to the heart, he wrote: "It would seem that such people are unaware that the essence of the nous is one thing, its energy another"[79].

Nous and heart

The nous is also called the essence of the soul, that is to say the heart. In many passages of Holy Scripture and in the Fathers there is this identification of nous and heart, since these terms are used interchangeably. The Lord blesses the pure in heart: "Blessed are the pure in heart, for they shall see God" (Matt. 5, 8). God is revealed in the heart and it is there that man comes to know Him. The Apostle Paul writes that God's illumination is there: God has caused His light to shine "in our hearts to give the light of the knowledge of the

---

77. 150 chapters, ch. 27
78. EF p. 410, 3
79. Triads, 1, 2, 5. CWS p. 44

glory of God in the face of Jesus Christ" (2 Cor. 4, 6). The same Apostle prays "that the God of our Lord Jesus Christ, the Father of glory, may give to you the spirit of wisdom and revelation in the knowledge of Him, the eyes of your hearts being enlightened that you may know..." (Eph. 1, 17-18). The heart receives the revelation of the knowledge of God. Elsewhere this heart is replaced by the nous. When the Lord was among his disciples after his resurrection, "He opened their understanding ('nous') that they might comprehend the Scriptures" (Lk. 24, 45). Since man comes to know God through opening the eyes of his heart and purifying his heart, the phrase "He opened their understanding" is the same as "He opened their hearts". Likewise "Blessed are the pure in heart, for they shall see God" is, I believe, linked with the apostolic passage: "...be transformed by the renewing of your mind (nous)..." (Rom. 12. 2).

So in this sense the nous is also called heart and the two terms nous and heart interchange. St. Maximus the Confessor, interpreting Christ's saying: "Give alms from what is inside, and you will find that everything is clean for you" (Luk. 11, 41), says: "This applies to those who no longer spend their time on things to do with the body, but strive to cleanse the nous (which the Lord calls 'heart') from hatred and dissipation. For these defile the nous and do not allow it to see Christ, who dwells in it by the grace of holy baptism"[80]. So the nous is called the essence of the soul, that is, the heart. In this conception nous and heart are identical, since Christ dwells in the nous.

Nous and reason

However, the energy of the nous, "consisting of thoughts and conceptual images", is also called nous. The Apostle Paul writes to the Corinthians: "If I pray in a tongue, my spirit prays, but my nous is unfruitful. What am I to do? I will pray

---

80. Philok. 2, p. 109, 73

with the spirit and I will pray with the nous also; I will sing with the spirit and I will sing with the nous also" (1 Cor. 14, 14-15). In this passage the spirit is the gift of tongues, and the nous is reason. So here 'nous' is identified with reason, intelligence. There are many passages in Holy Scripture with this meaning.

Beyond these things St. Maximus the Confessor, giving the name nous to the intelligence and the heart, which is the centre of our being, through which we acquire knowledge of God, presents the distinction and energy of each function. "A pure nous sees things correctly. A trained intelligence puts them in order"[81]. The nous (heart) is that which sees things clearly and therefore should be purified, and the intelligence is that which formulates and expresses what has been seen. With this passage we come to the point of asserting that in order to be a Father of the Church it is necessary to have not only a clear nous but also expression, that is trained speech, in order to express these supranatural realities as far as is possible.

Nous and attention

Other Fathers use the term 'nous' to define attention, which is more subtle than reason[82]. Theoleptos of Philadelphia links nous with attention, word with invocation, spirit with compunction and love. When the powers of the soul function in this way, then "the whole of the inner man serves the Lord. But it sometimes happens that while the mind is offering the words of prayer, the nous (the more subtle attention) does not go with it, does not fix its gaze on God, with whom the words of the prayer are speaking, but it is distracted by different thoughts without realising it. So the mind says the words from habit, but the nous is taken away

---

81. Philok. 2, p. 82, 97
82. Triads, 1, 2, 7. CWS p. 46

from knowledge of God. Therefore the soul too then seems not to be aware or organised, since the nous is scattered in various fantasies and is engaged in things which deceive it or in things which it desires"[83].

So the nous itself, which is not simply the thoughts, but the subtler attention, should return to the heart, to the essence of the soul, which is located, as in an organ, within the bodily organ of the heart, since this bodily organ is the seat of intelligence and "the first intelligent organ of the body". Thus we should concentrate our nous, which is scattered abroad by the senses, and bring it back again "to the selfsame heart, the seat of thoughts"[84].

We have not exhausted the subject of the nous. In this section we simply wanted in some way to distinguish the terms nous, heart and soul and to point out their relations and differences. We shall return to these concepts when we speak at greater length about nous, heart and thoughts.

In this section we want briefly to emphasise that the term 'nous' has many meanings in the biblico-patristic tradition. The nous is identified with the soul, but at the same time it is also an energy of the soul. Like the soul, the nous too is in the image of God. And just as the soul is divided into essence and energy, the same is true of the nous. And just as in God essence and energy are separated inseparably, so it is with the nous. That is why in some places the Fathers characterise nous as essence, that is the heart, in which case the nous is identified with the heart, and in other passages they characterise nous as energy, conceptual images and thoughts and the subtler attention which is poured out through the senses, when it should return to the heart. The Fathers mainly refer to the nous more generally as the heart and the soul, without excluding the other names which we mentioned before.

---

83. Philok. 4, p. 8 (in Gk.). Writings, p. 388f
84. Triads, 1, 2, 3. CWS p. 43

We have lost our tradition relating to it, and many of us identify the nous with intelligence. We do not at all suspect that aside from intelligence there is also another power which has greater value: the nous, the heart. The whole of civilisation is a civilisation of the loss of the heart. And a person cannot understand what he has not in his heart. The heart has died, the nous has been darkened, and we cannot perceive their presence. That is why this clarification has been necessary. A person who has the Holy Spirit within him, who is "in the revelation", does not need many clarifications, because he himself knows from experience the presence and existence of the nous, the heart.

3. Nous, heart and thoughts

What has been said so far is introductory to our analysis and interpretation of the inner life of the soul. The sickness and cure of the soul is mainly the sickness and cure of the nous, heart and thoughts. What follows will revolve around this topic. We shall study separately the nous, heart and thoughts. I think that this analysis will help us to examine our inner self.

a) The nous

We have already emphasised that the term 'nous' has many meanings in the works of the Fathers of the Church. Sometimes it is identified with the soul, sometimes it is an energy of the soul, the eye of the soul, sometimes the term suggests the essence of the soul, sometimes its energy, and sometimes it means the attentiveness which is subtler than mind. In this section, in studying the sickness and healing of the nous, we shall regard it as the eye of the soul. We shall take the term chiefly to mean the power of the soul[85] as well as the purest

---

85. Ibid. CWS p. 42

part of the soul, which is the eye of the soul, in accord with the words of St. John of Damascus: "It does not have the nous as something distinct from itself, but as its purest part, for, as the eye is to the body, so is the nous to the soul..."[86]. This eye of the soul, nous, which acts through the senses is what becomes contaminated, falls ill and needs to be healed. Just as when the eye of the body is ill the whole body is darkened, so when the eye of the soul, which is the nous, is ill, man's entire soul is darkened. This is what the Lord meant when he said: "If the light that is in you is darkness, how great is that darkness!" (Matt. 6, 23). When the nous has gone out of the heart, withdrawn from God, it sickens and dies, whereupon the whole soul is deadened. We shall see this more analytically in what follows.

The natural life of the nous

The Fathers define the natural life of the nous clearly. According to Nicetas Stethatos, "God is dispassionate nous, above all nous and all dispassion. He is light and the source of good light, He is wisdom, word and knowledge, as well as giver of wisdom, word and knowledge"[87]. And man, as the image of God, has a dispassionate nous when his nous is "in its natural state and does not move beyond its own rank and nature". Therefore man's nous desires and seeks to be united with God, "from whom it had its beginning", and by its natural qualities it traces back to him and "longs to imitate him in simplicity and love for man". And as the Nous-Father begets the Word, who begets and re-creates men, so also the soul's nous begets the word, and "recreates the souls of men of the same race like other heavens and makes them strong to persevere in the active virtues". And not only does the nous recreate the souls of other men through the word, but it gives

---

86. The Orthodox Faith. FC vol. 37 p. 236
87. Gnostic chapters, 1. Gk. Philok. 3 p. 326, 1

them life "by the breath of its mouth". Thus the nous of a man who is moving towards God re-creates other souls, and imitating him "is himself shown to be a creator of the intelligible creation and the great universe"[88]. This passage from Nicetas Stethatos shows that when the nous moves naturally towards God and is united with Him, it too becomes by grace what the Heavenly Nous is by nature.

The union of the nous with God is a standing, but at the same time it is also motion, since perfection in general can never be completed. St. Maximus writes of ever-moving standing and stationary motion. While man remains in God he is in constant motion. Nicetas Stethatos says the same thing about the nous: "All the nouses in this First Nous have both constant standing and endless motion." This is not the case with an impure nous, but with a nous which is pure and undefiled[89]. The nous united with the First Nous becomes good and wise. "God alone is good and wise by nature; but if you exert yourself, your nous also becomes good and wise by participation"[90].

In describing the natural state of the nous we have to define clearly what its natural, unnatural and supranatural movements are. St. Mark the Ascetic describes the three motions of the nous. "The nous changes from one to another of three different states: that according to nature, above nature, and contrary to nature". When it enters the state according to nature, it finds that it is itself the cause of evil thoughts, and confesses its sins to God, clearly understanding the causes of the passions. When it enters the state contrary to nature, it forgets God's justice and fights with men, believing itself unjustly treated. But when it is raised to the state above nature, it finds the fruits of the Holy Spirit"[91]. It is the life of

---

88. Ibid. p. 329, 12
89. Ibid. p. 332, 28
90. St. Thalassios. Philok. 2, p. 315, 37
91. Philok. 1, p. 132, 90

the Spirit which manifests the natural state of the nous and portrays its natural development. When a person perseveres in keeping his nous moving according to nature, he remains pure from the material sphere and "is adorned with gentleness, humility, love and compassion, and is illuminated by the light of the Holy Spirit"[92].

According to St. Maximus the Confessor, "The nous functions in accordance with nature when it keeps the passions under control, contemplates the inner essences of created beings, and abides with God"[93]. The holy Fathers also emphasise the fact that the nous is changed by every conceptual image of things which it accepts. If it contemplates the conceptual images of things spiritually, "it is transformed in various ways according to which of them it contemplates". When it is united with God it loses form and configuration altogether[94]. Therefore it is very important for the nous to learn to receive conceptual images of things spiritually, for otherwise it does not live in its natural state, it is distorted, and when the nous, which is the eye of the soul, is distorted, then the whole soul is automatically distorted. For when one power of the soul is defiled and becomes sick, all the other powers are distorted and sickened, since "the soul is single"[95].

The nous is what determines one's whole condition, since it is the nourisher of the soul. Our nous is between two things, virtue and vice, angel and demon, each of which works for its own ends. The nous joined with freedom "has both the authority and the power to follow or resist whichever it wishes to"[96]. The nous is what divides the soul. First the nous sickens and then it defiles the whole soul and leads it astray. "The soul

---

92. Nicetas Stethatos, Gnostic chapters, 13. Gk. Philok. 3. p. 329
93. Philok. 2, p. 105, 45
94. Ibid. p. 98, 97
95. St. Gregory Palamas. EF p. 410, 3
96. St. Maximus. Philok. 2. p. 98, 92

goes wherever the nous gives impetus to any human passion"[97]. It is characteristic of the nous that where something becomes its constant concern, there it prospers, and as a result it turns desire and love in that direction. This can be either towards what is divine, intelligible and proper to its nature or towards the passions and things of the flesh[98]. The passion of love, when reprehensible, occupies the nous with material things, but when rightly directed "unites it with the divine"[99]. Therefore Orthodox ascesis attaches great importance to the progress and movement of the nous. For when the nous turns and gazes at material things and is defiled by the conceptual image of those things, it falls ill, and it transmits that illness to all the powers of the soul.

In general we can say that the movements of the nous are according to nature, above nature and contrary to nature. With the freedom which it has, the nous moves according to its own desire and is changed according to the path followed and the place where it stays, and then it changes the soul either negatively or positively. "Men turn their minds either to their sins, or to Jesus, or to men"[100]. We trust that this will become clearer in what follows, when we speak of the sickness and healing of the nous.

St. Gregory of Nyssa teaches: "...the nous is not confined to any one part of us, but is equally in all and through all...". The communication of the nous with the body presents an ineffable and inconceivable contact, "not being within it (for the incorporeal is not enclosed within a body) nor yet surrounding it without (for that which is incorporeal does not include anything), but approaching our nature in some perplexing and incomprehensible way, and coming into contact with it, is

---

97. Nicetas Stethatos. Gnostic chapters, 17. Gk. Philok. 3, p. 330
98. St. Maximus. Philok. 2, p. 94, 71
99. Ibid.
100. Abba Ilia. Sayings. p. 60, 5

to be regarded as both in it and around it, neither implanted in it nor enfolded with it"[101].

St. Gregory Palamas, explaining the passage from St. Makarios which teaches that the nous and all the thoughts of the soul are in the heart as in an organ, and the passage in St. Gregory of Nyssa which teaches that the nous, being bodiless, is not in the body, writes that these two passages are not contradictory, but complete each other in a unity. St. Makarios and St. Gregory of Nyssa had different anthropological presuppositions. That is to say, it is in one sense that Macarius speaks of the nous as in the body and it is in another sense that St. Gregory speaks of it as outside the body. Just as anyone who states that God, being bodiless, is not in a specific place is not contradicting one who states that the Word was once in the pure virgin Mother of God, so it is in these passages in the Fathers referring to the nous. Man's nous, being bodiless, is outside the body but also in the body, using the heart ineffably as the first organ of flesh[102]. We have explained in another section that the nous has essence and energy and that as essence it is in the heart, while as energy it works in thoughts, and thus it comes out of the body and conceives the conceptual image of things. In the natural state the nous enters the heart, the energy enters the essence, and thus it rises towards God. This is the circular motion of the nous about which we shall speak later.

The nous as the image of God has life only when it is united with God and is made wise and good. This is the life of the nous. The Apostle Paul writes: "For who has known the nous of the Lord so as to instruct him? But we have the nous of Christ" (1 Cor. 2, 16). The natural state of the nous is for it to be united with the nous of Christ. Then it is illuminated and enlightened. The "real life and true energy of the nous" are present when the soul's intelligence is occupied with divine

---

101. The Making of Man, ch. 15. NPNFns vol. 5. p. 403f. PG 44, 177BC
102. St. Gregory Palamas. Triads, 2, 2, 29

visions and sends up praise and thanksgiving to God and when it attaches itself to Him by constant remembrance[103]. Withdrawal from God deadens the nous, while the life of the nous is association and union with Him. According to St. Maximus, the light of spiritual knowledge is the nous's life, and since this light is engendered by love for God, there is nothing greater than love for God[104].

As the body needs bread to live and the soul needs virtue to live, so too spiritual prayer is the nourishment of the nous[105]. Prayer feeds the nous and gives it life. When the nous is moving towards God and is united with Him, it is healthy, vital. And in this state it receives God's consolation. In God the nous acquires health, perception. And this perceptive faculty of the nous consists in "the power to discriminate accurately betwen the tastes of different realities"[106]. In the spiritual life it is essential that the nous should have life, so as to be able to distinguish the actions and consolations of God from the actions of the devil. In a healthy nous which devotes itself continually to divine realities, "the soul's passible aspect becomes a godlike weapon"[107]. Then the whole soul is healthy. The nous is a chariot drawing the soul either to God or to the devil and deeds of sin. In any case, when the nous is healthy, it is given assurance by God. The Apostle Paul's commandment about having a pure and living nous is clear: "Let every one be fully convinced in his own nous" (Rom. 14, 5).

Although the nous is a power of the soul in the sense which concerns us in this section, it does have other powers and energies. Nicetas Stethatos teaches that the nous has four powers: understanding, acuteness, apprehension and quick-

---

103. Ibid. 2, 2, 23
104. Philok. 2, p. 54, 9
105. Evagrius. Philok. 1, p. 67, 101
106. St. Diadochos of Photiki. Philok. 1, p. 261, 30
107. St. Thalassios. Philok. 2, p. 315, 49

wittedness. These four powers of the nous must be united with the four general virtues of the soul: the nous's understanding must be united with the soul's self-restraint, acuteness with moral judgement, apprehension with justice and quick-wittedness with courage. This forms the "chariot of fire traversing the heavens" which confronts the three passions of avarice, sensuality and ambition[108].

These divisions of the nous in us are no doubt incomprehensible to us, but the Fathers, through their struggles, and by the illumination of the Holy Spirit, distinguished and traced these powers and became familiar with the whole inner make-up of the soul. A person living "in the revelation", illuminated by the Holy Spirit, comes to know all the depths of the soul and all the powers of the nous, which are unknown and inconceivable to anyone who is far from grace. Moreover, to anyone far from God the whole man is obscure and unknown.

All these things which we have mentioned show the natural state of the nous as it functions in the natural man, in the man of God. "The nous's task is to reject any thought that secretly vilifies a fellow being"[109]. In the natural state the nous repulses the thoughts which proceed from the devil and in general repulses every thought which is contrary to love. Likewise the nous is perfected when it grows rich with knowledge of God. "The nous is perfect when transformed by spiritual knowledge"[110]. This knowledge is knowledge of God and of things created, in a way transcending knowledge. "A perfect nous is one which by true faith and in a manner beyond all unknowing supremely knows the supremely Unknowable and surveys the entirety of God's creation"[111].

---

108. Practical chapters, 12. Gk. Philok. 3, p. 275
109. St. Thalassios. Philok. 2, p. 327, 38
110. Ibid. p. 316, 54
111. St. Maximus. Philok. 2, p. 99, 99

Sickness of the nous

The nous was blackened, darkened, sickened by the fall. It ceased to be perfect. The same thing happens every time man commits sin.

The devil's first battle is with the nous. The demons try to enslave it when a man subsequently gives his consent and commits sin. St. Maximus teaches that the demons, taking advantage of the passions which exist in the soul, arouse impassioned thoughts, through which they fight the nous and force it to give its assent to sin. A great battle is waged by the demons to capture the nous and attract it to the impassioned thought. When the nous has been defeated, "they lead it to sin in the mind and, when this has been done, they induce it, captive as it is, to commit the sin in action". But the evil does not stop there. After having desolated the heart by means of passionate thoughts, the demons retreat. Yet in spite of that, the idol of sin remains in the nous. St. Maximus, referring to the Lord's words: "when you see the 'abomination of desolation'... standing in the holy place..." (Matt. 24, 15), says that man's nous is a temple of God in which the demons, having desolated the soul by means of impassioned thoughts, "set up the idol of sin"[112].

This is the sickness of the nous. Not only is it captured but it also falls ill, since the idol of sin remains as a continuing wound and a cause of new sin. We say that in this situation the nous has been captured by the devil and the passions, and "a nous dominated by the passions thinks base thoughts". This is manifested by words and deeds[113]. All that a man says and does manifests the sickness or health of his nous. Therefore those who have the gift of discrimination discern the condition of every man's nous by his outward movements and his words. Attachment of the nous to the senses "enslaves it

---

112. Ibid. p. 70, 31
113. St. Thalassios. Philok. 2, p. 319, 4

to bodily pleasure"[114]. The nous, instead of turning towards God and uniting with Him, turns to unite with the senses and so becomes a slave. This slavery, this captivity is sickness of the nous. And naturally this sickness causes the death of the nous.

In what follows we shall cite patristic passages to describe some **conditions** and **characteristics** of the sickness of the nous.

Holy Scripture speaks of the depraved nous, the mind of flesh: "men of corrupt nous and destitute of the truth" (1 Tim. 6, 5). All who resist the truth are "men of corrupt nous" (2 Tim. 3, 8). The Apostle Paul, referring to a heretic of his time, says that he is "puffed up by his fleshly nous" (Col. 2, 18). This passage clearly implies that when a man is sensuous, deprived of the operation of the Holy Spirit, as is mentioned in the Apostle Paul's theology, he has a fleshly nous. Elsewhere the nous which is far from God is characterised as "debased" (Rom. 1, 28). The Apostle Paul does not want the Christians to live as the Gentiles "in the futility of their nous" (Ephesians 4, 17). And the Fathers, such as St. Thalassios, speak of how the nous moves away from the realm of spiritual knowledge when the passible part of the soul departs from its virtues[115].

The sickness of the nous is also characterised by the word "darkening". The nous as an image of God is "luminous". But when it withdraws from God and loses its natural state, it is blackened, darkened. Hesychios the Presbyter teaches that the eight principal thoughts of evil, under which every evil thought is subsumed, approach the entrance to the heart. And if they find the nous unguarded, they enter the heart one by one, each in its own time. Whichever of them enters, "introduces a swarm of other evil thoughts as well; and having thus darkened the nous, it stimulates the body and provokes it to sinful actions"[116]. In another place too Hesy-

---

114. Ibid. p. 316, 55
115. Ibid. 56
116. Philok. 1, p. 194, 177

chios teaches that when a person leads a life of sin and dissoluteness, "he darkens his nous"[117]. Therefore patristic teaching advises us to keep watch over our thoughts so that our "nous
will not be darkened but, on the contrary, will see"[118].

So we can speak of the blindness and inability of the nous
to see things clearly. And when our nous is darkened, we do
not have a pure and open passage to our neighbour. Everything is defiled and darkened, with terrible and upsetting
consequences for our life. Just as clouds hide the sun, so evil
thoughts bring shadows to the mind and ruin it[119]. Our nous
is darkened and remains unproductive either when we speak
words of worldly import or, entertaining such words in our
mind, we associate with them, or when our body involves
itself with the nous in sensory things. Then we immediately
lose our fervour, compunction, intimacy with God and spiritual knowledge. Therefore "so long as we concentrate our attention on the nous, we are enlightened; but when we are not
attentive to it we are in darkness"[120].

Darkening is also called blindness, because it is real blindness of the nous. And the nous is made blind by the three
passions of avarice, self-esteem and sensual pleasure[121]. According to Nicetas Stethatos, the ignorance of an earthy nous,
which is fog and deep darkness, "covering the eyes of the soul,
makes it dark and obscures perception of the divine and the
human, so that it is unable to gaze upon the rays of divine
light or to delight in those good things which no eye has seen
nor ear heard nor the heart of man conceived"[122]. The nous,
and the soul in general, is incapable of contemplating God

117. Ibid. p. 174, 69
118. St. Thalassios. Philok. 2, p. 312, 86
119. Ladder. Step. 26, Summary. CWS p. 257
120. Hesychios the Priest. Philok. 1, p. 184, 127
121. St. Mark the Ascetic. Philok. 1, p. 184, 127
122. Natural chapters, ch. 87. Philok. 3, p. 320 (in Gk.)

and being illuminated. And this is its sickness and death. In this condition man cannot find the truth. St. Basil the Great teaches that as the eye cannot see an object clearly when it keeps shifting sometimes to the side and sometimes repeatedly up and down, so it is with the eye of the soul, that is, the nous. "Distracted by thousands of cares over the world, it cannot gaze clearly at the truth"[123].

Another sick state of the nous is callousness, insensibility, indifference: "To have an insensitive heart is to have dulled the nous," says St. John of the Ladder[124]. When the demons come to the soul and extinguish the light of the nous, there is no longer in us sobriety or discernment, self-knowledge or shame, and we are left with "indifference, insensitivity, want of discernment, and blindness"[125].

The ailing nous is a captive, a prisoner. "Reprehensible passions chain the nous, binding it to sensible objects"[126]. St. Maximus says that just as a sparrow tied by the leg cannot fly, much as it tries, because it is pulled down to the ground, "similarly, when the nous that has not yet attained dispassion flies up towards heavenly knowledge, it is held back by the passions and pulled down to the earth"[127]. No matter how hard it tries to fly to heavenly knowledge, it cannot do so unless it frees itself from the passions. The passions bind it and hold it captive to the earth. The nous is made coarse by the various passions and cannot pray purely to God[128].

"A conceited nous is a waterless cloud carried along by the winds of self-esteem and pride"[129].

---

123. St. Basil the Great. FC vol. 13, p. 9. Letter 2
124. Ladder. Step 6. CWS p. 133
125. Ibid. Step. 26. CWS p. 230
126. St. Thalassios. Philok. 2, p. 321, 41
127. St. Maximus. Philok. 2, p. 63, 85
128. Evagrius. Philok. 1, p. 61, 51
129. St. Thalassios. Philok. 2, p. 326, 26

A nous which is sick with the passion of self-esteem is under an illusion, trying to enclose the Deity in shapes and forms[130].

Hesychios the Priest also describes the way in which the nous becomes a captive. If it is inexperienced and lives without watchfulness, it at once begins to entertain whatever impassioned fantasy appears in it, that is, what the fantasy brings with it, and then it converses with it and makes responses. In this way "our own thoughts are conjoined to the demonic fantasy". And as fantasy waxes and burgeons so the nous sickens[131].

Apart from the sick states of the nous already mentioned, there is also defilement. The Apostle Paul says: "To the pure all things are pure, but to those who are defiled and unbelieving nothing is pure; but even their nous and conscience are defiled" (Tit. 1, 15). The nous can be defiled not only by a great, deadly sin, but also with one careless word. But this happens mainly to one who has tasted the joy and effect of prayer[132].

St. John of the Ladder speaks of a flick of the nous in which, without passage of time, without word or image, a sudden passionate urge lays hold of the victim. The passion in a man's soul may be evoked by a simple move without any previous complex thought[133].

So the nous's sickness, from what has been said, is corruption, darkening, blindness, indifference and insensitivity, bondage and captivity, illusion, defilement and a flick of the mind. Everything which expels the nous and turns it aside from its natural motion is a disease resulting in the nous's death. In this state the whole man is sick, defiled and dead.

---

130. Evagrius. Philok. 1, p. 68, 116
131. Philok. 1, p. 187, 144
132. Ladder. Step 28. CWS p. 279f
133. Ibid. Step. 15. CWS p. 182

Healing of the nous

Orthodox living presupposes above all that the noetic faculty of the soul should be healed. Since, when the nous is darkened, the whole soul is darkened and defiled, the curing of the nous results in the curing of our whole being. We now turn to the subject of healing the nous.

In order to clarify the subject, we shall limit ourselves to two basic points: first, how this healing is achieved and then what are the results.

It is a basic teaching of our saints that the nous is healed through guarding the nous; this is called watchfulness. The guarding of the nous is a "watchtower commanding a view over our whole spiritual life"[134]. The guarding of the nous has been called "light-producing and lightning-producing and light-giving and fire-bearing" and it surpasses many virtues. The guarding of the nous is that which by Christ's power can change men from being sinful, indecent, profane, ignorant, uncomprehending and unjust to being just, responsive, pure, holy and wise. Beyond these things, guarding the nous can enable men to "contemplate mystically and to theologise"[135]. Through guarding the nous a man is purified, is made holy and becomes capable of theology. According to Philotheos of Sinai, we should be extremely strict in guarding our nous. When we see an evil thought we must rebut it and immediately call upon Christ. "Jesus in his gentle love will say: 'Behold I am by your side and ready to help you'". But it is also necessary and required to guard the nous[136].

However, guarding the nous is not only the effort not to let evil thoughts come and capture the nous, but it is a variety of actions. Since evil thoughts come from the passions, the guarding of the nous begins with self-control in food and

---

134. Hesychios the Priest. Philok. 1, p. 175, 76
135. Ibid. p. 192, 171
136. Philok. 3, p. 26, 26

drink, rejection of all kinds of evil thoughts, and stillness of heart[137]. The guarding of the nous is combined with watchfulness and the Jesus Prayer, because "there is no progress whatsoever in guarding the nous without watchfulness, humility and the Jesus Prayer"[138]. This means that this guarding cannot achieve its end unless one makes the effort to be freed from passions and to acquire the virtues.

To heal a deadened nous takes courage. The Fathers lay great stress on the importance of courage for the spiritual life. A brave athlete does not give up or lose heart even in a circumstance where he bows to the devil, but he hopes in God. "A courageous soul resurrects his dying nous"[139]. A good horse, when mounted, warms up and quickens its pace. The singing of psalms is the pace and a resolute nous is the horse[140]. It is only courage that gives a man heart to revive his nous, dead from sin.

However, the nous has many tasks: all of Christ's commandments must be kept if it is to be revived. For if death comes to the nous through not keeping the commandments, its resurrection and restoration to life will come through keeping them. One must be concerned to love God, remember God, remember the Kingdom, remember the zeal of the holy martyrs, remember God's very presence, remember the holy and spiritual powers, remember departure from this life, remember judgement, sentence and punishment[141]. Stillness, prayer, love and self-control are "a four-horse chariot bearing the nous to heaven"[142]. The nous is illumined when a person does not neglect the practice of virtues[143].

Nicetas Stethatos, disciple of St. Symeon the New Theolo-

---

137. Hesychios the Priest. Philok. 1, p. 191, 165
138. Ibid. p. 192, 168
139. Ladder. Step 13. CWS p. 161
140. Ibid. Step. 28. CWS p. 279
141. Ibid. Step 6, CWS p. 134
142. St. Thalassios. Philok. 2, p. 308, 24
143. St. Thalassios. Philok. 2, p. 309, 48

gian and in the same tradition, states that "the short way for beginners to acquire virtue is silence of the lips and closed eyes and ears". This stillness of the senses through closing the entrances helps the nous to see itself clearly and to discern movements. Thus the nous "like a commander stands independently between ideas, judging and separating the good thoughts from the bad ones", accepting the good ones and "laying up spiritual goods" by which it is nourished and strengthened and filled with light, and casting the other thoughts into the abyss of oblivion, "shaking off their bitterness"[144].

This passage deserves our full attention. We see clearly that a nous which is freed from enslavement to the senses by silencing the lips and suspending external stimulation becomes the regulator of the soul. It does not allow putrid and satanic thoughts to enter the so-called unconscious, the depth of the soul. Good thoughts which nourish and give life to the person enter the depth of his soul. Thus all the conceptual images and actions of a man whose thought is the ruling emperor are pure.

St. Maximus further exhorts the spiritual combatant: "Bridle your soul's incensive power with love, quench its desire with self-control, give wings to its intelligence with prayer, and the light of your nous will never be darkened"[145]. It is a basic instruction of the Fathers that at the beginning of our inner spiritual work to heal the nous we must keep it pure. Of course this must also be continued afterward. St. John of the Ladder instructs: "Control your impetuous nous in your distracted body... fix your nous to your soul as to the wood of a cross, strike it with alternating hammer blows like an anvil... hold back your nous, so busy with its own concerns"[146]. But this work must be joined with the effort to protect God's claims on one's life. It should be emphasised that the practical man subjects his nous in a different way from the illuminated

---

144. Practical chapters, ch. 26. Gk. Philok. 3, p. 278
145. Philok. 2, p. 110, 80
146. Ladder. Step 4. CWS p. 104

man. Similarly there is a difference according to the man's spiritual age and the work that he is doing to control his nous. "The man engaged in ascetic practice can readily submit his nous to prayer, while the contemplative can readily submit prayer to his nous"[147].

This work achieves that healing of the nous which is called purification in the language of the Fathers. A nous that has been defiled by passions must be purified. This work of purification is performed by the Holy Spirit. "Only the Holy Spirit can purify the nous." Therefore it is necessary above all that the Holy Spirit should dwell in us, "so that we may have the lamp of spiritual knowledge always burning within us". When the mighty one enters the soul and overthrows the despoiler, then what has been taken captive can be set free, otherwise this is impossible[148].

Nicetas Stethatos describes how the nous is purified. "As we have five senses, so we also have five corresponding ascetic practices. The five ascetic practices are vigils, meditation, prayer, self-control and hesychia. One needs to join sight with vigils, hearing with meditation, smell with prayer, taste with self-control, and touch with hesychia. In this way the nous is quickly purified, refined, and becomes dispassionate and perspicacious[149].

Hesychios the Priest gives greater attention to the Jesus Prayer, because it purifies the nous from foul thoughts. Anyone troubled by sickening food takes the appropriate remedy and gets rid of it. The same is also done by prayer with regard to the defiled nous. When the nous, having received evil thoughts, swallows them and feels their bitterness "it can easily expel them and get rid of them completely by means of the Jesus Prayer uttered from the depths of the heart"[150].

---

147. Ilias the Presbyter. Philok. 3, p. 48, 9
148. St. Diadochos of Photiki, Philok. 1, p. 260, 28
149. Practical chapters, ch. 91. Gk. Philok. 3. p. 295
150. Philok. 1, p. 196, 188

So purifying the nous is not a matter simply of finding the thoughts which have entered it, but of expelling them, which is not achieved by rational thoughts and analyses, but only by the Jesus prayer. And when we say 'prayer' we mean the action of the Holy Spirit which comes into the heart when Christ is remembered in the heart. St. Gregory Palamas emphasises that the action of the nous, consisting of thoughts, is very quickly purified "by devoting time to prayer, especially prayer of a single word". When a man devotes himself to prayer, the action of his intellect is cured. The evil thoughts cease, but the whole soul is not pure. The power which produces the action cannot be purified unless "all the other powers of the soul" are also purified. All those powers must be purified by self-control, love, and so forth, because otherwise the man is deluded if he thinks that he has been purified[151]. To limit sleep, that is to keep vigil, contributes to this purification: "A vigilant eye makes the nous pure"[152].

If the nous's ignorance, which is a deep darkness covering the soul's vision, makes it dim and obscures the understanding of things divine and human, repentance cures it. Here we can also see the great value of repentance. Therefore St. Nicetas Stethatos, who describes the darkening of the nous, also offers us healing through repentance. "But when its eyes have been uncovered through repentance, the soul sees these things clearly, gives ear to them with knowledge and grasps them with understanding." At the same time it acquires knowledge of God and as a result "through God's wisdom it tells the good wonders of God to all"[153]. Repentance which takes place in deep mourning and joined with confession is what unveils the eyes of the soul to see the great things of God.

---

151. EF p. 410, 3. Gk. Philok. 4, p. 133, 3
152. Ladder. Step 20. CWS p. 196
153. Practical chapters, ch. 87. Gk. Philok. 3, p. 320

In the writings of the Fathers much is said about the return of the nous to the heart, the return of energy to the essence. A letter of St. Basil the Great to his friend St. Gregory contains the famous passage: "For when the nous is not engaged by external affairs nor diffused through the senses over the whole world, it retires within itself. Then it ascends spontaneuously to the consideration of God. Illumined by that splendour, it becomes forgetful of its own nature. Since, then, it does not drag the soul down either to the thought of sustenance or to a solicitude for bodily apparel, but enjoys freedom from earthly cares, it turns all its zeal to the acquisition of eternal goods"[154]. I have quoted this whole passage because it is expressive and was therefore used by St. Gregory Palamas in his dispute with Barlaam. St. Basil the Great says that the nous which is not scattered among things of the senses in the world outside returns to itself and through itself rises to the vision of God. Then, illumined and shining with beauty, it is not interested in earthly things and forgets even its own nature.

The return of the scattered nous to the heart – that is, the return of the energy to the essence – is the cure of the nous. There the nous finds its real place. On its return it first finds the physical heart and then the metaphysical, spiritual heart. The ascetic "descends into his inmost heart, into his natural heart first, and thence into those depths that are no longer of the flesh. He finds his deep heart – reaches the profound spiritual, metaphysical core of his being; and looking into it he sees that the existence of mankind is not something alien and extraneous to him but is inextricably bound up with his own being"[155]. The return of the nous to the heart is in reality a unifying of the nous, that is, a union of nous and heart. This union is confirmed by tears of compunction and a sweet sense of the love of God. "Tears of compunction during prayer are a

---

154. Letter 2. FC vol. 13, p. 7
155. Archim. Sophrony: Saint Silouan. p. 47

sure sign that the nous is united with the heart, and that pure prayer has found its prime place û the initial step in ascent to God. This is why ascetics rate tears so highly"[156]. On entering the heart, the nous detaches itself from every image, both visual and mental[157]. The doors of the heart are closed to every foreign element and "the soul penetrates into the 'darkness' of a quite especial nature, and is subsequently deemed worthy of standing ineffably before God with a pure nous"[158].

In discussing the return of the nous to the heart, of the nous's energy to its essence, we should speak of the three motions of the nous as described by St. Dionysios the Areopagite. He says that the soul and the nous have three movements. The first is the circular one, "the entrance into itself and away from what is outside, so there is an inner concentration of its spiritual powers". In this movement the soul first returns to itself, assembles all its powers and in that way rises towards the God who is without beginning or end and who is beyond all things. This way is fixed, it does not let the mind wander, and thus concentrated it rises to God. The nous is released from everything created, it discards every notion of creation, every fantasy, it is united with the heart through repentance, and there God is revealed, since the nous is united with Him. This is the motion of what is called apophatic theology. The second movement is in a straight line, when the soul, "progressing towards the things around it, rises from things outside, as if from some colourful and multiple symbols, to simple and unified contemplations". This is what is called natural theoria or cataphatic theology, which sees God in nature. Through contemplation of nature the soul is lifted up towards God. It is a method which is open to delusion, because many people who have learned in this way to look straight at God's creatures are deluded and come

---

156. Ibid. p. 133
157. Ibid. p. 151
158. Ibid. p. 145

to worship created things more than Creation and the Creator. The third movement, called the spiral one, is a link between the previous two movements. The Fathers give priority to the first movement, called the circular one, because it forms a circle. The nous returns to the heart and through the heart is lifted up to vision of God. in this way delusion is avoided[159]. This circular motion is attained through noetic prayer, in which the athlete of the spirit struggles "to return the nous to itself, to propel it not in a straight line but in the circular motion that is infallible"[160].

The return of the nous to the heart is achieved by prayer, especially noetic prayer, when the nous, pure from any thoughts and ideas prays to God without distraction. Therefore Neilos the Ascetic blesses the nous which prays without distraction and immaterially to God: "Blessed is the nous that is completely free from forms during prayer. Blessed is the nous that, undistracted in its prayer, acquires an ever greater longing for God. Blessed is the nous that during prayer is free from materiality and stripped of all possessions. Blessed is the nous that has acquired complete freedom from sensations during prayer"[161].

Since we have seen the ways in which healing of the nous takes place, in what follows we shall look at the results of healing. That is to say, we shall see from the works of the Fathers what happens to the nous directly after the cure or during that process.

One of the first fruits is dispassion. A dispassionate nous is "one which has conquered its passions and transcended grief and joy". In this state, when tribulations come, it rejoices, and when high spirits and joys come, it is self-controlled, not going beyond the bounds[162]. This dispassion is the life-giving

---

159. St. Dionysios the Areopagite. Divine Names, ch. 4, 8f. CWS p. 78
160. St. Gregory Palamas. Triads, 1, 2, 8. CWS p. 46
161. Philok. 1, p. 68, 117-120
162. Nicetas Stethatos. Practical chapters, ch. 92

death of the Lord (cf. 2 Cor. 4, 10), which comes about through the work of the Holy Spirit[163]. When the nous is freed from external stimuli and cleansed from the defilements of sin, it sees things more clearly. It sees all the methods of the evil one, even the moment when he is preparing for warfare. It has a clear knowledge of all the wiles of the evil one[164]. The dispassionate nous "forms conceptual images that are also passion-free, whether the body is asleep or awake"[165]. The clearest conscience is not troubled with impassioned thoughts during sleep when the mind is inactive..

Purification too is very closely connected with dispassion. "A pure nous is one divorced from ignorance and illumined by divine light"[166]. Purification of the nous is important because in this way a person acquires knowledge of God. The pure nous is taught sometimes by God, sometimes by the angelic powers, and sometimes "by the nature of the things that it contemplates"[167]. The pure nous, according to St. Maximus, "is occupied either with passion-free conceptual images of human affairs, or with the natural contemplation of things visible or invisible, or with the light of the Holy Trinity"[168]. It understands the Scriptures: "And he opened their under-standing, that they might comprehend the Scriptures" (Luke 24, 45).

According to St. Maximus there is an attraction between a pure nous and knowledge. "Through love knowledge of God naturally draws to itself the pure nous"[169]. The Holy Spirit finds the pure nous and "initiates it accordingly into the mysteries of the age to be"[170]. In this way the person becomes

---

163. Ibid. Natural chapters, ch. 20
164. St. Mark the Ascetic. Philok. 1, p. 121, 167
165. St. Thalassios. Philok. 2, p. 310, 54
166. St. Maximus. Philok. 2, p. 56, 33
167. Ibid. p. 98, 94
168. Ibid. p. 64, 97
169. Ibid. p. 56, 32
170. St. Thalassios. Philok. 2, p. 329, 75

a theologian. For theology is not given by human knowledge and zeal, but by the work of the Holy Spirit which dwells in the pure heart. The nous which has been purified "becomes for the soul a sky full of the stars of radiant and glorious thoughts, with the sun of righteousness shining in it, sending the beaming rays of theology out into the world"[171]. Therefore Abba Sisoes, in answer to Abba Ammon's question as to whether, in reading Scripture, it was necessary to concentrate on the words so as to be ready to answer questions that one might be asked, said "That is not necessary; it is better to possess yourself through purity of spirit and to be without anxiety and then to speak"[172].

Real theology is not a fruit of material concentration but a manifestation of the Holy Spirit. When a man's nous is purified, then he is illuminated and if his nous has the capacity, that is, wisdom, he can theologise. Therefore we say that his whole life, even his body itself, is theology. The purified man is wholly a theology. The Fathers sometimes made use of the earlier Fathers, not because they did not have experience themselves, but in order to confirm this experience, especially at the time when there were men who denied it.

Through purification of the nous we also gain real knowledge of ourselves. The philosopher Barlaam maintained that holiness and perfection cannot be found "without division, reasoning and analysis", so he held that anyone desiring to possess perfection and holiness must be taught "methods of distinction, reasoning and analysing". But St. Gregory Palamas opposed this view as "a heresy of the Stoics and Pythagoreans". We Christians, he taught, do not regard as true knowledge that which is found in words and reasonings, but that demonstrated by deeds and life, which is not only true but also sure and irrefutable". He goes on to say that no one can know himself through distinctions, reasonings and ana-

---

171. Nicetas Stethatos. Natural chapters, ch. 67
172. Sayings. p. 181, 17

lyses unless his nous has been made free of conceit and evil by severe penitence and intensive asceticism. No one who has not freed his nous from conceit and evil, that is to say, who has not purified his nous, is going to be aware of his poverty, which is a useful beginning for self-knowledge[173].

This passage is very important, because many people today teach that one can come to self-knowledge through self-analysis and psychoanalysis. But this is a delusion and can lead one to frightful results. When someone analyses himself, he is most likely to end in schizophrenia. The ascetic method is simple. Using the methods which we have described – that is, guarding the nous, purifying it and returning it to the heart through penitence and noetic prayer, and keeping Christ's commandments – we try to free the nous from its images and its captivity to sensual things so that as it returns to the heart it can see its inner desolation. Self-knowledge comes through the work of the Holy Spirit. It is only when the grace of God, along with our own work, has illumined our soul that we know accurately every detail of our being. Therefore the healing of our nous reveals the existence of the passions, whereupon, illumined by the Holy Spirit and empowered by it, we can wage war against them.

When the nous is healed it is left pure and free from fantasy and debility[174].

Another fruit of the cure of the nous is freedom. Previously a prisoner, now it is freed and "full of joy, winging its way towards the heavenly realm that is its native land"[175]. When it is freed of passions, whatever it does will be counted as a pure offering to God[176].

When the nous is released from the passions, which are its deadness, it is resurrected. So one can speak of the resurrec-

---

173. Triads, 1, 3, 13
174. St. Diadochos. Philok. 1, p. 267, 49
175. Ilias the Presbyter. Philok. 3, p. 61, 113
176. Ibid. p. 48, 10

tion of the nous. Nicetas Stethatos relates this resurrection to the miracle of the raising of Lazarus. Just as Lazarus died, so the nous dies of sin and is buried. As Christ comes to Bethany to raise up Lazarus, so He comes to our dead nous to raise it from the decay caused by passions. And just as Lazarus' sisters Martha and Mary go in tears and lamentation to meet Him, so "prudence and justice, plunged into grief over the death of our nous go in tears to meet Him". Justice is hardship and spirited work, while prudence is spiritual work and contemplation[177].

We find this correlation between the two miracles, that is, the raising of Lazarus and the raising of the dead nous in many of our Orthodox hymns sung in the church. I should like to quote two of them.

"Let us hasten to send forth our theoria and praxis yoked together in a prayer to Christ, that through His awesome authority to give life, we may offer Him our nous dead and buried like Lazarus, as a palm of righteousness and cry: 'Blessed is He that comes'"[178]. In this troparion it seems that Martha is the praxis and Mary is the theoria through which Christ is called to resurrect the dead nous.

"Let us in faithful imitation of Martha and Mary send inspired deeds as a delegation to the Lord asking Him to come and raise our nous lying horridly dead in the tomb, senseless with neglect of the fear of God, now utterly feelingless and without vital energy, and cry: 'Behold, Lord, just as of old in Your compassion You raised Your friend Lazarus with awesome authority, so in your great mercy give life to us all'"[179]. The nous is dead in the tomb and has no vital energy, therefore we exhort ourselves to send Martha and Mary, that is, actions, to Christ to resurrect it. A nous in control of itself (resurrected) becomes a temple of the Holy Spirit[180].

---

177. Gnostic chapters, ch. 98f
178. Thursday Matins before Palm Sunday. Gk. Phos edition, p. 357
179. Wednesday Vespers before Palm Sunday. Ibid. p. 355
180. St. Thalassios. Philok. 2, p. 322, 55

In this state the pure nous is illuminated[181] and seized with rapture. It delights in the vision of God and talks with the Lord. When the Fathers speak of the rapture and ecstasy of the nous they do not consider that the nous goes out of the body as happened to Pythia, but that it is freed from bodily and worldly care and offers itself to God, without losing consciousness of the world. He who has unceasing prayer experiences ecstasy of the nous. This ecstasy is called rapture and is a form of theoria.

The pure nous is illuminated, illumined. At this point we regard it as essential to speak about this light, especially the light of the nous, because it is spoken of in the patristic writings.

St. Diadochos, an expert in mystical theology, refers to this light of the nous: "You should not doubt that the nous, when it begins to be strongly energised by the divine light, becomes so completely translucent that it sees its own light vividly." But he means that this takes place "when the power of the soul gains control over the passions"[182]. Likewise in another place he says: "Those who meditate unceasingly upon this glorious and holy name in the depths of their heart can sometimes see the light of their own nous"[183].

This teaching of St. Diadochos is embraced also by Kallistos and Ignatios Xanthopoulos[184].

St. Neilos the Ascetic teaches that "when the angel of God comes to us, with his presence alone he puts an end to all adverse energy within the nous and makes its light energise without illusion"[185].

The nous is in the image of God. And inasmuch as God is light, the nous too has light. In this sense the saints say that

---

181. Nicetas Stethatos. Gnostic chapters, ch. 18
182. Philok. 1, p. 265, 40
183. Ibid. p. 270, 59
184. Writings, p. 265, 95
185. Philok. 1, p. 64, 75

man can see the light of his nous. But these things happen to the natural man, while in the fallen man the nous is blackened; it is darkened and hidden by the passions. However, when a man is freed from the passions and illumined by God, then during prayer he is able to see the light of his nous.

In his "Triads" St. Gregory Palamas refers to this subject in many places. Citing various words of the saints, he ends by saying: "Do you understand clearly, brother, that the nous freed from passions can see itself as a light during prayer and shines with divine light?"[186]. Indeed, "the nous, seeing itself, sees itself as light"[187], but St. Gregory continues: "Such is every purified nature not covered with the veil of evil". When it is not wearing the veil of evil, "it sees itself as a spiritual light"[188]. This vision of the light of the nous comes through the work of the Holy Spirit. "The purified and illuminated nous, when clearly participating in the grace of God, also beholds other mystical and supernatural visions – for in seeing itself, it sees more than itself: It does not simply perceive some other object, or simply its own image, but rather the glory impressed on its own image by the grace of God"[189].

This teaching indicates that the purified nous sees, not its own image, but the glory of Christ mirrored in it by the grace of God. The saints see this image changed from glory to glory, "that is, in quality of brightness in us, as the divine radiance becomes more and more distinct"[190]. Just as the sensory eye cannot be active unless light shines on it from outside, so the nous cannot see with its noetic sense unless the divine light shines on it[191].

---

186. Triads, 1, 3, 7
187. Ibid. 1, 3, 8
188. Ibid.
189. Ibid. 2, 3, 11. CWS p. 58
190. Ibid. 1, 3, 7
191. Ibid. 1, 3, 9

Briefly we can say that according to the teaching of St. Gregory Palamas, the nous, as the image of God, is light, but it is darkened by passions. It is only when the divine light shines and the nous is purified, that it can see not just its own light, but the shining which is formed in its image by the grace of God. Sensory vision in itself cannot be of any help at all to a person unless there is also a sensory light. The same is true of the vision of divine light in the nous of man. St. Gregory Palamas developed all this teaching because the philosopher Barlaam maintained that through human knowledge, by the elaboration of human thought, one can see God and acquire knowledge of God. But this is entirely mistaken.

In his book 'Saint Silouan the Athonite' Archimandrite Sophrony writes as follows about this natural light of the nous: "Attaining these bounds where 'day and night come to an end' (Job 26, 10), man contemplates the beauty of his own nous which many identify with Divine being. They do see a light but it is not the True Light in which there 'is no darkness at all'. It is the natural light peculiar to the nous of man created in God's image. This light of the nous, which excels every other light of empirical knowledge, might still just as well be called darkness, since it is the darkness of divestiture and God is not in it. And perhaps in this instance more than any other we should listen to the Lord's warning, 'Take heed therefore that the light which is in you be not darkness' (Luke 11, 35). The first prehistoric, cosmic catastrophe – the fall of Lucifer, son of the morning, who became the prince of darkness – was due to his enamoured contemplation of his own beauty, which ended up in his self-deification"[192]. In another place the same monk writes about the natural light, which is the darkness of divestiture: "If we would 'situate' the spiritual whereabouts of this darkness we could say that it is to be found on the outskirts of uncreated Light. But when hesy-

---

192. Archim. Sophrony, Saint Silouan, p. 162

chastic prayer is practised without due repentance and without the prayer being wholly directed up to God, the soul, denuded of all imaginings may abide for a brief while in this 'darkness of divestiture' without having beheld God, for God ipso facto is not yet in this darkness.

"Dwelling in the darkness of divestiture, the nous knows a peculiar delight and sense of peace. If at this point it turns in on itself it can perceive something akin to light, which, however, is not yet the uncreated light of Divinity but a natural attribute of the nous created in the image of God.

Clearing the frontiers of time, such contemplation approaches the nous to knowledge of the intransitory, thereby possessing man of new but still abstract cognition. Woe to him who mistakes this wisdom for knowledge of the true God, and this contemplation for a communion in Divine being. Woe to him because the darkness of divestiture on the borders of true vision becomes an impenetrable pass and a stronger barrier between himself and God than the darkness due to the uprising of gross passion, or the darkness of obviously demonic instigations, or the darkness which results from loss of grace and abandonment by God. Woe to him, for he will have gone astray and fallen into delusion, since God is not in the darkness of divestiture. God reveals Himself in light and as light"[193].

It is difficult for us to make a comparison between the texts of St. Gregory Palamas and Archimandrite Sophrony on the subject of the light of the nous, for we lack the relevant experience. While externally there appear to be differences, we believe that the difference is a matter of style. We firmly believe that both Fathers have experiences of these states and only express a different aspect of this experience. We have the feeling, without being absolutely sure, that Archimandrite Sophrony is referring more to the intelligence which man deifies and loves in himself. Therefore he emphasises

---

193. Ibid. p. 179

epigrammatically that the darkness of divestiture constitutes an "impenetrable covering of Divinity and a wall" separating man from God more than the passions, the darkening of the demonic suggestions or abandonment of God. In reality this light of the nous is darkness, and in saying this he agrees absolutely with St. Gregory Palamas, as he also agrees absolutely with Palamas's teaching that theoria is pure action of God in man. "...the vision of Uncreated Divine Light is impossible unless one is in a state of illumination by grace – a state in virtue of which the act of beholding God is itself, above all, 'fellowship with God', union with Divine Life"[194]. Personally we cannot find a disagreement between these two eyewitnesses. They simply express themselves in different words, having in mind different conceptions which they wanted to confute.

Anyway it is a fact that when man's nous becomes one spirit with the Lord, "he sees spiritual things clearly"[195]. Dispassion of the nous stimulates it to attain spiritual knowledge of created beings[196]. The nous, freed from the passions and unceasingly illumined through contemplating created beings, becomes like light[197].

The healed nous is also granted vision of God. Naturally it does not see the essence of God, but His energy. When the saints see the light, they see it "when they acquire the divinising communion of the Spirit". That is to say, whenever they are united with God, they see the garment of their deification, "their nous being glorified and filled by the grace of the Word, beautiful beyond measure in His splendour"[198]. This is how the nous is glorified.

Then spiritual delight blossoms in the nous because "when

---

194. Monk of Mt. Athos p. 113. cf. Saint Silouan p. 173
195. St. Gregory Palamas. Triads, 1, 3, 17
196. St. Thalassios. Philok. 2. p. 326, 20
197. Ibid. p. 310, 50
198. St. Gregory Palamas. Triads, 1, 3, 5. CWS p. 33

the nous is engaged in the vision of intelligible realities, its delight in them is such that it can hardly be dragged away"[199]. United with God it becomes "wise, good, powerful, compassionate, merciful and long-suffering; in short, it includes within itself almost all the divine qualities. But when the nous withdraws from God and attaches itself to material things, either it becomes self-indulgent like some domestic animal, or like a wild beast it fights with men for the sake of these things"[200].

As a result of the healing of the nous, the body too is healed. Naturally, when we say that the body is healed we do not mean that it is freed from illnesses, even if this can succeed up to a point. We say 'up to a point' because many illnesses, especially of a nervous nature, originate from deadness of the nous, but the body is mainly freed from the passions of the flesh. St. Maximus says: "When you see that your nous reflects upon its conceptual images of the world with reverence and justice, you may be sure that your body too continues to be pure and sinless"[201]. The nous which meditates on divine things also keeps the body pure from the so-called bodily passions. First the nous is receptive to the pledge of the good things to come, then it rises towards the First Nous, and being sanctified "is itself transformed with the body which is attached to it, to make it more divine". Thus it too is prepared "for the absorption of the flesh by the Spirit in the age to come". Since the body will taste the eternal good things it is essential that it too is prepared by this life[202].

All the saints who live this life follow the same method for healing and purifying the nous and so they acquire the same teaching. We believe that the saints do not have their own particular views, they do not have different dogmatic posi-

---

199. St. Thalassios. Philok. 2, p. 315, 46
200. St. Maximus. Philok. 2, p. 74, 52
201. Ibid. p. 91, 52
202. Triads, 1, 3, 33

tions. Since they have the same experience, they have the same teaching. If we see differences at some points, it is because we interpret their teachings with erroneous presuppositions. If we try to see the different expression of each saint – since although they all have the same knowledge of God, they do not have the same wisdom – if we try to detect the real sense of each word, we will not find different teachings. In fact we ourselves are fragmented and inexperienced in spiritual matters, cut off from the living tradition of the Church, and therefore we see differences in the holy Fathers.

The Apostle Paul writes: "...be perfectly joined together in the same nous and in the same judgement" (1 Cor. 1, 10). The saints think the same. St. Gregory Palamas emphasises that "this suprarational knowledge is common to all those who have believed in Christ above concept"[203].

All that we have cited shows that the nous which has been affected by the passions is sick, weak, dying, deprived of its natural state and in need of healing. The Orthodox ascetic method describes how the nous is cured. This cure is indispensable, because with it the nous is purified and acquires spiritual knowledge of God, and this spiritual knowledge constitutes the salvation of man.

b) The Heart

One of our basic pleas to God is for salvation. "For peace from above and for the salvation of our souls let us pray to the Lord." Likewise most of the troparia end with the words "pray that our souls may be saved".

The salvation of the soul is not the stripping off of something but the putting on of Christ. It is not a negative state, but positive, chiefly communion and union with Christ. This communion takes place primarily in the heart. Therefore to

---

203. Ibid. 2, 3, 66

attain salvation is mainly to find the heart. When God grants us to find our heart, we are walking the path of salvation. Abba Pambo's words are characteristic: "If you have a heart, you can be saved"[204]. To have a heart means to find one's heart, within which one will be guided by God.

St. Mark the Ascetic, interpreting the Lord's words: "The kingdom of God is within you" (Luke 17, 21), says: "It is necessary in the first place to have the grace of the Holy Spirit energising the heart and so, in proportion to this energising, to enter into the kingdom of heaven"[205]. Therefore many Fathers regard it as essential to find the place of the heart, which is energised by the uncreated grace of God, because then the Christian has God as his teacher and is safely directed by the Holy Spirit.

What the heart is

When Holy Scripture and the Fathers speak of the heart they mean the metaphysical (spiritual) heart, but also the bodily heart. The heart is both the bodily organ and the centre of our being, in which we have communion and union with God. These two meanings of the heart meet at a point but at the same time they are differentiated. We shall look at this more analytically in what follows.

First of all let us consider the **metaphysical (spiritual) heart**. It is difficult enough for anyone to give a definition of the spiritual heart, because "truly the heart is an immeasurable abyss"[206]. Especially for the man of flesh who is ruled by logic and is living in the darkness of the life after the fall, it is impossible to know this spiritual heart. Therefore no definition can be found that will be able to describe the reality

---

204. Sayings, p. 166
205. Philokalia 1, p. 138, 149
206. St. Makarios. Philok. 3, p. 321, 83

which the spiritual man experiences. One can only formulate characterisations and images.

The spiritual man who lives by prayer "discovers that his heart is not just a physical organ or centre of his psychic life but something indefinable yet capable of being in contact with God, the Source of all being"[207]. The heart is the place where the entire spiritual life develops, the place energised by God's uncreated energy. In many people this "deep heart" is unknown not only to others but also to the person himself. For the grace of God effects the salvation of man hiddenly in his heart. What Archimandrite Sophrony says is characteristic: "The battle-ground of the spiritual struggle is, first and foremost, man's own heart, and he who would explore his own heart will appreciate the prophet David's reflection that 'the heart is deep' (Ps. 64, 6). The real life of the Christian is lived in this deep heart, hidden not only from alien eyes but also, in its fullness, from the owner of the heart himself. He who enters these secret recesses finds himself face to face with the mystery of being. Anyone who has ever given himself over with a pure heart to contemplation of his inner self knows how impossible it is to detect the spiritual processes of the heart, because in its profundity the heart touches upon that state of being where there are no processes"[208].

The Apostle Peter calls the heart a hidden person, "the hidden person of the heart" (1 Pet. 3, 4). It is really the place where God is sanctified: "Sanctify the Lord God in your hearts" (1 Pet. 3, 15). The grace of God dawns in the heart: "...until the day dawns and the morning star rises in your hearts" (2 Pet. 1, 19). In spite of man's union with God in the heart, the heart remains the "lesser" and God the greater, "God is greater than our heart" (1 Jn. 3, 20).

These scriptural passages have been pointed out, not in order to show how the Scriptures and the Fathers charac-

---

207. Archim. Sophrony. Saint Silouan. p. 233
208. Ibid. p. 10

terise the heart, which we can do in another section, but in order to show that many passages in the Scriptures and the Fathers speak about the heart.

We have already said that the nous is the eye of the heart, and pointed out that in many places the Fathers link the nous with the heart. In fact the heart is identified with the nous. St. Maximus the Confessor is characteristic: "...to cleanse the nous, which the Lord calls 'heart'"[209]. The nous is the eye of the soul, the heart is the centre of man's being, the centre of the spiritual world, but it seems that these two are linked together. It is very significant that St. Gregory Palamas, while speaking of purity of heart, goes on to analyse the nous and its purity[210].

We must certainly also keep in mind what we examined in the last section, that the Fathers call nous both the essence of the soul, which is in the heart, and the activity of the soul, which consists of thoughts. "The activity of the nous, consisting of thoughts and conceptual images is also called nous. Nous is also the power energising these things, which Scripture calls 'heart'"[211]. Nicephoros the Solitary, analysing and describing attention, says that some of the Fathers characterise attention as guarding the nous, others call it guarding of the heart, others watchfulness and others spiritual stillness. "But all these names mean the same thing. Just as of bread one can say a round, a slice, a piece, so also understand about this"[212]. Therefore, according to Nicephoros the Solitary, whether we say keeping the nous or guarding the heart, it is the same thing. This means that in patristic theology the nous is linked and identified with the heart. Therefore all that we wrote in the previous section about the nous is true of the heart as well, but here we shall say more about the heart.

---

209. Philokalia 2, p. 109, 73
210. EF p. 409-10
211. Ibid. p. 410, 3
212. Writings, p. 32. Gk. Philok. 4, p. 26

The connection between nous and heart appears also in the teaching of St. Diadochos of Photike. He teaches that from the moment of baptism the grace of God "is hidden in the depths of the nous", at the same time concealing its presence from the perception of the nous. When a person begins to love God "with full resolve", then "by means of the nous's perception, grace communicates something of its riches to his soul". But when he rids himself of all his material wealth, "then he discovers the place where the grace of God is hidden"[213]. In another chapter St. Diadochos says that through baptism grace comes to dwell in the depths of the soul, "that is to say, in the nous". And when we fervently remember God, "we feel divine longing well up within us from the depths of our heart"[214]. Here in these passages we see the linking of nous, soul and heart.

Since in the time of St. Diadochos the heretical idea of the Messalians predominated – the idea that the grace of God and Satan exist together in the same place in the soul – Diadochos made a distinction between what is known from Scripture and what is sensed by the nous. He emphasises that "before holy baptism, grace encourages the soul towards good from the outside, while Satan lurks in its depths, trying to block all the nous's ways of approach to the divine. But from the moment that we are reborn through baptism, the demon is outside, grace is within"[215]. So grace and Satan do not co-exist in the same place. Divine grace, through the perceptive faculty of the nous, delights the body with an ineffable joy, while the demons capture the soul by force through the bodily senses, especially when they find us lax in the spiritual struggle[216].

When we act according to the desires of the flesh, the grace

213. Philok. 1, p. 279, 77
214. Ibid. p. 280, 79
215. Ibid. p. 279, 76
216. Ibid. p. 280, 79

of God which has been in the depths of our spiritual heart since baptism, is hidden by the passions, so our effort is to try to uncover this grace through living an ascetic life in grace. This means that our effort must be to drive away the clouds which conceal our heart. St. Diadochos asks, since the devil is driven out of the heart by baptism, "How, then, can such an intruder, cast out in this shameful way, return and dwell together with the true Master who now lives freely in his own house?"[217].

This teaching of St. Diadochos is put here in order to make it clear that through baptism the grace of God enters into the deep heart, into the depth of the spiritual heart. And when this heart is hidden by the passions, we then have a great struggle to uncover it.

Theoleptos, Metropolitan of Philadelphia, teaches that the heart, that is to say the nous, is revealed when one lives by the hesychastic method. "When, having put an end to external distractions, you also master inner thoughts, the nous will begin to rise to spiritual words and actions"[218]. He urges us: "Put an end to conversations with the outer world and wrestle with your inner thoughts until you find the place of pure prayer and the home in which Christ dwells"[219].

From this passage it seems that the heart is the place which is revealed through asceticism in grace and the place in which Christ is made manifest. This is known to the man who is cleansed from the passions and from all sinful acts. To fallen man who lives far from God, the heart is hidden, completely unknown – he does not know whether it exists, whereas for the man who lives a godly life, the heart is known, a reality.

This teaching leads us to the view that the disclosure of the heart is in fact a disclosure of the person. When someone,

---

217. Ibid. p. 285, 84
218. Writings, p. 385f, 8. Gk. Philok. 4, p. 6
219. Ibid. p. 386, 9

through asceticism in grace, discovers the heart, where Christ is revealed and is King, he becomes a person, since the person is properly the 'likeness'. Thus to disclose the heart is to disclose the person.

It is not our intention at this point to develop the ontology of the person as it is presented in the teaching of the Fathers of the Church. They have written important studies on this subject. We believe, in accord with the Fathers' teachings, that the image of God is the potential likeness of God and the likeness of God is the image in action. In the same way man, created by God and re-created through holy baptism by the Church, is potentially a person. And when, through personal struggle and mainly by the grace of God, he attains the likeness, then he is an actual person. Therefore we maintain that ontologically all people are persons, even the devil himself, but soteriologically we are not all persons, since we have not all attained the likeness of God. Without wanting to disregard the ontology of the person, at this point we want to stress particularly the person's ascetic life, which is usually overlooked by contemporary theologians.

All that Archimandrite Sophrony says about this is characteristic: "In the Divine Being the Hypostasis constitutes the innermost esoteric principle of Being. Similarly, in the human being the hypostasis is the most intrinsic fundamental. 'Persona' is 'the hidden man of the heart, in that which is not corruptible...which, in the sight of God, is of great price' (1 Pet. 3, 4) – the most precious kernel of man's whole being, manifested in his capacity for self-knowledge and self-determination; in his possession of creative energy; in his talent for cognition not only of the created world but also of the Divine world. Consumed with love, man feels himself joined with his beloved God. Through this union he knows God, and thus love and cognition merge into a single act"[220].

The person is the "hidden man of the heart". This is the

---

220. Archim. Sophrony. His life is mine, p. 44

only formulation that can be made about the person, because it cannot be defined in scientific terms, since it is a mystical communion and union with Christ. Just as a definition cannot be given of the Church, but only that it is the Body of Christ, the same is true of the human person, the heart, in which there is mystical communion between God and man. "Scientific and philosophical knowledge may be formulated but the 'persona' is beyond definition and therefore incognisable from without, unless he himself reveals himself. Since God is a Secret God, so man has secret depths. He is neither the author of existence nor the end. God, not man, is the Alpha and Omega. Man's godlike quality lies in the mode of his being. Likeness in being is the likeness of which the Scriptures tell"[221]. Inasmuch as the person is not defined, the heart which is the person is also not defined.

The person is a reality which is born by the grace of God. "The 'persona' is born from on High and so is not subject to the laws of nature. The 'persona' transcends earthly bounds and moves in other spheres. It cannot be accounted for. It is singular and unique"[222]. Since the person is the heart, we can say that the heart too is reborn from on High. It is not a natural state. It is only by the grace of God that one can discern the place of the heart.

This rebirth of the person is in reality a revelation. The person is "a new birth from on high. An exquisite flower unfolds within us: the hypostasis – 'persona'. Like the Kingdom of God the 'persona' 'cometh not with observation' (Luke 17, 20). The process whereby the human spirit enters into the domain of divine eternity differs with each one of us"[223]. Thus the 'persona', like the heart, is born from above.

The heart is the place where God is revealed as love and light. "God reveals Himself mainly through the heart, as Love

---

221. Ibid. p. 43
222. Ibid. p. 43
223. Ibid. p. 42

and Light. In this light man contemplates the Gospel precepts as the reflection on earth of celestial Eternity, and the glory of Christ as the only-begotten of the Father û the glory the disciples saw on Mount Tabor. The personal revelation makes the general revelation of the New Testament spiritually familiar"[224].

We have examined these things in order to make it understandable that when a man discovers his heart, he is then properly a person. We also wanted to make it clear that the heart is the place which is disclosed through the ascetic life in grace and in which God is revealed. It is there that a man perceives the light of God and there that he overflows with God's love and with love for God. A man attains perception of the heart, but it is impossible to comprehend the whole life that is there.

According to the teaching of the Fathers, this spiritual heart is located in the **bodily heart** as in an organ. We have said what needed to be said when we studied the place of the soul and the nous. The same things are true of the spiritual heart as well. St. Gregory Palamas, referring to the Lord's words "out of the heart proceed evil thoughts, murders, adulteries, fornications, thefts, false witness, blasphemies" (Matt. 15, 19) and to the saying of St. Makarios: "the heart directs the entire organism, and when grace gains possession of the heart, it reigns over all the thoughts and all the members, for it is there, in the heart, that the mind and all the thoughts of the soul have their seat", writes that "our heart is the place of the rational faculty, the first rational organ of the body"[225]. In support of the teaching that the spiritual heart is in the heart, the bodily organ, St. Gregory refers to the words of the Apostle Paul – "you are our epistle written in our hearts... you are manifestly an epistle of Christ ministered by us, written not with ink but by the Spirit of the living God, not on tablets

---

224. Ibid. p. 44
225. St. Gregory Palamas. Triads, 1, 2, 3. CWS p. 43

of stone but on the tablets of flesh, that is, of the heart" (2 Cor. 3, 2-3) – and to the teaching of St. Maximus the Confessor: "When God comes to dwell in such a heart, He honours it by engraving His own letters on it through the Holy Spirit, just as He did on the Mosaic tablets"[226].

When the nous returns from its dispersion, it first finds the physical heart, and then it enters the spiritual heart, the deep heart. This is the common experience of all who practise the Jesus prayer and the holy work of the return of the nous to the heart. "The ascetic learns the great mysteries of the Spirit through pure prayer. He descends into his inmost heart, into his natural heart first, and thence into those depths that are no longer of the flesh. He finds his deep heart – reaches the profound spiritual, metaphysical core of his being; and looking into it he sees that the existence of mankind is not something alien and extraneous to him but is inextricably bound up with his own being"[227]. Consequently the athlete of this hesychastic method can clearly distinguish the spiritual from the bodily heart. He perceives the existence and the energy of both these hearts. In the beginning the nous finds the bodily heart and then it also discovers the spiritual heart, and it is able to perceive the movements of both hearts at the same time. So there is no confusion in this situation.

St. Nicodemos of the Holy Mountain, who belongs organically within the Orthodox tradition, says that the bodily heart is a natural, para-natural and supranatural centre[228]. It is a natural centre because, of all the members of the human body, it is the heart that is fashioned first. St. Basil said: "In the creation of animals the heart is the first to be founded by nature, in accordance with the animal that must be analogous to it"[229]. It is the para-natural centre because

---

226. Triads, 1, 3, 41
227. Archim. Sophrony. Saint Silouan. p. 47
228. Handbook of Council. CWS p. 154-157
229. Ibid. CWS p. 154

from there come all the passions and blasphemous thoughts.
Certainly this must be interpreted to mean, in accordance
with what has been said, that after holy baptism the grace of
God is present in the centre of the heart, while the devil
works from outside. The Apostle Peter said to Ananias: "Ananias, why has Satan filled your heart to lie to the Holy
Spirit...?" (Acts 5, 3) Satan invaded the heart of Judas: "And
supper being ended, the devil having already put it into the
heart of Judas Iscariot, Simon's son, to betray him..." (Jn 13,
2). Likewise the Lord's teaching is well known: "Out of the
heart proceed evil thoughts, murders, adulteries, fornications, thefts, false witness, blasphemies" (Matt. 15, 19). The
heart is the supranatural centre as well, because the grace of
Christ is active there. The Apostle Paul says: "God has sent
forth the Spirit of his Son into your hearts, crying out: 'Abba,
Father!'" (Gal. 4, 6) And in another place he writes: "The love
of God has been poured out in our hearts" (Rom. 5, 5). St.
Thalassios writes that a good heart produces good thoughts
because its thoughts correspond to its store of treasure[230].

The fact that good and evil thoughts come from the heart
does not mean that grace and Satan are in the same place at
the same time. "The heart produces good and bad thoughts
from itself" but the evil ideas are not born of its nature but as
a result of the remembrance of evil. The heart conceives most
of its evil thoughts from the attacks of the demons. In any
event we feel that they arise from the heart[231]. St. Diadochos
emphasises further that the grace of God which comes at
baptism conceals its presence in those who have been baptised "waiting to see which way the soul inclines". When one
keeps the commandments of Christ and remembers the
Name of Christ unceasingly, the fire of divine grace spreads
even to the heart's more outward organs of perception and
burns up "the tares in the field of the soul". The breath of the

---

230. Philok. 2, p. 312, 85
231. St. Diadochos of Photiki. Philok. 1, p. 284, 83

Holy Spirit in this state extinguishes the arrows of the devil before they reach the body, it extinguishes the fiery darts while they are still in mid-air[232].

Therefore the greatest battle takes place in the heart. When Christ has conquered there and the devil has been defeated, inner and outer peace comes. Thus the most important work of the combatant is "to enter his own heart and there to wage war with Satan, to hate him"[233]. The heart, which is the natural, para-natural and supranatural centre, is the source of the bodily and spiritual life, but it can also become the source of spiritual death.

Characterisations of the heart

From what we have written it is evident that while an exact definition of the spiritual heart cannot be given, it can be said that the heart is that place which is revealed through the ascetic life in grace and in which God Himself is revealed and dwells. This place is perceptible to the person who is organically and essentially within the Orthodox tradition.

The holy Fathers who experienced this fact have given several characterisations and images of this life. In what follows we shall try to look at these characterisations û definitions, which show the heart and its role in the whole spiritual life more clearly.

The heart is the **place** where God dwells: "That Christ may dwell in your hearts through faith" (Eph. 3, 17). "The love of God has been poured out in our hearts by the Holy Spirit who was given to us" (Rom. 5, 5). Just as coal engenders a flame, "so will God, who from our baptism dwells in our heart". And if He finds the air of our thought free from the winds of evil and if it is protected by the guarding of the nous, then He will

---

232. Ibid. p. 285, 85
233. St. Makarios. Gk. Philok. 4, p. 24

kindle our nous to theoria as a flame lights a candle[234]. Since God dwells there, all "the treasures of wisdom and spiritual knowledge" are hidden there. "They are revealed to the heart in proportion to our purification by means of the commandments"[235]. In the mirror of the soul "Jesus Christ, the wisdom and power of God the Father, is typified and luminously reflected". We must seek the kingdom of God inside our heart and if we cleanse the eye of our nous we will really find there the kingdom of God, the seed, the pearl, the leaven and many other things. We will find the Divinity in our hearts. "Christ said that the kingdom of heaven is within us, indicating that the Divinity dwells in our hearts[236].

Dwelling in our hearts, God **teaches** and **writes** His doctrines and His law. Therefore the heart is the place where God's commandments are written. The Apostle Paul speaks of those "who show the work of the law written in their hearts" (Rom. 2, 15). "God writes his own laws in the heart"[237]. There the person not only knows "the essences, but also, after passing through all of them, he will in some measure see God Himself"[238]. When God comes to dwell in such a heart, "He honours it by engraving His own letters on it through the Holy Spirit"[239]. Thus the saints, having God in their hearts and being worthy of having God's law written in their hearts, acquire the nous of Christ in accordance with what the Apostle said: "But we have the nous of Christ" (1. Cor. 2, 16). Christ's nous which the saints receive does not bring with it a loss of noetic power, nor does it come "as a supplementary part added to our nous", nor "does it pass essentially and hypostatically into our nous. Rather, it illumines the power of

---

234. Hesychios the Priest. Philok. 1, p. 180, 104
235. St. Maximus. Philok. 2, p. 109, 70
236. Philotheos of Sinai. Philok. 3, p. 25, 23
237. Maximus, Philok. 2, p. 158, 81
238. Maximus, Philok. 2, p. 158, 80
239. Ibid.

our nous with its own quality and conforms the activity of our nous to its own." That is to say, the power of our nous, without being lost, is illumined by the energy of Christ. To "have the nous of Christ" means, according to St. Maximus, "apprehension in accordance with that of Christ, and apprehending Christ through all things"[240]. The person thinks in accordance with the will of God, has perpetual remembrance of God. The same applies to the desiring power. The person constantly desires what God desires, and desires Him insatiably. St. Peter of Damascus refers to St. Basil the Great, who says that when God finds a heart free from all worldly matters and worldly learning, He then "writes on it His own doctrines as if it were a clean slate"[241]. Thus in this state it is a matter of 'doctrinal consciousness'. The person knows the doctrines of the Church from experience, since he has the life of God in his heart. We must struggle to have Christ dwelling in our heart, because then God Himself will "teach us how to hold fast to His laws"[242].

The heart is the hell into which Christ descends and frees man's soul. Just as He descended into hell and freed the souls of the righteous, so Christ descends into the depth of the heart. St. Makarios teaches that when we hear that the Lord went down into hell and freed the souls, we should not think that these things are far from what happens now. The tomb is the heart. The Lord comes "to the souls in hell that call upon Him", that is, into the depths of the heart, and after a dialogue with death, "lifting up the heavy stone that oppresses the soul, and opening the tomb, He resurrects us – for we were truly dead – and releases our imprisoned soul from its dark prison"[243].

The heart is the earth where the grain of mustard seed is

---

240. Ibid. 83
241. Peter of Damascus. Philok. 3, p. 154
242. Abba Philemon. Philok. 2, p. 349-350
243. Philok. 3, p. 337

sown by the Lord. According to St. Maximus, "The grain of mustard seed is the Lord, who by faith is sown spiritually in the hearts of those who accept Him"[244].

The heart is the **church** and the **altar**, that sacred place where the Lord is glorified and sanctified. The Apostle Peter instructs: "Sanctify the Lord God in your hearts" (1 Pet. 3, 15). All visible things, according to St. Makarios, are reflections of hidden things. The visible church figures and reflects the church of the heart. The priest who celebrates the sacraments is a figure of "the true priest of Christ's grace"[245]. In this spiritual and true church which is the depths of the heart, an eternal liturgy goes on in the resurrected man: "Speaking to one another in psalms and hymns and spiritual songs, singing and making melody in your heart to the Lord" (Eph. 5, 19). The heart which does not have evil thoughts and is energised by the Spirit is "a true sanctuary, even before the future life"[246]. The heart is a church and an altar. St. John of the Ladder teaches: "To keep a regular watch over the heart is one thing; to be a bishop over the heart is another". In the first case the nous is a ruler, in the second case the nous is a bishop who offers spiritual sacrifices[247]. The heart is also the sanctuary where the fire is[248]. It is what the two disciples felt on their journey to Emmaus when Christ was speaking to them: "Did not our hearts burn within us while He talked with us on the road, and while He opened the Scriptures to us?" (Lk. 24, 32) The heart is "the Lord's reception room"[249].

The heart is the **vessel** which holds the oil of divine grace. According to St. Makarios of Egypt, "The five watchful virgins who bore in the vessels of their hearts the oil that was not

---

244. Philok. 2, p. 140, 11
245. Philok. 3, p. 334, 113
246. St. Gregory of Sinai. Acrostics, 7. Writings, p. 38
247. John of the Ladder. Step 28. CWS p. 280
248. Ibid. Step 26. CWS p. 230
249. The Art of Prayer. p. 187

inherent in their nature – for it is the grace of the Holy Spirit – were able to enter with the bridegroom into the bridal chamber"[250]. Thus the heart is the vessel in which the prudent person keeps the grace of the Holy Spirit and so enters the bridal chamber to rejoice at the bridegroom's celebration.

The heart is **the field** where the treasure is hidden, for which the finder sells everything in order to buy it[251].

The heart is **the image** of the **New Testament**, or rather the New Testament typifies purity of heart and the watch and guard of the nous[252]. The Old Testament is an icon of outward and sensory, bodily asceticism. "The Holy Gospel, or New Testament, is an icon of attentiveness, that is, of purity of heart"[253].

The heart is **heaven**. Where there is humility and remembrance of God "established through watchfulness and attention, and also with recurrent prayer inflexible in its resistance to the enemy, there is the place of God, the heaven of the heart"[254].

Within the heart is **the guarantee** of the Spirit: "God, who also has sealed us and given us the Spirit in our hearts as a guarantee" (2 Cor. 1, 22).

The heart is **the tablets** on which God's letter is written: "You are our epistle written in our hearts, ...written not with ink but by the Spirit of the living God, not on tablets of stone but on tablets of flesh, that is, of the heart" (2 Cor. 3, 2-3).

The heart is the place where shines **the Light of God**, "who has shone in our hearts to give the light of the knowledge of the glory of God in the face of Jesus Christ" (2 Cor. 4, 6).

In the heart man is assured of **sonship** and there the voice of God is heard clearly, saying "because you are sons, God has sent forth the Spirit of His Son into your hearts, crying out, "Abba, Father!" (Gal. 4, 6) Since God resides there, it is there

---

250. Philok. 3, p. 313, 65
251. Matt. 13, 44 and St. Maximus, Philok. 2, p. 109, 71
252. Hesychios the Priest. Philok. 1, p. 181, 113
253. Ibid. 112
254. Philotheos of Sinai. Philok. 3, p. 17, 4

that He speaks with man. There the word of God is heard clearly and distinctly.

In the pure heart are also the eyes with which to see the mysteries of God: "that the Father of glory may give you a spirit of wisdom..., the eyes of your hearts being enlightened, that you may know what is the hope to which He has called you" (Eph. 1, 17-18).

The peace of God prevails in the heart: "And let the peace of God rule in your hearts" (Col. 3, 15).

The heart is **the lyre**, its strings are the feelings, the plectrum is the mind which through intelligence constantly moves the plectrum with remembrance of God, "from which ineffable sweetness fills the soul, and the pure nous is lit up by divine illuminations"[255].

The heart is **the spring** from which, through prayer and warmth of feeling, water comes "from the life-giving Spirit"[256].

The heart is **our inner man**[257].

The Apostles and Fathers use these many images and characterisations to present and express the heart. We can say in brief that the heart is "our inner man", the place which is revealed through the ascetic life in grace and in which God is revealed and dwells. It is the spiritual church where a perpetual divine Liturgy is celebrated, a perpetual doxology is offered to God. This place, unknown to many, but known to the saints, gives life to man.

Sickness of the heart

It is well known throughout the Biblico-patristic tradition that when the heart of man ceases to conform to the will of God and does the desires of the devil, it sickens and is made dead. One speaks of the sickness, hardening, uncleanness,

---

255. Callistos the Patriarch. Writings, p. 271, 2
256. St. Gregory of Sinai. Writings, p. 82f
257. St. Gregory Palamas. To Xeni. Gk. Philok. 4, p. 109

spiritual death of the heart. In this section we shall look at some manifestations of the sick heart.

The devil enters the heart of man and takes it captive: "And supper being ended, the devil having already put it into the heart of Judas Iscariot, Simon's son, to betray Him..." (Jn. 13, 2). No doubt his nous had been in captivity for many years before this. "Just as it is impossible for fire and water to pass through the same pipe together, so it is impossible for sin to enter the heart without first knocking at its door in the form of a fantasy provoked by the devil"[258]. Fantasy is what leads the devil's provocation into the heart. In fallen man fantasy, which is more subtle than thought and coarser than the nous, is the beginning of evil. Therefore the Fathers advise us to keep our fantasy pure, or better, to live in such a way as not to activate fantasy, but rather to mortify the fantastic. It is only when that is made dead by great penitence and much inward grief that one can theologise.

The Fathers write about the perdition of the heart. This is taken to mean that the grace of Christ is not acting in the heart and that the supranatural centre has become a paranatural centre. Perdition of the heart is the loss of salvation.

One of the diseases of the heart is **ignorance** and **forgetfulness of God**. When it has lost the grace of God, the heart becomes clouded, dark, hidden. This is what was seen in the Jews and heretics. They read the Scripture but they did not understand it at all because their hearts were veiled. "Even to this day, when Moses is read, a veil lies on their heart" (2 Cor. 3, 15). It is through the heart that one acquires certainty of God, it is in the heart that God is revealed, that He speaks and interprets His word. When it is hidden, a man is in deep darkness. And a heart which has ignorance is hell. "Hell is ignorance, for both are dark; and perdition is forgetfulness, for both involve extinction"[259].

---

258. Hesychios the Priest. Philok. 1, p. 170, 45
259. St. Mark the Ascetic. Philok. 1, p. 114, 62

Hardness and **hardening** is another disease of the heart. Because it does not accept the grace of God, which changes everything, it remains hard. "You stiff-necked people, uncircumcised in heart and ears!" said the Protomartyr Stephen to the Jews (Acts 7, 51). This hardness is what arrogance stores up, and a man will be judged for it. "By your hard and impenitent heart you are storing up wrath for yourself on the day of wrath when God's righteous judgement will be revealed" (Rom. 2, 5). A hard heart is an iron gate to the city. When closed the gate does not allow one to enter the city. But the heart of one who suffers hardship and affliction will open of its own accord as it did to Peter[260]. It is our duty not to create the preconditions for hardening of the heart. "Do not harden your hearts as in the rebellion" (Heb. 3, 8). The Lord many times encountered such callous hearts. After the miracles of the multiplying of the five loaves and the storm "their hearts were hardened" (Mark 6, 52). In another connection the Lord said to the people: "Is your heart still hardened?" (Mark 8, 17) When confronted with men who were observing whether He would heal on the Sabbath, the Lord "looked around at them with anger, grieved by the hardness of their hearts", and healed the man who had a withered hand (Mark 3, 5).

Uncleanness is another sickness of the heart. When the heart has lost the grace of God and the evil demons are working in it, it is naturally unclean. According to Nicetas Stethatos, uncleanness of the heart is not only that the person has unclean thoughts, but also that he boasts of his successes, is puffed up about his virtues, has great thoughts, that is to say, is proud of his wisdom and his knowledge of God, and blames those of his brothers who are indolent and careless. This is shown in the parable of the Publican and the Pharisee[261]. Every desire that comes to his heart, even if it is

---

260. Ibid. p. 111, 21
261. Nicetas Stethatos. Practical chapters, ch. 48

not carried out externally, is impurity and adultery. The Lord said: "Everyone who looks at a woman to lust for her has already committed adultery with her in his heart" (Matt. 5, 28). But also every other desire which is not carnal in the narrow sense of the term but goes against the will of God is a defilement of the heart and hence a sickness. The heart is then sick.

Likewise the **foolish** heart is sick. Of the idolators who worship created things more than the Creator, we are told "their foolish hearts were darkened" (Rom. 1, 21).

Lack of uprightness is another sickness of the heart. The heart which does the will of the evil one is not upright, since uprightness of heart is possible only when the heart is in its natural state, that is, when it is the dwelling-place of God. The Apostle Peter said accusingly to Simon the Sorcerer, who wanted to acquire the grace of God with money: "Your heart is not right in the sight of God" (Acts 8, 21).

Rudeness too is a sickness of the heart. The passions in the heart make it rude, and this rudeness is manifested outwardly as well. Therefore in the Orthodox tradition kindness is clearly spoken about – not so much outward as inward kindness. The heart must be simple, refined. A man with a simple heart is also outwardly kind. Thus there is an outward kindness which does not come from kindness of heart, or rather is in clear contrast to a rudeness existing in the heart, and there is also an outward kindness which flows from and reflects inner gentleness. Archimandrite Sophrony writes about St. Silouan: "Even the most perceptive intuition brought into contact with Father Silouan, whatever the circumstances, could have found nothing ignoble in him. He did not know what it was to spurn or disregard. He was a stranger to affectation. He was a really noble spirit in the way only a Christian can be noble"[262]. So when there is affectation, hypocrisy, sarcasm, antipathy, it is certain that the heart is sick, since its behaviour is rude.

---

262. Archim. Sophrony. Saint Silouan. p. 53

Another sickness of the heart is **inward self-indulgence**. The heart's pleasure, instead of centring on and delighting in the love of God, revolves around and enjoys carnal things, things displeasing to God. A self-indulgent heart is a prison of the soul, especially at the hour of death. According to St. Mark the Ascetic, "A self-indulgent heart becomes a prison and chain for the soul when it leaves this life"[263]. The passions of the soul are satisfied as long as there is a body. But when the soul has been released from the body it will not be able to be satisfied, since it will lack material things. Therefore these passions, mainly self-indulgence of the soul, not finding satisfaction, will strangle the soul. These are the demons spoken of in the patristic writings. This is why a self-indulgent heart is a prison and chain for the soul at the time of departure from this life.

A man's sick and dead soul transmits the sickness and darkening to his whole psychosomatic being. Whatever he thinks and desires is dead. Therefore Abba Dorotheos says that as long as we are subject to passion we must not trust our heart at all. For a crooked ruler makes even straight things crooked[264]. And St. Mark the Ascetic advises: "Until you have eradicated evil, do not obey your heart"[265].

The sick heart must be healed. If it is not healed, man's whole organism is sick.

Curing of the heart

The highest aim of man is to attain knowledge of God, for this is his salvation. Naturally when we say 'knowledge of God' we do not mean knowledge in the head, but 'communion in being'. That is, knowledge of God is communion with God. Where this communion is attained, there is salvation. But

---

263. Philok. 1, p. 111, 20
264. Abba Dorotheos. SC p. 526, 202, 2. cf. CS 22, p. 251
265. Philok. 1, p. 122, 177

this communion takes place in the depths of the heart. There God meets with man, there He imparts His knowledge, there man gains a sense of His being. In order for this communion and vision of God to come about, the heart must be pure. The Lord affirmed this: "Blessed are the pure in heart, for they shall see God" (Matt. 5, 8). The heart which has fallen ill and been made dead needs to be cured and purified in order to offer knowledge of God. The pure heart is the organ of knowledge, the organ of Orthodox epistemology.

In what follows we shall concern ourselves with how the heart is cured.

Repentance is the first healing medicine. The heart has to repent and come to its natural condition. If a life of sin has led it to the unnatural state, a life of repentance will bring it back to its right state, will give it life. St. John of the Ladder offers precise definitions of repentance: "Repentance is the renewal of baptism. Repentance is a contract with God for a fresh start in life. Repentance goes shopping for humility. Repentance is ever distrustful of bodily comfort. Repentance is critical awareness and a sure watch over oneself... Repentance is reconciliation with the Lord... Repentance is the purification of conscience..."[266]. In another place the same saint tells how all who have been defiled after baptism must be purified and must remove the pitch from themselves with the unceasing fire of the heart and the oil of divine compassion[267]. God's compassion and the heart's fire heal a person of his sickness.

The deeper the repentance, the more **contrition** increases. A contrite heart is one which lives in repentance. The prophet king David says: "The sacrifice acceptable to God is a broken spirit. A broken and contrite heart God will not despise" (Ps. 51, 17). God dwells in a contrite heart. Everyone who comes to the King to receive remission of his debt needs to have

---

266. Ladder. Step. 5. CWS p. 121
267. Ibid. Step 7. CWS p. 144

"unutterable contrition"[268]. According to St. Nicetas Stethatos, the distinguishing marks of truth are not in faces, forms
and words, nor does God reside in those things, but truth as
well as God resides "in contrite hearts, in spirits of humility
and in souls enlightened by the knowledge of God"[269].

In speaking of contrition of heart we must describe how
the heart is made contrite and what this contrition is. St.
Mark the Ascetic, beginning by saying that it is impossible for
a person to be rid of evil without contrition of heart, defines
precisely what makes it contrite. "The heart is made contrite
by threefold self-control: in sleep, in food, and in bodily relaxation"[270]. Bodily relaxation produces self-indulgence, which is
receptive to evil thoughts. Contrition is also created by "wise
solitude and complete silence"[271]. And St. Mark the Ascetic,
coming back to this theme, emphasises that vigil, prayer and
patient acceptance of what comes constitute a breaking that
does not harm but benefits the heart[272]. Bodily labour and
being deprived of necessities produce a pain in the heart
which is useful and salutary to the person. St. Philotheos of
Sinai, who lays stress on the fact that we must do all we can
to humble the arrogance of our heart, underlines ways to
achieve this. The heart is crushed and humbled by remembrance of our former life, that is Adam's life before the fall,
and by recalling all the sins we have committed since childhood, except of course carnal sins, "for the remembrance of
these is harmful". The memory of sins engenders tears and
moves us to give heartfelt thanks to God; and perpetual and
vivid mindfulness of death gives rise to godly sorrow. Likewise
the soul is humbled by the recollection of our Lord's Passion

---

268. Ibid. Step 28. CWS p. 277
269. Natural chapters, ch. 32
270. Philok. 1, p. 143, 210
271. Gregory of Sinai. Acrostics, 104. Writings, p. 59
272. Philok. 1, p. 111, 19

and the many blessings we have received from God[273]. The carnal man, that is the man who is far from God, is distinguished by the hardness and coarseness of his heart. The man of God, who receives the Holy Spirit, is distinguished by the refinement of his heart. The heart is sensitised and softened when it has been purified of passions and is contrite.

The Fathers also describe harmful contrition. According to Mark the Ascetic, "there is a breaking of the heart which is gentle and makes it deeply penitent, and there is a breaking which is violent and harmful, shattering it completely"[274]. The good kind of breaking happens in a spirit of compunction and in an atmosphere of prayer. That is to say, a contrite heart prays unceasingly to God. It does not despair but hopes in God's great love for man. So it is marked by hope. St. Symeon the New Theologian, an experienced spiritual physician, recognised that long and untimely sorrowing of the heart "darkens and disturbs the mind", it banishes pure prayer and compunction from the soul and creates a painful pining of the heart which results in hardness and extreme callousness. This is how the demons bring about despair[275]. Thus a breaking that is not enclosed in compunction and prayer darkens the person further and is a favourable climate for the devil's injection of despair and hopelessness. Genuine heartbreak, which, as we said, is not injurious to the heart, is marked by the presence of prayer, compunction and hope in God.

A broken heart comes with prayer and has very many results. An anonymous hesychast presents the benefits of this salutary method: "1. Break your heart with prayer, oh monk, so that the power of the devil may be completely broken away from your heart by perfection...

7. Just as a man fears to take hold of a fiery and sparking

---

273. Philok. 3, p. 20, 13
274. Philok. 1, p. 111, 18
275. CS 41, p. 49. Ch. 1, 63. Gk. Philok. 3, p. 244, 46

iron, so the devil fears the breaking of a heart. For the breaking of the heart breaks his cunning completely.

8. In the relaxed and unbroken heart, as soon as it is confronted with the devil's fantasy, the heart accepts it at once and is deeply impressed by the idea of the fantasy, but in a broken heart there is no room for any fantasy.

9. Where there is contrition of heart all satanic evil is put to flight and every demonic action is set ablaze.

14. Break your heart with prayer so that sin may be broken away from your heart...

25. Did the devil see a heart wounded by the contrition of prayer? He at once remembered the blows which Christ endured from man, and therefore he took fright and lost courage.

26. Beloved one, break the devil with the contrition of your heart so that you may enter triumphant into the joy of your Lord.

27. Break your heart with prayer so that Satan who deceives you may be broken to bits[276].

In order in some way to interpret the heart's contrition we must speak of **pain in the heart**. We must say from the start that when we speak of pain in the heart we are mainly referring to the spiritual heart. The spiritual heart aches, is in pain. When this arises by the grace of God it has no tragic consequences for the physical heart. That is to say, while the spiritual heart is breaking, is crushed, is suffering from the joyful sorrow of living in repentance, the physical heart continues its natural course without any ill effects. In most cases cardiologists cannot detect the illness, for the simple reason that the physical heart of the person with heartache is not sick.

Heartache is necessary because even the strictest ascetic life is bogus and fruitless without it[277]. And certainly in order

---

276. Anonymous hesychast: Neptiki theoria, p. 171-174 (in Greek)
277. John of the Ladder. Step 7. CWS p. 144

for this heartache, so essential for the spiritual life, to exist, one must not fully satisfy bodily hunger. For "just as a sheep does not mate with a wolf, so suffering of the heart does not couple with satiety for the conception of virtues," says St. Mark the Ascetic[278]. All the virtues are conceived through heartache. A Christian life without pain is bogus.

Pain of the heart is essential for salvation: "It must be realized that the true sign of spiritual endeavour and the price of progress is suffering pain, that is the sense of our shameful sinfulness, when with sorrow and weeping we fall down at the feet of Jesus like the sinful woman at the house of Simon the Leper in Bethany. She heard Him say: 'Your sins are forgiven.' He who is without pain bears no fruit, because: 'prayer without pain is counted as a miscarriage', according to St. Isaac the Syrian. Pain of the heart and physical striving bring to light the gift of the Holy Spirit, bestowed in holy baptism upon every believer, buried in passions through our negligence in fulfilling the commandments, and brought once more to life by repentance, through the ineffable mercy of God.

"Do not, because of the suffering that accompanies them, cease to make painstaking efforts, lest you be condemned for fruitlessness and hear the words, 'Take the talent from him' (Matt. 25, 28). Every struggle in the soul's training, whether physical or mental, that is not accompanied by suffering, that does not require the utmost effort, will bear no fruit. 'The kingdom of heaven suffers violence, and the violent take it by force' (Matt. 11, 12). Many people have worked and continue to work without pain, but because of its absence they are strangers to purity and out of communion with the Holy Spirit, because they have turned aside from the severity of suffering.

"Those who work feebly and carelessly may go through the motions of making great efforts, but they harvest no fruit, because they undergo no suffering. According to the prophet,

---

278. Philok. 1, p. 144, 217

unless our loins are broken, weakened by the labour of fasting, unless we undergo an agony of contrition, unless we
suffer like a woman in travail, we shall not succeed in bringing to birth the spirit of salvation in the ground of our heart",
for it is written: 'We must through many tribulations enter
the kingdom of God' (Acts 14, 22)"[279].

This pain in the spiritual heart, which is also felt physically without being injurious when it is in accord with what is
emphasised by the Orthodox tradition, is essential for our
salvation, because it helps all the powers of our soul to be
concentrated there. The nous is then more easily attached to
the heart and returns to it. This pain, which in some way
creates a wound, is often connected with weeping. This is
called tears. A person bursts loudly into tears. This is called
mourning. And we know from the works of our Fathers that
this wound, which contributes to salvation, is felt more keenly
than a bodily wound. But, as we shall see in what follows,
heartbreak creates an ineffable pleasure.

St. Theophan the Recluse writes characteristically about
this wound which creates metaphysical pain: "Take care that
your attention is in your heart and not in your head, and hold
to this not only when you are standing in prayer but at all
other times as well. Try to acquire a kind of soreness in your
heart. Constant effort will achieve this quickly. There is nothing peculiar in this: the appearance of this pain does not have
the meaning of a wound, while it is essentially a pain. This
wound is not a physical wound and a physical pain, which
would discourage and threaten life. It is a wound from the
intoxicating love felt by the penitent soul, like that of the
Prodigal Son, in the union of the divine embrace. It is an
expiatory suffering and an insatiable sweetness, an inexpressible mystical contemplation, an inseparable bond with
God, a desire to leave this life, and a loving conversation with
God. This pain will help you to gather all the powers of your

---

279. The Art of Prayer. cf. p. 117

soul into this beloved labour, and God, seeing your effort, will give you what you seek. Then certain changes and divine states will occur in your heart"[280].

St. John of the Ladder witnesses to the fact – which is probably his own experience – that in some people this metaphysical pain was so great, the heart ached so much that blood literally poured from the wounded heart and mouth: "I have seen men who reached the ultimate in mourning, with the blood of a suffering and wounded heart actually flowing out of their mouths, and I was reminded of the saying: 'Like grass I am cut down and my heart is dried up' (Ps. 102, 4)"[281].

The outpouring of **tears** is another result of this suffering. The Lord blessed those who mourn: "Blessed are they that mourn, for they shall be comforted" (Matt. 5, 4). So godly mourning and the tears that come from it are a commandment of Christ. Tears are a way of life. Just as repentance and mourning are a way of life, so are the tears which pour from the repentant and broken heart. In speaking of tears, we must point out that there are inner tears of the heart and outward tears of the body. The heart often weeps, is washed by a river of tears. The spiritual combatant who lives in the spirit of the Orthodox tradition often "catches' his heart weeping. Usually these tears of the heart appear outwardly. Sometimes they are in secret. But let us look at the value of tears.

The saints urge the Christian to weep, because in that climate the heart is purified and acquires spiritual sensitiveness, overcoming its hardness. St. Isaac urges: "Drench your cheeks with the weeping of your eyes"[282]. He urges us particularly to call upon Mary and Martha to teach us "mournful cries"[283]. St. Neilos the Ascetic teaches us to pray first for the

---

280. Ibid. p. 127
281. Step 7. CWS p. 144
282. St. Isaac the Syrian. Ascetical homilies, p. 91
283. Ibid.

gift of tears[284]. Likewise if we pray with tears all we ask will be heard[285].

The value of tears is great. The Fathers, who experienced this fact, are typical. Tears are a baptism. "Greater than baptism itself is the fountain of tears after baptism, even though it is somewhat audacious to say so"[286]. Tears are a sign of a man reborn. According to Abba Poemen, "Weeping is the way which the Scriptures and our Fathers give us, when they say, 'Weep!' Truly there is no other way than this"[287]. It is, as we said, a way of life. It is impossible for us to know ourselves without tears. That is to say, if we realise our sinfulness, which is a sign of divine grace in us, if we have acquired the gift of self-knowledge and self-reproach, then we spontaneously begin to weep. Therefore "No one should leave himself dead and go and weep for another"[288]. Tears in a man show that Christ "has touched his eyes and given him spiritual sight"[289]. Tears open the eyes of the soul. It is necessary too, because, as Abba Arsenios teaches, a man will have to weep at some time in any case. He who weeps voluntarily here on earth will not weep in the next life. On the contrary, he who does not weep here will "weep eternally hereafter"[290].

St. Symeon the New Theologian, who, with the others, can be characterised as a theologian of tears, says that tears are a sign of life. As babies cry when they come from their mother's womb and this is a sign of life, so it is with spiritual birth. Tears are a part of human rebirth. If the baby does not cry, it is not said to be alive. Therefore, according to St. Symeon, "human nature has mourning and tears as a concomitant

284. St. Neilos the Ascetic. Gk. Philok. 1, p. 177, 5
285. Ibid. 6
286. Ladder. Step 7. CWS p. 137
287. Sayings. p. 155, 119
288. Barsanuphius and John. Q. 341. (In Gk.)
289. St. Mark the Ascetic. Philok. 1, p. 111, 15
290. Sayings. p. 16, 41

from birth"[291]. He said this because many people in his time maintained that not all people have the same nature and therefore they cannot all shed tears. But this is not so. The saint adds that tears are just as necessary for the soul as food and drink are for the body. He who does not weep every day or every hour "will destroy his soul and cause it to perish from hunger"[292]. When a person has acquired a preference for goodness, zeal, patience, humility and love for God, the soul that at present is like rock "will become a fountain of tears"[293]. St. Symeon has recorded the information, found also in Scripture, that "some adults at the moment of their baptism have shed tears, having been smitten with compunction by the coming of the Holy Spirit; yet not painful tears of suffering, but such as were sweeter than honey... They were shed from their eyes without pain and without sound"[294].

All these things show on the one hand that tears are necessary for our spiritual life, and on the other hand that they are a way of life, that they are what nourishes the soul. And further, they have many forms. It is to this that I wish to direct attention in what follows.

Nicetas Stethatos, disciple of St. Symeon the New Theologian, teaches that tears of repentance are one thing and tears that come from holy compunction are another. The former are like the river which overflows and sweeps down all the walls of sin, whereas the latter are to the soul like rain falling on the fields and like snow on the grass: "they nourish the grain of knowledge, and make it luxuriant and fruitful"[295]. He also emphasises that the taste of tears sometimes brings bitterness and pain, sometimes joy and gladness, to the noetic feeling of the heart. The tears of repentance create bitterness and

---

291. CWS p. 314
292. Ibid.
293. CWS p. 313
294. Ibid.
295. Practical chapters, ch. 70

pain; the tears of the pure heart, the heart which has attained its freedom from passions, are tears of pleasure and indescribable sweetness[296]. Almost the same difference is found between tears from the fear of God and tears from the love of God[297].

Tears have many effects. They purify a person's heart from the stain of sins and then enlighten his heart. The Fathers teach that when the devil comes to a person's soul, he drops various images and then withdraws, leaving the idol of sin in the heart. Tears clean this idol away: the place of the heart is washed and the cloud which covered it disappears. Abba Poemen teaches: "He who wishes to purify his faults purifies them with tears"[298]. In another place he says: "In all our afflictions let us weep in the presence of the goodness of God until He shows mercy on us"[299]. So where there is mourning there is not a trace of slander or criticism[300]. Actually it has been confirmed by our experience in the Church that tears can wash away sins as water washes away something written[301]. At our tears the Holy Spirit comes and rests upon our heart, purifies us and washes us from the filth of wickedness[302].

Tears not only purify but they also illumine the soul. In reality the grace of God which comes through repentance brightens and sanctifies the heart of man. The abyss of mourning, that is, great mourning, sees consolation. With purity of heart comes illumination. "Illumination is an ineffable energy which is unknowingly perceived and invisibly seen." Mourning brings comfort, according to Christ's beatitude. This comfort is the solace of a sorrowing soul. Divine help is the renewal of a soul depressed by grief which, "in a wonderful

---

296. Ibid. 69
297. Callistus and Ignatius. Writings, p. 231, 58
298. Sayings. p. 155, 119
299. Ibid. 122
300. Ladder. Step. 10. CWS p. 156
301. Ibid. Step 26 summary, CWS p. 259
302. St. Isaac the Syrian, The Ascetical Homilies, p. 91

way, transforms painful tears into painless ones"[303]. And Nicetas Stethatos teaches that no one can attain the potential likeness to God unless he has previously, through hot tears, purified the filth existing within him and kept the commandments of Christ. In this way we cast off deformity[304] and become capable of enjoying the glory of God.

The Fathers do also point to tears of delusion. It is possible for some tears to be activated by the devil. When a person weeps and then boasts, he is deluded. Therefore the Fathers warn us: "Do not grow conceited if you shed tears when you pray"[305]. No one should boast and think that he is superior to many others. The aim of our tears is that through them we should be cleansed of the filth of passions. When we forget the purpose of tears and become proud, we can lose our head: "Many people, shedding tears for their sins, forget what tears are for, and so in their folly they go astray"[306].

There are many kinds of tears, such as sentimental tears, egoistic tears, tears of Satan, tears of God, and so on. But we should strive to transform those sentimental tears as well. The Fathers of the Church urge us to weep, even if our weeping has in it elements of egoism. Then through self-reproach, through turning our attention to ourself and our sins, by ceasing conversations with others and by talking with God, looking at our own wretchedness, we can be transformed and find salvation.

I believe that the terrible condition in which many people find themselves is due to the fact that we have become estranged from weeping: we do not cry. Therefore when we are burdened with various difficulties, when our nerves are strained, when our whole inner atmosphere is in a wretched

---

303. Ladder. Step 7. CWS p. 143
304. Gnostic chapters, ch. 34
305. St. Mark the Ascetic. Philok. 1, p. 111, 15
306. Evagrius. Philok. 1, p. 58, 8

state, then with a thought of self-reproach we should try to weep. If we make an attempt, God will send His grace and the tears will become a way of life and so our heart will be purified of passions.

Repentance, mourning, contrition, tears are closely connected with the **fire** which is **engendered** in the heart. Repentance is helped by the fire which the Holy Spirit kindles in the person's heart. The Lord, referring to this fire which He kindles in the heart, said: "I came to cast fire upon the earth; and would that it were already kindled!" (Lk. 12, 49) As Christ approaches the heart, the heart is set on fire because of the existence of the passions, as we shall analyse in what follows. This is the burning which the disciples felt as they were journeying towards Emmaus: "Did not our hearts burn within us while he talked to us on the road, while he opened the Scriptures to us?" (Lk. 24, 32).

This fire burning up the passions of the heart is experienced as light. When the Apostle Paul had this experience, he wrote: "...before the Lord comes, who will bring to light the things now hidden in darkness and will disclose the purposes of the heart" (1 Cor. 4, 5). And the Apostle Peter expresses his own experience when he writes: "until the day dawns and the morning star rises in your hearts" (2 Pet. 1, 19). The heart experiences the grace of God first as a fire, a fire which burns up sin and the passions, and then when the passions burn away, it experiences God's grace as light illuminating our whole inner man.

This teaching that we first experience God's grace as a fire and then as light is analysed by St. John of the Ladder. He says that when the supercelestial fire comes to dwell in the heart, it burns some because they still lack purification and it enlightens others "according to the degree of their perfection". This same thing is called "both the fire which consumes and the light which illuminates". That is why some people come from their prayer as if from a fiery furnace, and feel a relief from defilement, while others, when prayer is ended, feel as if they were coming out resplendent with light and clothed in a garment of humility and joy[307]. This fire which the heart of man perceives is often perceived by the body as well. Thus the person thinks that he is in hell and burning with the flames of hell. This is important and salutary. For such repentance heals the soul. And we know very well that the greater the repentance, the more effective the healing. Also the more the fire of repentance is experienced, the more the preconditions are created for the vision of uncreated Light.

According to the Apostle Paul, God is a consuming fire (Heb. 12, 29). Our whole labour, says St. John of the Ladder, continues until the fire of God enters our sanctuary, that is, our heart. This God, Who is fire, consumes "all lusts, all stirrings of passion, all predispositions, and all hardness of heart, both within and without, both visible and spiritual"[308].

Repentance is a deed and moment of grace, but we too must help true repentance to come, that is, help God's fire to come into our heart. Besides, the whole ascetic life is a cooperation, a synergy of the divine and human wills. The Fathers teach that we are cleansed from the passions "either through voluntary sufferings or through involuntary misfortunes". Voluntary suffering is godly sorrow, repentance, the sense of the fire of repentance. Involuntary misfortunes are the various trials of our lives. "When the voluntary ones come first, involuntary ones do not follow"[309]. Therefore we must strive to let repentance, God's fire, develop in us so that we may be delivered from involuntary misfortunes. We must always keep in our hearts this fire of repentance and the warmth that comes from it. The devil is afraid of a monk living in mourning and does not dare to approach him. Therefore a faithful and prudent monk is one "who has kept unquenched the warmth of

307. Ladder. Step 28. CWS p. 280
308. Ibid. Step 26. CWS p. 230
309. Nicetas Stethatos. Natural chapters, ch. 9

his vocation, who adds fire each day to fire, fervour to fervour, zeal to zeal"[310].

Pure prayer is born in the heart of him who has this fire. Therefore one of the requirements of our prayer is that this fire should come, on the one hand, to burn the sins and passions, and on the other hand, to give us pure prayer. "When fire comes to dwell in the heart, it resurrects prayer" and as a result of this the fire of the Holy Spirit descends into the upper chamber of our soul[311]. Therefore the order is clear: "Do not stop praying as long as, by God's grace, the fire (of fervour) and the water (of tears) have not been exhausted"[312].

This blessed fire, kindled in our heart with the coming of grace in connection with repentance and tears, is what brings about our spiritual rebirth. With the help of this fire our whole inner condition is transformed, and many expressions of our body also change. St. Theophan the Recluse writes: "From the moment when your heart starts to be kindled with divine warmth your inner transformation will properly begin. This slight flame will in time consume and melt everything within you, it will begin and continue to spiritualise your being to the full. Indeed until this flame starts to burn, there will be no spiritualisation, in spite of all your strivings to achieve it. Thus the engendering of its first flicker is all that matters at this moment, and to this end be sure to direct all your efforts. But you must realise that this kindling cannot take place in you while the passions are still strong and vigorous, even though they may not in fact be indulged. Passions are the dampness in the fuel of your being, and damp wood does not burn. There is nothing else to be done except to bring in dry wood from outside and light this, allowing the flames from it to dry out the damp wood, until this in its turn is dry enough to begin slowly to catch alight. And so little by

---

310. Ladder. Step 1. CWS p. 80
311. Ibid. Step 28. CWS p. 279
312. Ibid.

little the burning of the dry wood will disperse the dampness and will spread until all the wood is enveloped in flames.

"All the powers of the soul and activities of the body are the fuel of our being, but so long as man does not pay heed to himself these are all saturated and rendered ineffective by the soggy dampness of his passions. Until the passions are driven out, they obstinately resist spiritual fire. Passions penetrate into both the soul and the body, and overpower even man's spirit itself, his consciousness and freedom; and in this manner they come to dominate him entirely. As they are in league with devils, through them the devils also dominate man, although he falsely imagines that he is his own master. Delivered by the grace of God, the spirit is the first to tear itself out of these fetters. Filled with the fear of God and under the influence of grace, the spirit breaks every bond with passion, and repenting of the past, firmly resolves henceforward to please God alone in everything, to live only for Him, to walk according to His commandments"[313].

St. Theophan writes about this blessed fire: "According to St. Barsanuphios, when we receive in our heart the fire which the Lord came to send on earth, all our human faculties begin to burn within. When by long friction fire is ignited and logs begin to burn with it, the logs thus kindled will crackle and smoke until they are properly alight. But when they are properly alight they appear to be permeated with fire, and produce a pleasing light and warmth without smoke and crackling. So it happens within men.

"They receive the fire and begin to burn – and how much smoke and crackling there is, only those who have experienced it can know. But when the fire is properly alight the smoke and crackling cease, and within reigns only light. This condition is a state of purity; the way to it is long, but the Lord is most merciful and all powerful. Thus it is clear that when a man has received the fire of conscious communion

---

313. The Art of Prayer. p. 204f

with God, what lies before him is not peace but great labour. But from this point onwards he will find the labour sweet and full of fruit, whereas before, the work was bitter and bore little fruit or none"[314].

The more the blessed fire burns up the passions, the more it is experienced as a light which illumines the heart. Hesychios the Priest teaches that just as when a person looks at the sun, he cannot but fill his eyes with light, "so he who always gazes intently into his heart cannot fail to be illumined"[315]. The heart which does not receive images, forms, and the fantasies of evil spirits is conditioned by nature to give birth from within itself to "thoughts filled with light". Coal produces a flame. Much more will God, who dwells in our heart from our baptism, "kindle our mind to contemplation" if He finds it free from the winds of evil and protected by the guarding of the nous[316]. A heart that is emptied of fantasies "gives birth to divine, mysterious conceptual images that sport within it"[317]. The heart becomes an instrument of the Holy Spirit and acquires knowledge of God. All the thoughts and actions of the person who has rid himself of passions and fantasies are theological. The whole person is a theology. Theology gushes up from word, silence, action and stillness. In the pure heart, which is "the heaven of the heart", "the place of God"[318], shines the sun of righteousness.

We spoke before about the fire which comes into the heart, the "sanctuary of God". The existence of the fire creates **warmth** in the heart and the body. And one energy of fire is warming. St. Diadochos of Photike is expressive about this warmth which is created in the heart. When the soul, he says, acquires knowledge of itself, there flows from it a certain

---

314. Ibid. p. 156
315. Philok. 1, p. 180, 108
316. Ibid. 104
317. Ibid. p. 190, 156
318. Philotheos of Sinai. Philok. 3, p. 17, 4

feeling of warmth for God. This warmth very easily exhausts itself. But the warmth engendered by the Holy Spirit is peaceful and enduring. It is not dispersed outside the heart, but through the heart it makes "the whole man rejoice with a boundless love". The first warmth is a natural warmth, while the second is spiritual[319]. The warmth which gushes up like a spring focuses one's nous so that pure prayer comes into being. The athlete of this spiritual exercise must know that spiritual warmth comes neither from the right nor the left, nor from above, but "issues forth in the heart like a spring of water from the life-giving Spirit". It exists in the heart. "It is this prayer alone that you should wish to find and possess in the heart, always keeping your nous free from fantasy and stripped of conceptual images and thoughts"[320]. The coming of this warmth into our heart is important because in this way the powers of the soul will be concentrated there and will become undistracted prayer. St. Theophan the Recluse teaches: "This flame is the work of the grace of God; not a special grace, but one common to all. It appears when a man has attained a certain measure of purity in the general moral order of his life. When this small flame is kindled, or a permanent warmth is formed in the heart, the ferment of thoughts is stilled. The same thing happens in the soul as happened to the woman with an issue of blood: 'Her blood stanched' (Luk. 8, 44). In this state prayer comes near to permanency, and for this the Jesus prayer serves as an intermediary. This is the limit to which prayer performed by man himself can rise. I think that this is very clear to you.

"Further on in this state, another kind of prayer may be given, which comes to man by grace instead of being performed by him. The spirit of prayer comes upon man and drives him into the depths of the heart, as if he were taken by the hand and forcibly led from one room to another. The soul

319. St. Diadochos. Philok. 1, p. 278, 74
320. St. Gregory of Sinai. Gk. Philok. 4, p. 86ff

is here taken captive by an invading force, and is kept willingly within, as long as this overwhelming power of prayer still holds sway over it. I know two degrees of such invasion. In the first, the soul sees everything and is conscious of itself and of its outer surroundings; it can reason and govern itself, it can even destroy this state if it so desires. This too should be clear to you.

"But the Holy Fathers, and especially St. Isaac the Syrian, mention a second degree of prayer which is given to or descends upon a man. St. Isaac considers that this prayer, which he calls ecstasy or ravishment, is higher than that described above"[321].

As St. Diadochos mentioned above, it is possible to kindle a natural warmth. That is to say, there are two kinds of warmth, natural and supranatural. St. Theophan the Recluse writes again about this and about the effects of supranatural warmth: "Real warmth is a gift of God; but there is also natural warmth which is the fruit of your own efforts and passing moods. The two are as far apart as heaven and earth. It is not clear in the early stages which kind of warmth you have; later on it will be revealed. You say that your thoughts tire you out, that they do not allow you to stand firmly before God. This is a sign that your warmth comes not from God but from yourself.

"The first-fruit of the warmth of God is the gathering of thoughts into one, and their ceaseless concentration upon God. Think of the woman whose issue of blood suddenly dried up. In the same way, when we receive warmth from God, the flux of thoughts is halted. What then is necessary? Keep your natural warmth but set no value on it, and consider it only as a kind of preparation for God's warmth. And then, grieved over the faintness of the echo of God's warmth in your heart, pray to Him unceasingly and with suffering: 'Be merciful! Turn not Thy face from me! Let Thy face shine on me!' Along

---

321. The Art of Prayer. p. 65f

with this, increase bodily privations in food, sleep, work and so on. And place everything in the hands of God"[322].

Moreover it must be pointed out that, as in many other matters, here too the devil is able to bring about a warmth in the heart in order to distract our attention from God. When the kindled warmth distracts attention from God and prayer ceases to be pure, so that one tends to be excited, it is a sign that it is satanic. The wise and good spiritual athlete does not admire himself, he does not let his nous flee from the sense of sin, the experience of repentance and the insatiable remembrance of God in deep humility.

In any case, warmth of heart is communicated to the body as well. St. Gregory Palamas, opposing Barlaam's claim that the body does not participate in prayer, says that this is not Orthodox patristic teaching. Not only does the soul receive a pledge of the good things to come, but the body does as well[323]. The rebirth of the soul involves the rebirth of the body. Mourning does not end in the soul, but "from the soul it passes to the body and to the bodily senses"[324]. The grace of God which is in the soul also passes to the body. St. Gregory uses as arguments from Scripture the case of Moses, whose face shone, and of Stephen, whose face became the face of an angel[325]. This happens also with warmth. The warmth of the soul passes to the body. During continuous prayer, when the noetic lamp is lighted and when through spiritual theoria the nous raises up love into a tall flame, then "the body too in a strange way is lifted up and warmed. To those who see it, it seems to come from the fire of a visible furnace"[326]. And Christ's sweat is equally a sign of the perceptible warmth

322. Ibid. p. 159
323. Triads, 1, 3, 33
324. Ibid.
325. Triads, 1, 3, 31
326. Triads, 1, 3, 32

which "continued supplication to God can in itself communicate to the body"[327].

This warmth is so indispensable for the spiritual life that St. John of the Ladder states that if we lose this blessed and beloved fervour, we must carefully find out why, and let our soul "arm itself with all its longing and zeal" in order to get it back[328].

The presence of grace in the heart is manifested also by a **leap of the heart**. St. Gregory Palamas, with St. Basil the Great and St. Athanasius the Great, says that leaping of the heart is a sign of grace: the heart leaps "in the enthusiasm of love for the good"[329]. And in another place he says that when the soul leaps with love for the Only Desired One, then "the heart too is set in motion, indicating by spiritual leapings that it is in communion with grace, as if rushing up from here below to meet the Lord when He comes with his body in the clouds, according to the promise"[330]. The heart is preparing now to receive the heavenly King.

In these ways the heart is being purified and healed from the existing filth of sin. The passions are being transformed. Instead of serving the devil and his works of sin they serve the Lord. Thus the heart of man is being **purified** and prepared to see God. In what follows we shall look at this purification of the heart and the results which it offers to man.

The Lord said: "Blessed are the pure in heart, for they shall see God" (Matt. 5, 8). James, the Lord's brother, urges: "Purify your hearts, you men of double mind" (Jas. 4, 8). And the Apostle Peter commands: "Love one another fervently with a pure heart" (1 Pet. 1, 22).

The pure heart sees God and "the riches that are in

---

327. Ibid.
328. Ladder. Step 1. CWS p. 76
329. Triads, 1, 3, 2
330. Ibid. 1, 3, 32

Him"[331]. It sees God, who is the "supreme consummation of all blessings"[332]. The Old Testament is an icon of outward bodily asceticism, while the Gospel, or the New Testament, is an icon of purity of heart. Fasting, self-control, sleeping on the ground, standing, vigils and all the other bodily ascetic practices are good because they keep the passible part of the body from committing sinful acts. It is education of our outer man and a guard against active passions. At the same time it is protective against sins in thought. But "purity of heart or watch and guard of the nous, whose image is the New Testament, will not only uproot all passions and evils from our hearts; it will also introduce joy, hopefulness, compunction, sorrow, tears, an understanding of ourselves and of our sins, mindfulness of death, true humility, unlimited love of God and man, and an intense and heartfelt longing for the divine"[333].

The Holy Fathers, without overlooking the outward ascetic practices, which are educational anyway, give greater attention to inner purity, to purity of heart. Outward ascetic practices prepare the ground for developing the inner struggle. If a person stays in the outward ascetic practices and does not go on to the inward as well, he is living in the Old Testament period. The effort to purify the heart involves dispelling the clouds of evil from the air of the heart, so that we may see the sun of righteousness, Christ, "and so that the principles of His majesty may shine to some extent in the nous"[334].

But what is a pure heart? What kind of heart is pure? St. Symeon the New Theologian describes the pure heart. He says that a pure heart is one which is not troubled by passion; it also involves avoiding any inclination of mind to whatever is evil or profane, and having within oneself one thing alone:

---

331. St. Maximus. Philok. 2, p. 109, 72
332. Ibid. p. 158, 80
333. Hesychios the Priest. Philok. 1, p. 181, 112f
334. Philotheos of Sinai. Philok. 3, p. 18, 8

recollection of God in irrepressible love[335]. A pure heart is one which is seized in rapture and "looks upon the pledges of the good things promised to the saints and those eternal goods in so far as human nature is capable..."[336]. Other Fathers too speak of the pure heart. A pure heart is one which has no natural propulsion towards anything and in which God writes His laws as if on a writing-tablet[337]. A pure heart is one which does not allow any evil thoughts to enter the soul[338]. He is pure in heart whose heart does not condemn him for having rejected a commandment of God, or for negligence, or for accepting a hostile thought[339]. A person is pure in heart when he strives not to pass judgement on the prostitute, sinners or disorderly persons, but looks upon them all with a pure eye: "never to despise or judge or abhor anyone or to divide people according to categories"[340]. St. Makarios establishes what indicates a pure heart: "if you see a man with one eye, do not make any judgement in your heart, but regard him as whole. If someone has a maimed hand, see him not as maimed. See the crippled as straight, the paralytic as healthy"[341].

How does one gain purity of heart, which really means its healing from passions? St. Gregory Palamas, analysing the theological teaching that the energy of the soul is in its thoughts and the essence of the soul is in the heart, says that the energy of the nous in thoughts is easily purified by the prayer of a single word. But in this case let no one think that he has been completely purified unless all the other powers of the soul have also been purified, unless the essence of the nous, which is in the heart, has been purified. If he thinks so, he is deluded. When a person sees the impurity of his heart,

335. Practical and theological chapters, ch. 3, CS 41, p. 81, 32
336. Ibid. p. 81f, 35
337. St. Maximus. Philok. 2, p. 159, 81
338. Hesychios the Priest. Philok. 1, p. 196, 193
339. St. Theodoros, Gk. Philok. 1, p. 171, 193
340. St. Macarius. CWS p. 111. Hom. 15, 8
341. Ibid.

then he must in prayer apply all the other powers. He cleanses the active part by practice, the cognitive part by knowledge, the contemplative part by prayer, and so through them reaches "the true, perfect and stable purity of heart and mind, which no one ever gains except by perfection in actions, constant contrition, theoria and prayer in theoria"[342]. According to St. Symeon the New Theologian, purity of heart is achieved not by just one commandment, but by all the commandments. And the heart cannot be purified without the working of the Holy Spirit. Just as the smith uses his tools, but fire as well, because he cannot produce anything without it, "in the same way a man can do all things using the tools of the virtues, but they will not clean away dirt and corruption from the soul. Without the presence of the fire of the Spirit they will be feeble and useless"[343].

Abba Poemen emphasises particularly the action of the word of God. As water which drips little by little on stone, so the word of God is soft while the heart is hard. "When a person hears the word of God over and over, his heart is opened to fear God"[344].

The Holy Fathers lay great stress on the power of prayer and especially prayer of a single word, the Jesus prayer. Through this prayer a person is purified with the cooperation of the Holy Spirit. Hesychios the Priest says that it is impossible for us to cleanse our hearts, to drive out of it impassioned thoughts and spiritual enemies "without frequent invocation of Jesus Christ"[345]. Invocation of the Name of Jesus creates joy and tranquillity in the heart. "But it is Jesus Christ, the Son of God and Himself God, cause and creator of all blessings, who completely purifies the heart"[346]. Many

---

342. EF, p. 410f
343. CS 41, p. 80. 3, 29
344. Sayings. p. 162, 183
345. Philok. 1. p. 166, 28
346. Ibid. p. 177f, 91

Fathers emphasise the value of prayer for transforming the passions and purifying the heart[347]. St. Gregory of Sinai says that there are two ways of inner prayer and union, "or rather two entrances, one from each side of the noetic prayer which is activated by the spirit in the heart". In other words, there are two ways of noetic prayer and union of the nous and heart. One is when, through the constant invocation of the Name of Christ and through the warmth that arises, energy is produced in the heart and the passions diminish. The second way is when "the spirit draws the nous to itself and confines it to the depth of the heart, limiting its usual movements"[348]. Anyway it is a fact that when the heart is purified, a perpetual divine Liturgy goes on in it, and hymns are sung to God. What the Apostle Paul stressed applies here: "speaking to one another in psalms and hymns and spiritual songs, singing and making melody in your heart to the Lord" (Eph. 5, 19). This prayer is the most acceptable to God.

Of course when a person's heart has been purified, he must not be proud of it, for no creatures are purer than the bodiless ones, the angels, and yet Lucifer, by exalting himself, became the devil and is unclean. "His pride was reckoned by God as impurity"[349]. Thus purity of heart is a very delicate thing and is achieved with great labour and mainly with God's help and energy. An impure heart, even if the impurity is from arrogant thoughts, is blind.

The results of impurity of heart are many. We shall underline only a few of them.

He who is struggling to keep his heart pure has Christ Himself, the heart's Lawgiver, as his teacher, who secretly communicates His will to him[350].

---

347. See Hesychios Ibid. p. 192, 170; p. 172, 62; p. 195, 184. Callistus and Ignatius, Writings p. 243, 75
348. Philok. 4 in Gk. , 15 Chapters, ch. 1, p. 71, 1
349. Philotheos of Sinai. Philok. 3, p. 19, 11
350. Hesychios the Priest. Philok. 1, p. 195, 186

The pure heart experiences what is called hesychia of the heart[351]. It lives in the peace of God. "And let the peace of God rule in your hearts" (Col. 3, 15). It conquers cowardice. "If a man has achieved purity of heart, he has conquered cowardice"[352]. He fears nothing, not even death, for the fear of death is a consequence of impurity of heart. He is freed from demonic thoughts, words and actions[353]. He possesses inner silence of the heart and hesychia free of all thoughts[354]. His heart becomes "completely receptive to the Holy Spirit" and mirrors God clearly[355]. It dismisses the congestion which bodily cares create and opens itself, and this is hope in God. "Ample room in the heart denotes hope in God; congestion denotes bodily care"[356]. "He who cultivates good and immortal plants in his heart has a cheerful and bright countenance. His tongue sings hymns and prayers and is very kindly in conversation"[357]. The pure heart which has rid itself of fantasy does not sin. "It is impossible for sin to enter the heart without first knocking at its door in the form of a fantasy provoked by the devil"[358].

The purification of the heart, also in view of the results which we have presented before, seems to be a healing of the heart. The sickness, which is the passions, is expelled. The heart becomes well. But the Fathers advise that before, during and after purification, attention and guarding on our part are necessary. There has to be continuous watchfulness and guarding of the heart. We must be attentive to our heart, because if it is wounded, the whole body withers, just as when we injure the heart of a plant, the whole plant withers[359].

---

351. Ibid. p. 179, 100
352. St. Symeon the New Theologian. CS 41, p. 51. 1, 67
353. Hesychios the Priest. Philok. 1, p. 183, 122
354. Ibid. p. 179, 100
355. Abba Philemon. Philok. 2, p. 354
356. St. Mark the Ascetic. Philok. 1, p. 134, 114
357. Nicetas Stethatos. Practical chapters, ch. 33
358. Hesychios the Priest. Philok. 1, p. 170, 45
359. Ibid. p. 175, 78

Isaiah the Solitary urges us to examine ourselves daily and understand our heart and cast out everything evil: "Examine yourself daily in the sight of God, brother, and discover which of the passions is in your heart. Cast it out, and so escape His judgement. Be attentive to your heart, brother, and watch your enemies, for they are cunning in their malice"[360]. This attention is necessary even while the person is still very sinful. For when he abandons the sins and turns to God, "his repentance regenerates him and renews him entirely"[361]. "Holy Scripture, old and new, speaks everywhere about the guarding of the heart"[362]. And he cites such passages. "He who dwells continually within his own heart is detached from the attractions of this world, for he lives in the Spirit and cannot know the desires of the flesh"[363]. After attempting to keep our nous pure and to drive away evil thoughts and fantasies, in order to keep our heart pure we must control our tongue and belly. For wordiness and gluttony are the things which defile the nous with our breath and then also defile the heart, since the nous is the supplier of food for the heart. "A brother asked Abba Tithoes, 'How should I guard my heart?' The old man said to him, 'How can we guard our hearts when our mouths and our stomachs are open?'"[364].

I believe that all these things have shown clearly that in order to seek a conscious Christian life and to attain salvation, we must find the place of the heart. One ascetic used to give this answer to different people's questions: "Ask your heart. What does your heart say to you?" And as we have explained, the heart is not simply the feelings, but the place which is revealed by grace through asceticism and in which God is revealed.

---

360. Philok. 1, p. 26, 20f
361. Ibid. 22
362. Ibid. 23
363. St. Diadochos. Philok. 1, p. 270, 57
364. Sayings. p. 198, 3

We must acquire a sense of this. The entire ascetic life in Christ is aimed at this. And when we find the heart we must make every effort for it to be cured of its spiritual sicknesses. We are all sick in heart. And we must be cured. Finding and curing the heart is essentially finding salvation.

c) Intelligence (logiki) and Thoughts (logismoi)

Intelligence and thoughts play a leading role in the sickness and cure of the soul. It is in them that one is provoked to evil, that simple thoughts become compound, and as a result a desire is conceived which leads one to commit sin. Therefore an Orthodox therapeutic method must look into the subject of thoughts and the meaning of intelligence. This is why we are now going to examine intelligence on the one hand and thoughts on the other, in order to see how the curing of our souls takes place.

I. Intelligence

We have already said that the soul of man, created by God, is intelligent and noetic. St. Thalassios writes that God created intelligent and noetic beings "with a capacity to receive the Spirit and to attain knowledge of Himself; He has brought into existence the senses and sense objects to serve such beings"[365]. While the angels have intelligence and nous, men have reason, nous and senses, since man is a microcosm and a summing up of the whole creation. So it is through the nous and the intelligence that man knows God. The intelligent energy of the soul is linked with the noetic energy. There is no identity between the two, as we shall see in what follows.

When we spoke of the soul we saw that it was created in

---

365. Philok. 2, p. 326, 13

the image of God. And since God is Trinitarian: Nous, Word
and Spirit, the same is true of the soul as well: it has nous,
word and spirit. To say that the soul has nous, word and
spirit is to make certain presuppositions. The first presupposition is that, according to the teaching of St. Gregory Palamas, man's representation of the trinitarian mystery is not
meant in the sense that the Trinity should be understood
anthropomorphically, but man is to be understood in a trinitarian way[366]. That is to say, the Trinitarian God is not
interpreted on the basis of man, but man is interpreted on the
basis of the Trinitarian God. And this interpretation is not
merely psychological and human, but revelatory. This means
that it is only when a person is within the revelation, as all
the saints lived, that he can grasp this fact. The second
presupposition is that while man has nous, word and spirit in
accordance with the trinitarian mode of being, man's nous,
word and spirit are not hypostases, as is the case with the
Persons of the Holy Trinity, but energies of the soul. So "these
three are 'inseparable from one another' but they do not have
a personal character"[367].

The nous is the eye of the soul, which some Fathers call the
heart. The word is spiritual knowledge "implanted in the
nous as always co-existing with it"[368]. As Christ the Word is
He who reveals the will of the Nous, that is, of the Father, so
also the word of man is that which reveals what the nous
perceives and experiences. And just as it is impossible to con-
ceive of a word without spirit, so also in man the word is linked
with the spirit[369]. And just as the Spirit, which is a particular
hypostasis, is "an ineffable love of the Begetter towards the

366. Amphilochiou Rantovits. The Mystery of the Holy Trinity in St. Gre-
     gory Palamas. p. 47. In Gk
367. Ibid. p. 50
368. Ibid.
369. St. Gregory Palamas. 150 Chapters, ch. 36, p. 121ff

ineffably begotten Word himself"[370], so also the spirit in man is a certain impulse of the nous, "which involves an extension in time, in conjunction with our word, and requires the same intervals and proceeds from incompletion to completion"[371].

These things have been said in order to show the position and value of the word in man's soul. The word is that which expresses the experience and life of the nous, and this takes place in the spirit.

In many Fathers, as in St. Maximus the Confessor, the word is also called the 'logistikon', intelligence. The word in man is said inwardly but also expressed outwardly. Outward silence does not mean that there is not an inner word. But after a study of the works of the Fathers it can be asserted with some caution that the word is inward and outward and is united with the nous, while the intelligence which is connected with mind is the organ through which the word is expressed. Thus it can be stated that there is a subtle difference between the word and intelligence, just as there is between word and mind. St. Thalassios teaches that "the intelligence by nature submits to the Logos"[372]. The intelligent man must submit to the Word. The mind, according to St. Gregory Palamas, is not the eye of the soul. The nous is the eye of the soul, while the mind deals with the sensory and the intellectual. He writes: "When someone speaks of the 'eyes of the soul', which have experience of the heavenly riches, do not confuse them with 'mind'. The latter exercises its faculties on sensory and intellectual things"[373]. That is to say, it is not the mind but the nous which knows the heavenly treasures. The mind simply makes thinkable the things which man's nous lives experientially. God is revealed to the nous, but the mind records this experience in intelligent sentences.

---

370. Ibid.
371. Ibid.
372. Philok. 2, p. 313, 5
373. Triads. 1, 3, 34

It is usually said that man is an intelligent ('logiko') being, in the sense that he has intelligence and thinks. But in patristic theology an intelligent person is not one who simply has intelligence or speech, but one who, by means of the word and intelligence seeks to find God and to unite with Him[374]. A person who purifies his nous, where God is revealed, and afterwards, through the word and mind, expresses this inner experience, is intelligent. Apart from this setting man is without word and does not differ from the dumb animal. To be sure, he has intelligence and the word, but because he is not connected with God, he is dead. The dead soul manifests the dying of the word as well.

This is how the word functioned in man **before the fall**: the nous perceived God and the word expressed the experiences of the nous. "A pure nous sees things correctly. A trained intelligence puts them in order"[375]. According to the theology of St. Thalassios, which we mentioned before, the intelligence by nature submits to the word and disciplines and subjugates the body, while it is an insult to the intelligence to be subject to what lacks intelligence, that is, the body, and "concern itself with shameful desires". It is also an act of depravity for the soul to abandon the Creator and worship the body[376]. Thus man's nous before the fall had a relationship with God, and the word expressed this experience and life with the help of the mind, that particular instrument of the body.

But **after the fall** came the dying and death of the soul. As a result, it became impossible for the whole inner world of the soul to function naturally and for all the harmonised inner functions to go on. Man's nous was confused, hidden by the passions and overcome by impenetrable darkness. The word, not having to express the experiences of the nous, was identified with the mind. Thus the intelligence was raised above

---

374. St. Theognostos. Philok. 2, p. 367, 35
375. St. Maximus. Philok. 2, p, 82, 97
376. Philok. 2, p. 313, 5ff

the nous and now holds sway in fallen man. In fact this is the
sickness of the word and of the intelligence. The intelligence
is overnourished, it has been raised to a greater position than
the nous and has captured the word. The overnourished intelligence is the source of great abnormality in the spiritual organism. Arrogance, with all the energies of egoism, which is
the source of the abnormality, is raging there.

What Archimandrite Sophrony writes about the movements of the intelligence in fallen man and about the abnormality which this creates in the whole spiritual organism is
characteristic. I quote it in its entirety because it is very expressive. "The spiritual struggle is a manifold struggle but
the struggle with pride strikes deepest and is the most
grievous. Pride is the supreme antagonist of divine law, de-
forming the divine order of being and bringing ruin and death
in its train. Pride manifests itself partly on the physical plane
but more essentially on the plane of thought and spirit. It
arrogates priority for itself, battling for complete mastery,
and its principal weapon is the reasoning mind.

"Intelligence, for example, will reject the commandment
'Judge not, that ye be not judged' (Matt. 7, 1) as nonsensical,
urging that the faculty of being able to judge is a distinctive
quality in man, which makes him superior to the whole world
and affords him the power to dominate.

"In order to assert its superiority the intelligence points to
its achievements, to its creativeness, producing many con-
vincing proofs purporting to show that in the age-old experience of history the establishment or affirmation of truth
falls entirely within its province.

"Intelligence, functioning impersonally, is by nature only
one of the manifestations of life in the human personality,
one of the energies of the personality. Where it is allotted
priority in the spiritual being of man, it begins to fight
against its source – that is, its personal origin.

"Rising, as he thinks, to the furthest heights; descending,
as he believes, to the lowest depths, man aspires to contact

the frontiers of being, in order, as is his way, to define it, and when he cannot achieve his purpose he succumbs and decides that 'God does not exist'.

"Then, continuing the struggle for predominance, boldly and at the same time miserably, he says to himself:

"'If there is a God, how can I accept that I am not that God?'"

"Not having reached the frontiers of being and having attributed to himself this infinity, he stands up arrogantly and declares, 'I have explored everything and nowhere found anything greater than myself, so – I am God.'

"And it is a fact that when man's spiritual being is concentrated on and in the mind, reason takes over and he becomes blind to anything that surpasses him and ends by seeing himself as the divine principle.

"The intellectual imagination here reaches its utmost limits and, at the same time, its fall into the darkest night"[377].

No wise people without God can have pure word and pure intelligence. St. Gregory of Sinai says: "Only the saints, through purity, have become intelligent in accordance with nature. None of those wise in words have had pure intelligence, because they corrupted it from the start with evil thoughts"[378].

In order to see the corruption of intelligence in fallen man and what it does to our whole spiritual organism, we shall examine three levels on which fallen intelligence enters.

First, in our relationships with God. Whereas it was the nous that attained experience of God, now fallen intelligence undertakes to do this. Thus intelligence attempts to create arguments to demonstrate the existence of God, and this naturally is absolutely impossible to achieve. For the only argument for the existence of God is the pure nous's experience. Therefore in its attempt to advance alone on the path of the knowledge of God, fallen intelligence fails because

377. Archim. Sophrony: Saint Silouan. p. 165f
378. Acrostics, 2. Writings, p. 37

it either does not meet God at all or creates a false image of God. Thus from time to time various philosophical theories about God and various religions have been created. The heresies which have shaken the Church of Christ were due to this arrogant conceit of intelligence. Therefore it is emphasised by the Fathers that the saints do not theologise in the Aristotelian way, that is through intelligence and philosophy, but in the manner of a fisherman, that is, through experience (like the Apostles, through the Holy Spirit), after inner purification and disclosure of the nous.

On this point the dialogue which took place between St. Gregory Palamas and Barlaam the philosopher is characteristic. Barlaam asserted that man's intelligence alone is worthy of receiving knowledge of God. This is the noblest element in man's being. Then he claimed that what the prophets saw in the Old Testament and the apostles saw on Mt.Tabor was symbol, and therefore the philosophers had more authentic knowledge of God than the prophets and apostles. So he called vision of the uncreated light "inferior to our intellection". In reply St. Gregory taught that the saints' theoria is not from without, but from within, through inner transformation and purification. Therefore the light is not simply an external and material symbol, but a natural symbol, that is, energy of uncreated grace. The uncreated light is not a phantom and symbol which comes and goes, and so it is not "inferior to the energy of intellection", but it is "ineffable, uncreated, eternal, timeless, unapproachable, dazzling, infinite, unbounded, invisible to angels and men, archetypal beauty, immutable, glory of God, glory of Christ, glory of the Spirit, ray of divinity..."[379]. In reply to Barlaam's view that the uncreated light is "inferior to our intellection" he writes: "Oh earth and heaven and all those who see in them the light of the Kingdom of God, the beauty of the age to come, the glory of the divine nature û are they all lower than intellec-

---

379. Hagiorite Tome. Gk. Philok. 4, p. 191

tion?"[380]. The uncreated light is the glory of the divine nature, the beauty of the age to come.

Barlaam's mentality of raising philosophy higher than the vision of God, a thing which compelled St. Gregory Palamas to call him a philosopher rather than one who sees God, is the attitude of all heretics who have wanted to replace revelation by philosophy, and vision of God by knowledge coming from overuse of intelligent thought. Actually when human intelligence has dominion in a man, it leads him to a variety of heretical theories. Here the difference between philosophers and theologians is evident. The former philosophise about God. The latter, after purifying their nous, behold God. The former have a darkened nous and interpret everything onesidedly through intelligence, while the Holy Fathers, the real theologians, acquire experience of God through their nous; and then intelligence serves their nous by expressing this inner experience in propositions.

The way of knowing God in patristic theology is different from that of the philosophers. True knowledge of God is founded on humility: "Blessed are the poor in spirit, for theirs is the kingdom of heaven" (Matt. 5, 3). On purity of heart: "Blessed are the pure in heart, for they shall see God" (Matt. 5, 8). On keeping the commandments of Christ: "Anyone who transgresses and does not abide in the doctrine of Christ does not have God. He who abides in the doctrine of Christ has both the Father and the Son" (2 Jn. 9). On love: "If one loves God, one is known by Him" (1 Cor. 8, 3). It is not through human wisdom, through mental wealth and intelligence, that one can know God. The wisdom of God was unknown to "the rulers of the age, for had they known, they would not have crucified the Lord of glory" (1 Cor. 2, 8). In fact "the unspiritual man does not receive the things of the Spirit of God" (1 Cor. 2, 14).

Secondly, fallen intelligence affects our relation to our-

---

380. Triads. 3, 1, 23

selves, that is, our knowledge of ourselves. Many people influenced by Pythagorean self-knowledge try to find themselves and acquire knowledge of themselves through intelligence. But according to St. Gregory Palamas, this is a heresy of the Pythagorean and Stoic philosophers. The attempt to investigate oneself by intelligence can quickly end in schizophrenia. For one will attribute one's inner problems to other causes and so will fall into melancholy and anguish. The method of Orthodox therapeutic treatment and Orthodox self-knowledge consists in making the nous humble and guileless not by syllogistic, analytical and divisive methods, but by painful repentance and assiduous asceticism, as St. Gregory Palamas says and we have explained before[381]. Thus we acquire knowledge of our inner world not through intelligence, but through watchfulness, purification of the nous, ascetic living and repentance. In attempting to keep his nous pure a man becomes aware of his inner problems, he discovers the passions that hold sway in him.

Thirdly, disturbance of intelligence appears in the way in which we approach our fellow men. Usually psychiatrists observe the thinking of their patients and work their way into it in order to be able to identify their illness. Thus much intelligence is used which may lead to erroneous inferences. When this extends into interpersonal relationships it leads to their destruction, to the development of the passions of judgement and condemnation, which are not pleasing to God. Our own behaviour towards our fellow men is not characterised by intelligence but by love. We avoid judging others and classifying them in various categories. We try especially to do the reverse of what human intelligence dictates to us. We try not to see the sin and bad actions of our brother but to have love and compassion towards him. According to St. Makarios of Egypt, Christians should strive "not to pass judgement of any kind on anyone, neither on a prostitute nor on sinners nor on

---

381. Triads. 1, 3, 13

disorderly persons. But they should look upon all persons with a single mind and a pure eye...". We should behave in such a way that also if someone is suffering from a bodily ailment, we cannot look at it and pass judgement on it[382].

As spiritual fathers we face people personally. That is, we divest ourselves of every image, characterisation and idea and pray that God may reveal to us the person's real problem and guide us to give him the right therapeutic treatment. Each one interests us personally. In this way we avoid judging the one who's soul is ill, we avoid placing people in categories, we try to offer true personal therapeutic treatment. This means that we stand personally before the one who is making his confession.

From what has been said it is plain that fallen man is possessed by the power and authority of the intelligence in his relations with both God and his neighbour. The 'rule of reason', which is the basis of the whole of Western civilisation is the foundation of every internal and external anomaly. We who live in the Orthodox Church are trying to restore things. Our objective is twofold. We are striving on the one hand to limit the authority of intelligence, and on the other hand to discover our nous. We can see, from the fact that in fallen man the nous is in deep darkness and intelligence constitutes the only source of existence, that in order to arrive at the condition before the fall and to be guided to a life according to nature, the terms must be reversed, that is, nous and intelligence must each be put in its natural place, as we have described. In other words, the intelligence must be restricted, the nous must be developed, the word must be brought to birth by the illuminated nous, and then intelligence must formulate the nous's knowledge in words and sentences.

Obedience to the will of God has a significant role to play in restricting intelligence. We strive not to place trust in our

---

382. St. Macarius. Hom. 15, 8. CWS p. 111

own judgement and our own opinion, which comes from intelligence. Abba Dorotheos says: "In all things that come upon me I never desire to run around in quest of human wisdom, but I always act with the small power I have on whatever it is, and at the same time leave the whole to God"[383]. Indeed the same saint has a whole chapter entitled: "That a man ought not to rely exclusively on his own judgement"[384]. When the devil finds in someone one bit of self-will or self-righteousness, "he will cast him down through that"[385]. Similarly we are told to obey the will of God uncritically as it is expressed in Scripture and in the works of the Fathers of the Church. Our intelligence will certainly rebel and protest, but it is necessary to subject it to the will of God. And since it is possible not to know God's will in so many details of our daily life, we are required to obey a spiritual father who will guide us on our spiritual journey. According to Abba Dorotheos, "No one is more wretched, no one is more easily caught unawares, than a man who has no one to guide him along the road to God"[386]. Thus disobedience is death, while obedience is life. St. John of the Ladder writes: "Obedience is absolute renunciation of our own life, clearly expressed in our bodily actions. Or, conversely, obedience is the mortification of the limbs while the mind remains alive. Obedience is unquestioning movement, death freely accepted, a simple life, danger faced without worry... a safe voyage, a sleeper's journey. Obedience is the burial place of the will and the resurrection of humility... to obey is to put aside the capacity to make one's own judgement... Obedience is self-mistrust up to one's dying day, in every matter, even the good[387].

Obedience is mortification of one's own will, of one's own

---

383. Abba Dorotheos. CS Ch. 22, p. 252, 11
384. Ibid. ch. 5, p. 122
385. Ibid. p. 123
386. Ibid. p. 122
387. Ladder. Step 4. CWS p. 91f

understanding, not in order that passion should be mortified but that it should be transformed. Obedience practised in the way proposed by the Church does not destroy intelligence but heals it, placing it in its natural position. Therefore it is life. The Church's long experience has shown that anyone who can be obedient can be cured of his soul's inner sicknesses, that his whole inner world can be transformed. Obedience is a means of progress for man.

Along with restricting intelligence we try, through repentance and the ascetic life of the Church, to purify the nous so that it may be illuminated by God's uncreated energy. This is achieved by watchfulness, prayer – chiefly the noetic prayer of the heart – and by the whole active and contemplative life. Through all the means outlined by the Orthodox tradition, the nous receives grace, is vitalised, raised to its right position, and then sheds grace on the intelligence as well. In this way intelligence becomes a servant of the nous that is favoured with grace, and we return to our natural state.

Intelligence which is not subjected to this nous endowed with grace is sick and creates innumerable anomalies in our life, while, when it is subject to the nous it is healthy and natural. This is the aim of the ascetic therapeutic training of the Church.

II. Thoughts – Logismoi

It is in the intelligent part of the soul that evil thoughts operate which excite desire and attempt to capture man's nous so that sin is committed. The development of sin starts with thoughts. Therefore anyone who wishes to purify his inner world, to be released from sin, to be freed from the captivity of his nous must keep his intelligence safe from the impact of evil thoughts. So in this section we shall try to analyse what these thoughts are, what causes them, what results they produce in our spiritual organism, and finally what methods cure us of them. This is a very crucial matter because our spiritual death or spiritual life depend on our confronting them. Furthermore, as we shall see in what follows, many physical abnormalities and illnesses originate from unbridled thoughts.

What logismoi are

When the Fathers speak of 'thoughts' (logismoi), they do not mean simple thoughts, but the images and representations behind which there are always appropriate thoughts. The images with the thoughts are called 'logismoi'. "Images in some cases appear to take on visible form, while others are mostly products of the mind, but more often it is a combination of the two. As visible images also generate some thought or other, ascetics label all images 'intrusive thoughts'"[388]. The various satanic thoughts sometimes use as their vehicle what the senses bring to the nous, sometimes they mobilise fantasy and disjointed memory, and they attack the person with the ulterior aim of effecting his capture.

According to Hesychios the Priest, most people are unaware that these thoughts are nothing but "images of material and worldly things"[389]. As it appears from this text, imagination plays a very important role in the formation of the image in us. Thus one can say that logismoi are painters of various images and representations in our intelligence, most of them memories of the past. One brother who was being attacked by memories of the past said: "My thoughts are old and new painters: memories are troubling me, and idols of women"[390].

All things have their inner principles (words, logoi) with which they speak and communicate with man. According to St. Gregory of Sinai, Holy Scripture also calls these 'words' of

---

388. Archim. Sophrony: Saint Silouan. p. 134
389. Philok. 1, p. 189, 154
390. Sayings. p. 101, 1

things 'thoughts'. The words of things are also called conceptual images, and vice versa. Their action "is not material in itself, but it takes the form of material things, and its form changes"[391]. The words of things are used by the demons and therefore they can also be called the words of the demons[392]. St. Gregory of Sinai characterises evil thoughts, or rather their onslaught, as a "flowing river", which, through assent to sin, is transformed into a deluge that drowns the heart[393].

In speaking of 'thoughts' and trying to pinpoint exactly what they are, I think that we must refer to the division made by St. Maximus. He says that some thoughts are simple, others composite. Thoughts which are not linked with passion are simple. Passion-charged thoughts are composite, consisting "of a conceptual image combined with passion"[394]. The memory of a thing, when combined with passion makes the thought passion-charged or composite. I think that at this point it is well to outline the distinction between a thing, a conceptual image, and a passion as St. Maximus analyses them. Gold, a woman, a man, and so forth, are things. The simple memory of gold, a woman, or a man is a conceptual image. A passion is "mindless affection or indiscriminate hatred for one of these same things". An impassioned conceptual image is a thought compounded of passion and a conceptual image. Therefore we must strive to separate the passion from the conceptual image so that the thought remains simple. And this separation can be made through spiritual love and self-control[395].

Impassioned thoughts either stimulate the soul's desiring power or disturb its incensive power, or darken its intelligence[396].

---

391. Acrostics, 66. Writings, p. 49
392. Acrostics, 67. p. 49
393. Acrostics, 64. p. 48
394. Philok. 2, p. 79, 84
395. Ibid. p. 89, 42f
396. St. Maximus. Philok. 2, p. 85, 20

Evagrius emphasises that there are thoughts which cut off and there are thoughts which are cut off. Evil thoughts cut off good ones, but also evil thoughts are cut off by good ones. He offers an example. The thought of giving hospitality for the glory of the Lord is cut off by the tempter, who suggests a thought of hospitality for the sake of appearing hospitable in the eyes of others. Likewise the thought of giving hospitality to gain human recognition is cut off "when a better thought comes" which prompts us to be hospitable for the Lord's sake and for the sake of virtue[397]. So it is possible for one thought to start off as evil, but through our own effort and the inspiration of the Holy Spirit to be transformed into a good one, and vice versa. However, we shall look at this more analytically later, when we speak of curing from evil thoughts. At least we see here that there are thoughts which cut off and thoughts which are cut off, good thoughts and bad thoughts.

The cause of evil thoughts

What we have written about the nature of evil thoughts also shows their causes. According to St. Gregory of Sinai, the origin and cause of evil thoughts lies in "the splitting up, through man's transgression, of his single and simple memory"[398]. Before his transgression man's memory was simple, that is, it had no passion and it was turned entirely towards God. All the powers of the soul were centred on God. Immediately after the transgression this single memory was split up. St. Thalassios teaches that evil thoughts arise from three sources: the senses, the memory, and the body's temperament. The worst are those that come from the memory[399].

I think that St. Isaac the Syrian gives us a starting-point for seeing more clearly the causes of evil thoughts and what it

---

397. Philok. 1, p. 42, 6
398. Acrostics, 60. Writings. p. 48
399. Philok. 2, p. 309, 46

is that provokes them. He teaches that "the movement of thoughts in a man originates from four causes. Firstly, from the natural will of the flesh; secondly, from imagination of sensory objects in the world which a man hears and sees; thirdly, from mental predispositions and from the aberrations of the soul; and fourthly, from the assaults of the demons who wage war with us in all the passions. Therefore as long as a person remains in this world he cannot avoid thoughts and warfare"[400].

The basic cause of evil thoughts is the warfare of the devil. The majority of evil thoughts are from the devil. The devil's aim is to lead a man to sin either in thought or in action. He even waged war against Christ Himself, naturally without any success. The demons who are always trying to lay hold of our soul do so "by means of impassioned thoughts" so that they may cause it to sin either in the mind or in action[401]. When a man thinks evil, he sins in thought, whereas when he does the will of the devil and gratifies his desire, he sins in action. The committing of sin is called sinning in action. The demons constantly sow thoughts in order to capture the nous. The saints recognise "the seeds of the demons" and advise people accordingly[402].

St. Gregory of Sinai says that thoughts are the words of demons and the forerunners of passions. First comes the thought, and then the sin is committed[403]. According to Ilias the Presbyter, demons wage war against our soul first through thoughts and not through things. "Hearing and sight are responsible for the warfare waged through things, habit and the demons for that waged through thoughts"[404]. The demons constantly implant impure and shameful thoughts.

---

400. St. Isaac the Syrian. Ascetical Homilies, p. 20
401. St. Maximus. Philok. 2, p. 68, 20
402. Sayings. p. 9, 11
403. St. Gregory of Sinai. Acrostics, 67. Writings p. 49
404. Philok. 3, p. 36, 18

Each passion has its corresponding demon, and St. John of the Ladder emphasises that shameful and unclean thoughts in the heart come from the deceiving demon of the heart[405]. The cunning of the demons in this warfare is great, and only the saints whose nous is pure and who have the gift of insight can distinguish it. Thus St. John of the Ladder writes that he once noticed the demon of vainglory doing a double piece of work. In one brother he sowed thoughts of vainglory, and at the same moment he revealed those thoughts to another brother so that he would be praised as a thought-reader and thus fall into the sin and passion of vainglory[406]. Therefore the devil's warfare against us by means of thoughts is harder than that waged by means of material things[407].

But usually the devil takes his opportunity from the passions which exist in our soul in order to launch the appropriate warfare of thoughts. He knows the passions that are there and he excites the soul at those points. "The passions lying hidden in the soul provide the demons with the means of arousing impassioned thoughts in us"[408]. And since the most basic passion, from which all the others are engendered is self-love, it is in the passion of self-love that "the three most common forms of desire" have their origin[409]. When the heart of man inclines towards self-indulgence, it becomes a source of evil thoughts: "From a pleasure-loving heart arise unhealthy thoughts and words"[410]. Since there are voluntary and involuntary thoughts, that is, thoughts which come to us unsought and thoughts coming from our own will – for involuntary ones arise from previous sin, while voluntary ones are from our free will – therefore we can say that the voluntary

405. Ladder. Step 15. CWS p. 185
406. Ibid. Step 22. CWS p. 203
407. St. Maximus. Philok. 2, p. 63, 91
408. Ibid. p. 70, 31
409. St. Thalassios. Philok. 2, p. 324, 87
410. St. Mark the Ascetic. Philok. 1, p. 121, 162

thoughts are causes of the involuntary ones[411]. The causes of thoughts are the passions, and the causes of passions are sinful acts[412].

In general we can say that the thoughts which come from the demons capture the nous and lead it to commit sin in thought and deed. And when this sin is repeated many times and the organism acquires a habit, passion comes into being. Then from the passions, which in a way are the wounds of the soul, come the corresponding evil thoughts. It is the same as with wounds of the body. Something causes the body to be wounded, and as a result the wound causes an irritation, whereupon the problem continues and increases further.

At many points in His teaching the Lord mentions that the evil thoughts come from within the heart. "Out of the heart come evil thoughts, murder, adultery, fornication, theft, false witness, slander" (Matt. 15, 19). Luke the Evangelist mentions that an argument arose among Christ's disciples "as to which of them would be greatest". "But when Jesus perceived the thought of their hearts, he took a child and put him by His side" (Lk. 9, 46f). When the Lord appeared after the Resurrection, he said to His disciples: "Why are you troubled? And why do questionings arise in your hearts?" (Lk. 24, 38). All these passages show that questionings come from within the heart of man. Indeed the nous is the first to be attacked by the thought, but then passions work in the heart, and through them the devil takes the opportunity to put his own thoughts into play. Therefore it is said that questionings come from within the heart.

The teaching of St. Diadochos of Photike is related to this. The heart produces good and evil thoughts. However, it does not produce evil thoughts by nature, but from the memory of evil, of that first sin which it committed and which led to the habit. The heart conceives most of its evil thoughts as a result

---

411. Ibid. p. 142, 190
412. St. Gregory of Sinai. Acrostics, 62. Writings, p. 48

of the evil of the demons. However, we feel that they arise
from the heart. Man's nous, being highly responsive, makes
its own the thoughts sown in it by the evil spirits. The same
happens also with the flesh. Since the flesh delights in being
flattered by deception and since there is a union between the
soul and the body, the thoughts sown in the soul by the demons
seem to come from the heart[413]. The nous provides the nourishment for the heart. Whatever it has, good or bad, it transmits directly to the heart. Since most of us are inexperienced
in this spiritual combat and since this transmission takes
place very quickly, we feel that the thoughts are produced by
the heart.

Aside from the devil and the passions, things in themselves
engender thoughts. But, as St. Gregory of Sinai teaches,
things in themselves give birth to simple thoughts, while
suggestions of the devil engender evil thoughts[414]. So matter
is not bad; what is bad are the shameful desires within us, the
passions in us and the provocation on the part of the demons.
"Just as it is impossible to stop a watermill from turning" and
grinding the wheat or tares that we throw into it, so it is with
our mind; it is in constant motion. it depends on us whether
we give it spiritual meditation or works of the flesh. Therefore when we are occupied with worldly concerns and matters
of the flesh, and when we give ourselves over to pointless and
useless conversation, "these base thoughts multiply in us"[415].
So the use of the world and the being of the world are not bad,
but what is bad is our own disposition, our own self-will.

Certainly aside from evil thoughts there are good thoughts,
those coming from God. How can we distinguish these
thoughts? Those of us who are beginners in the spiritual life
should ask experienced spiritual fathers, and especially those
who have the gift of distinguishing spirits. In any case, one

---

413. St. Diadochos of Photike. Philok. 1, p. 284, 83
414. Acrostics, 68. Writings p. 49
415. St. Cassian of Rome. Philok. 1, p. 97f

general teaching is that when a thought suggests something to us and joy comes, it is a sign that the thought is from God. The thoughts of the devil are full of disturbance and dejection. St. Barsanuphios teaches: "When a thought suggests to you to do something according to the will of God, and you find in this matter joy, and at the same time sorrow which fights against it, know that this thought is from God... The thoughts which come from the devil are filled with disturbance and dejection, and they draw one after them secretly and subtly; for the enemies clothe themselves in sheepskins, that is, they instil thoughts which in appearance are right, but within are 'ravening wolves'"[416]. It must be noted that a thought is capable of evoking a joy which, however, comes from vanity and a self-indulgent heart. Therefore thoughts can be distinguished only by one who has tasted the grace of the Holy Spirit and has been cleansed from the passions which are found in the soul. Those who lack this experience should consult experienced spiritual fathers, because the devil suggests righteous thoughts, while he is unrighteous.

Now that we have pointed out what thoughts are and what causes give rise to them, we must look briefly at the different kinds of thoughts. Thoughts are analogous to the passions. For each passion there is a thought. St. Cassian of Rome divides them into eight and analyses at length the eight thoughts of evil. These are: "gluttony, unchastity, avarice, anger, dejection, listlessness, self-esteem and pride"[417].

St. Thalassios says that there are three basic thoughts: gluttony, self-esteem and avarice. All other impassioned thoughts follow in their wake[418]. These three thoughts correspond to the three great general passions: self-indulgence, love of glory, and avarice or love of possessions, to which the temptations of Christ refer.

---

416. Barsanuphius and John. Q59. ET p. 52f
417. Philok. 1, p. 73
418. Philok. 2, p. 324, 88

We must make mention of one great, disgraceful thought, that of blasphemy. St. John of the Ladder, recognising the wickedness and seriousness of thoughts of blasphemy, as well as the fact that they mainly attack those who are struggling in the spiritual life, devotes a whole chapter to describing them and presenting methods for ridding ourselves of these thoughts. He writes that the thought of blasphemy comes from pride. It attacks a man even during the Liturgy, even at the time of preparation for Holy Communion. It attacks the nous and distracts it from the words of the prayer. It stops many from praying and cuts many off from Communion; it causes the bodies of some to be worn away with grief. St. John of the Ladder advises us not to regard ourselves as the cause of thoughts of blasphemy. They are the demon's words intended to estrange us from God and His Church[419].

Yet evil thoughts are the beginning of the devil's warfare against us. A thought planted by the devil develops until the sin is committed and leads to passion. Therefore in what follows we shall try to see this development of evil thoughts in the light of the experience of the Holy Fathers.

St. Maximus teaches that the impassioned thoughts aroused by the passions lying hidden in the soul fight the nous and force it to give its assent to sin. When the nous has been overcome in this warfare "they lead it to sin in the mind; and when this has been done they induce it, captive as it is, to commit the sin in action". After the action the demons who have desolated the soul by means of these thoughts, retreat, but the spectre or idol of sin remains in the nous[420]. Thus thoughts take the nous captive and lead it captive into sin. If the idol of sin is not driven away by intense and lasting repentance, it is a source of abnormalities in the spiritual organism.

This in general outline is the development of an intrusive

---

419. Ladder. Step 23. CWS p. 211f
420. Philok. 2, p. 70, 31

thought and the course it takes. But we would do well also to see a few details about it, again as described by the Fathers.

The thought that has entered the soul's intelligence endeavours to capture the nous. To this end it prompts a feeling of the pleasure to be afforded by one or another passion which is in the soul. This stage is called temptation and is not to be reckoned as sin[421]. Prolonged delectation afforded by the passion attracts the attention of the nous[422]. If the nous does not tear itself away from the suggested delights, it finds itself attracted, favourable conversation with them begins, coupling follows, and it comes to assent. The increasing pleasure captures the whole nous, and the will as well. Thus the person's resistance becomes weak. Then the sin is committed. When the captures are repeated, the habit of a passion is formed, "and then all man's natural forces are at its service"[423]. The presence and prolongation of pleasure are very important for the capture and activation of passion. Therefore the Fathers advise mortifying the pleasure as far as possible, or better, its transformation, when it captures the person's nous. Abba Dorotheos says that whenever passionate desires reappear in the soul of those who put up a fight, they are immediately rejected[424].

Hesychios writes about the mingling and uniting of the soul's thoughts with the provocation of the demon through fantasy: "...its thoughts become entwined in the fantasy provoked by the devil", and so it comes to assent and to action[425]. Fantasy plays an important role, especially in cases where the object or person is far from us. But also when the person or object is seen, that is, when it is linked with the senses, then too fantasy magnifies things and increases their beauty

---

421. Archim. Sophrony. Saint Silouan. p. 134
422. Ibid.
423. Ibid. p. 134f
424. Abba Dorotheos. CS p. 197
425. Philok. 1, p. 169f, 43

in order to capture the nous and lead it to consent. From this point of view we can say that impassioned thoughts blur and confuse the nous, fill it with impure images and carry it "unwillingly and forcefully towards sinful acts"[426].

It seems that a man's freedom gives its consent not only at the time when it receives the temptation, the proposal from the demonic thought, but also beforehand, when, with freedom's consent, the eye and the ear of the soul are darkened. As Philotheos of Sinai teaches, the reason why a person looks on things adulterously is that "the inner eye has become adulterous and darkened" and the reason for wanting to hear about foul things is that "our soul's ears have listened to what the foul demons inside us have whispered to us"[427]. If a person is corrupted inwardly, the eye of his heart is defiled and then his outward bodily senses are also corrupted. That is why man's struggle must first be carried on inwardly.

Likewise when a person keeps thoughts within him and elaborates them, pleasure arises and the nous comes to assent and action. "As eggs warmed in dung hatch out, so unconfessed evil thoughts hatch evil actions"[428].

What has been said shows clearly the consequences of prolonged and elaborated thoughts. In the next section we shall present these consequences.

Consequences of evil thoughts

When a thought is prolonged in us we become enslaved to the attraction. "When a thought lingers within a man, this indicates his attachment to it"[429]. Attraction is a person's attachment to created things and his desire to realise them and acquire only those things. When the nous is disengaged

---

426. Abba Dorotheos. CS p. 195
427. Philok. 3, p. 29, 33
428. Ladder. Step. 26, Summary. CWS p. 257
429. St. Mark the Ascetic. Philok. 1, p. 132, 89

from heavenly food, from the remembrance of heavenly things, it constantly offers itself to the sensory and created things of the world. This is called attraction. It is led there by the thought which lingers within it.

The person becomes intemperate. He cannot control himself. "He whose mind teems with thoughts lacks self-control"[430].

"The person who in thought does not fight the thought of sin, saying nothing against it, commits it bodily"[431].

When an evil thought lingers in someone and is not opposed but put into action, it reinforces the passion in him, and then it fights and torments him further[432].

Thoughts rot us and crush us, also creating problems in interpersonal relations. "We spend all our time corrupting ourselves by the thoughts which we have against one another and tormenting ourselves..."[433].

Evil thoughts defile and pollute our soul[434], they damage it, they poison it. "Such is the cunning of the evil one, and with these arrows he poisons every soul"[435].

"A man who is carried away by his thoughts is blinded by them; and while he can see the actual working of sin, he cannot see its causes"[436]. This acceptance of thoughts gives the devil mastery over him and can lead him even to suicide, since he cannot resist the power of the devil.

An impure thought debases the soul[437], it throws a man's soul down on the ground.

Impassioned thoughts stimulate the soul's desiring power; they disturb the incensive power and the intelligence. "It is in

---

430. Ibid. p. 129, 40
431. Sayings. p. 101, 1
432. Abba Dorotheos. CS p. 242f
433. Ibid. SC p. 300, 86. CS p. 145
434. Sayings. p. 60, 4
435. Hesychios the Priest. Philok. 1, p. 170, 44
436. St. Mark the Ascetic. Philok. 1, p. 121, 168
437. St. Thalassios. Philok. 2, p. 312, 91

this way that the nous's capacity for spiritual contemplation and for the ecstasy of prayer is dulled"[438]. Without God a man is dead.

Anyone who continuously feels disturbed by thoughts and whose underbelly is aflame shows that he is far from the fragrance of the Spirit[439].

Intimacy with God is lost. "When the nous associates with evil and sordid thoughts it loses its intimate communion with God"[440]. God cannot have communion with someone whose nous is constantly defiled by evil and impure thoughts. And God is disgusted by a man who accepts unclean thoughts while standing at prayer, just as an earthly king would be disgusted by a man who in his presence turned his face away and talked to his master's enemies[441].

Not only does a man of unclean thoughts lose his intimacy with God and the fragrance of the Holy Spirit, but he is completely separated from God. "For unclean thoughts separate God from man." God does not disclose His mysteries to one who is possessed by evil thoughts[442]. Abba Dorotheos says very clearly, "A single evil thought can turn a man away from God when it is taken in and adhered to"[443].

Since thoughts separate a person from God, they are followed by other, bodily abnormalities. Anguish, insecurity and physical illnesses are caused by thoughts. Physicians too have become aware of this, so they advise us not to keep thinking about things and worrying. One thought can let a person lie sleepless for a whole night. So we say that thoughts disturb a man and even break his nerves. Abba Theodoros said: "A thought comes and bothers me..."[444].

---

438. St. Maximus. Philok. 2, p. 85, 20
439. Nicetas Stethatos. Practical chapters, ch. 57
440. St. Maximus. Philok. 2, p. 58, 50
441. Ladder. Step 28. CWS p. 280
442. Sayings. p. 135, 1
443. Abba Dorotheos. CS p. 190
444. Sayings. p. 68, 1

The results of evil thoughts are truly terrible. We have pointed them out very briefly, but we could have cited more patristic passages. We have tried to indicate the general abnormalities which they produce in our psychosomatic organism.

A psychotherapeutic method must, however, also describe the ways in which people are healed of evil, demonic thoughts. We now come just to this topic.

Curing of evil thoughts

As with all diseases of the soul and body, so also with thoughts there is preventive treatment as well as therapeutic treatment after the illness. We shall look at both.

The preventive work is to try not to let the thought enter us and capture our nous. This is achieved by **watchfulness, attentiveness, hesychia,** and **cutting off evil thoughts.** The Apostle Paul instructs his disciple Timothy to be constantly watchful: "As for you, always be watchful" (2 Ti. 4, 5). The patristic writings contain an extensive analysis of this struggle.

Watchfulness is also called guarding of thoughts. St. John of the Ladder teaches that it is one thing to guard thoughts and another to watch over the nous. Watching over the nous is higher than guarding thoughts[445]. This is true in the sense that we defined earlier, that the nous is the eye of the soul, the heart, while a thought is what functions in a man's mind. It is one thing to try to keep the mind pure and another to try to keep the nous, that is the heart, pure. Nevertheless purity of thoughts is needed, because it is impossible to keep one's inner self free from sin if one has evil thoughts[446]. The patristic commandment is to concentrate our nous (the soul's energy in its essence), to be watchful of thoughts and to fight

---

445. Ladder. Step 26. CWS p. 239f
446. Philotheos of Sinai. Philok. 3, p. 29, 33

against impassioned thoughts[447]. It is essential that we pay attention to our reflections, recollections and notions[448]. Indeed in this struggle to keep the nous pure and have constant remembrance of God, we have to discard the good thoughts as well, because even with good thoughts the nous gradually forms the habit of withdrawing from God. The monk Silouan taught: "The saints learned how to do battle with the enemy. They knew that the enemy uses intrusive thoughts to deceive us, and so all through their lives they declined such thoughts. At first sight there seems to be nothing wrong about an intrusive thought but soon it begins to divert the nous from prayer, and then stirs up confusion. The rejection of all intrusive thoughts, however apparently good, is therefore essential, and equally essential is it to have a nous pure in God"[449]. We should never have a single thought in our heart, whether senseless or sensible[450]. We should protect the eye of the soul from every thought, as we do the eye of the body from every harmful object.

When a person becomes accustomed to this holy struggle of laying aside all thoughts, then the nous tastes the goodness of the Lord and acquires purity so that it can distinguish thoughts and "store in the treasures of its memory those thoughts which are good and have been sent by God, while casting out those which are evil and come from the devil"[451].

This watchfulness of the soul, this guarding of thoughts, is called inner hesychia. Therefore in Orthodox teaching hesychia is not simply stillness from outward stimulations (this too is the beginning of hesychia, especially for the beginner), but it is mainly stillness of the heart. St. Thalassios advises: "Seal your senses with hesychia and sit in judgement upon

---

447. St. Thalassios. Philok. 2, p. 309, 45
448. Sayings. p. 60, 4
449. Archim. Sophrony. Saint Silouan. p. 168
450. Hesychios the Priest. Philok. 1, p. 171, 49
451. St. Diadochos of Photike. Philok. 1, p. 259f, 26

the thoughts that attack your heart"[452]. According to St. John of the Ladder, "stillness of the body is the accurate knowledge and management of one's feelings and perceptions, but stillness of soul is the accurate knowledge of one's thoughts and is an unassailable mind". Brave and determined thinking, watching at the doors of the heart, killing or driving off invading notions are the friends of hesychia[453]. When a person perseveres in this struggle, and especially when the nous has been captivated by the Kingdom of God, then the thoughts vanish just as the stars are hidden when the sun rises[454].

Apart from watchfulness and stillness of the nous, another way to prevent the nous from being irritated is **to avoid the causes** which evoke thoughts. St. Maximus gives an example to show how we must struggle to maintain purity of heart. As we know, the demons of passion either stimulate the soul's desiring power or disturb its incensive power and its intelligence. Therefore a monk should watch his thoughts and seek out and eliminate their causes. "The soul's power of desire is stimulated by impassioned thoughts of women. Such thoughts are caused by intemperance in eating and drinking and by frequent and senseless talk with the women in question; and they are cut off by hunger, thirst, vigils and withdrawal from society. The incensive power is disturbed by impassioned thoughts about those who have offended us. This is caused by self-indulgence, self-esteem and love of material things. It is on account of such vices that the passion-dominated person feels resentment, being frustrated or otherwise failing to attain what he wants. These thoughts are cut off when the vices provoking them are rejected and nullified through the love of God"[455].

Furthermore, in order to be rid of thoughts one should

---

452. Philok. 2, p. 308, 22
453. Ladder. Step 27. CWS p. 261f
454. Ilias the Presbyter. Philok. 3, p. 59, 91
455. Philok. 2, p. 85f, 20

struggle against passions, since it is from these that the demons find occasion to implant convenient thoughts. With regard to the passion of unchastity St. Maximus advises: "fast and keep vigils, labour and avoid meeting people". With regard to anger and resentment: "be indifferent to fame, dishonour and material things". With regard to rancour: "pray for him who has offended you and you will be delivered"[456].

Another struggle is to reduce the pleasure-loving of the heart[457], because thoughts try to kindle pleasure and attract the nous. Along with the pleasure-loving of the heart, it is necessary to tackle the pleasure-loving of the body as well. Everything which evokes bodily pleasure and bodily comfort must be driven away by the athlete of the inner struggle. For if a person gives in to bodily pleasure, "he will necessarily, even if he does not wish it, be led off by force to the Assyrians, to serve Nebuchadnezzar"[458]. If a person does not take a very firm stand towards himself on the subject of pleasure, he will not be able to maintain or acquire his inner freedom.

As we pointed out a little earlier, we must avoid things and people that evoke evil thoughts in us. One ascetic, answering the question of a brother who said that he was struggling with memories of women and the desires of the past, said: "Do not fear the dead, but flee from the living, and before all things persist in prayer"[459]. We surely are not asked to avoid all people. This is possible for a few who are seeking perfect purity in order to give themselves wholly to God, but we must avoid those people who are a temptation to us, not so much because they are bad, but because we ourselves are inwardly weak and susceptible to sickness. When a person makes it a principle to watch his nous and pay attention to matters and

---

456. Ibid. 84f, 13
457. St. Mark the Ascetic. Philok. 1, p. 121, 162
458. Abba Dorotheos. CS p. 195
459. Sayings. p. 101, 1

objects and people, he can learn for which of them he has a passion[460].

The fear of God helps to liberate us from warfare with thoughts. The fear of God is God's gift to man. He who receives this gift struggles all day not to do anything displeasing to God, or rather he does not simply struggle, but the fire of the fear of God melts every oncoming thought. But even if there is not this charismatic fear, let us at least of ourselves struggle to create the sense of the presence of God and of the judgement to come. "As wax melts before fire, so does an impure thought melt before the fear of God"[461]. The fear of God is the shepherd that leads the sheep, that is, thoughts. Without the shepherding fear, thoughts will be in confusion[462].

Parallel with these things, **toil** and the **ascetic life** are a method of therapy. Fasting, vigils and prayer help the nous to avoid capture by the oncoming thoughts. "Waste your body with fasting and vigils, and you will repulse the lethal thoughts of pleasure"[463]. "Keep your body under control, and pray constantly; in this way you will soon be free from the thoughts that arise from your prepossessions"[464]. St. Mark the Ascetic teaches that if we do not want to be moved by evil thoughts, we must accept humiliation of soul and affliction of the flesh. And this must not be just on particular occasions, but "always, everywhere and in all things"[465].

These things which have been mentioned can be used by a person to prevent sickness due to thoughts, but also if he is sick they are needed as a method of curing from thoughts. But let us look more analytically at how we can cure the soul which has been affected by thoughts.

---

460. St. Maximus. Philok. 2, p. 95, 78
461. St. Thalassios. Philok. 2, p. 308, 26
462. Elias the Presbyter. Philok. 3, p. 65, 136
463. St. Thalassios. Philok. 2, 308, 25
464. Ibid. p. 326, 17
465. Philok. 1, p. 143, 207

In the first place one must not be at all **agitated**. The demons' effort is to create agitation in a person and then in the confusion to interfere more actively in the soul and take it captive. Therefore St. Maximus teaches: "Stand up courageously against the thoughts that surge over you, especially those of irritation and listlessness"[466]. Facing thoughts with courage is a second martyrdom. The advice of all the Fathers is not to be agitated when we are attacked by satanic thoughts. St. Barsanuphios says: "If the thought comes, do not be alarmed but understand what it wants to do and counteract it without agitation, calling on the Lord." The bad thing is not that a thief enters the house, but that he takes what he finds in the house[467].

Some people allow the thought to enter their nous and heart in order to hold **a dialogue** with it and overcome it by the power of Christ. This is done by a few who are abundantly blessed with the grace of Christ and who want to enter into face-to-face combat with the devil in order to destroy him. However, this is not possible for most Christians, who are powerless to take up this strenuous and dangerous combat. So most of us have to scorn intrusive thoughts.

It must be said that the less experienced in spiritual matters a man is, the slower he is to perceive the entrance of the thought. Usually those who are practised spiritual athletes perceive the thought before it has entered their intelligence and even when it is preparing to wage war on the athlete. Some perceive the thought only when there is coupling or when there has already been assent, or on the very threshold of action or even after sin has been committed. "The spiritually inexperienced man generally encounters sinful thoughts only after they have progressed, unnoticed, through the first stages of development – that is, after they have acquired a measure of strength – when the danger approaches of actu-

---

466. Philok. 2, p. 58, 52
467. Barsanuphius and John (in Gk.) p. 223, Q. 448

ally sinning"[468]. In any case, wherever he meets it he must immediately fight against it. And the more practised he is in this holy game, the more he perceives the thought in the first stages of its development.

A better way than dialogue is **to scorn** the thoughts and **cut them off**. Archimandrite Sophrony presents the teaching of St. Silouan about the best method of fighting thoughts: "The Gerontas was saying that the experience of the Holy Fathers shows various ways of combating intrusive thoughts but it is best of all not to argue with them.

"The nous that debates with such a thought will be faced with its steady development, and, bemused by the exchange, will be distracted from remembrance of God, which is exactly what the demons are after – having diverted the nous from God, confuse it, and it will not emerge 'clean'.

"Stephen the Hermit (out of whose hands a leopard fed) as he lay dying (Ladder, Step 7), disputed with intrusive thoughts, as was his wont, and so found himself struggling against devils.

"St. Mark of Thrace for having tried to comfort his soul before departing from this life by enumerating his efforts was kept swinging in the air 'for an hour' – which suggests that it could have been for all time.

"Other Fathers were more discriminating in their spiritual struggle"[469].

So it is not safe, especially in the beginning of the spiritual life, to let thoughts enter the heart. "But as soon as we perceive them we should counter-attack and repulse them"[470]. To scorn a thought is a good way especially for beginners in this struggle.

Without entering into dialogue with the thought, we should refuse to do what it says to us and in that way also weaken the passion itself, and "fighting in this way little by little, and

468. Arch. Sophrony. Saint Silouan. p. 135
469. Ibid. p. 66
470. Hesychios the Priest. Philok. 1, p. 170, 44

with the help of God, he overcomes the passion itself"[471]. This is called resistance to a thought.

Someone said to Abba Poemen: "Abba, I have many thoughts and they put me in danger." The old man led him out and said to him: "Expand your chest and do not breathe in". To the man's answer that he could not do it Abba Poemen replied, "If you cannot do that, no more can you prevent thoughts from arising, but you can resist them"[472]. So we cannot prevent thoughts from coming to us.

We need to oppose them. And the opposition consists, on the one hand, in utter scorn, and on the other hand, in not doing what they say. "If we do not do anything about them, in time they are spoiled, that is to say, they disintegrate"[473]. Just as when someone shuts a snake or a scorpion in a bottle, in time it will die, "so it is with evil thoughts: they are suggested by the demons; they disappear through patience"[474]. When a thought led Abba Agathon to criticise, he said: 'Agathon, do not do that,' and so the thought was still"[475]. Likewise Abba Theodore and Abba Lucius spent fifty years mocking their temptations by saying to the thought of leaving the place of their asceticism: "After this winter we will leave here." When the summer came, they said, "After the summer we will go away from here." Thus they passed the whole time and mocked the demons[476]. Postponing the time of satisfying a thought helps us to be rid of it.

Another way of healing is the struggle not to let thoughts persist. The struggle lies in not letting a simple thought stir passion and not letting a passionate thought be given assent. "Both these two forms of counter-attack prevent the thoughts

471. Abba Dorotheos. CS p. 243
472. Sayings. p. 144, 28
473. Ibid. p. 142, 20
474. Ibid. p. 142, 21
475. Ibid. p. 20, 18
476. Ibid. p. 68, 2

themselves from persisting"[477]. For a thought which persists will engender other thoughts and create many problems in the inner world and will take our nous an unwitting captive.

Likewise we should not let the simple thought become a compound or passionate thought, but also a compound thought should be turned into a simple one. A compound thought is composed of passion and a conceptual image. It will be necessary with self-control and spiritual love to separate the passion from the conceptual image, and then the thought will become simple[478].

Since an intrusive thought tries to kindle sensual pleasure, which will then take the nous captive, the nous must cut off the intended pleasure[479]. St. Maximus teaches that we must become murderers not only of bodily passions but also of the soul's impassioned thoughts[480].

Apart from cutting off and scorning thoughts, it is necessary to chase them away, and this is done mainly by prayer. St. Gregory of Sinai teaches that a beginner cannot chase a thought away unless God does it. The strong can wage war with thoughts and chase them away, but again even they do it with God's help. "When thoughts come, call to our Lord Jesus, often and patiently, and they will retreat; for they cannot bear the warmth of heart produced by prayer, and they flee as if scorched by fire." In prayer the name of Jesus is pronounced, which flogs the devil, and the presence of divine grace creates warmth of heart. These things burn evil thoughts and drive them out of the nous. If anyone lacks the energy to pray, let him imitate Moses: lift his hands and eyes to heaven, and then God Himself will drive the thoughts away[481]. Just as

---

477. St. Maximus. Philok. 2 p. 97, 87
478. Ibid. p. 89, 43
479. Arch. Sophrony. Saint Silouan. p. 134
480. Philok. 2, p. 163, 97
481. Writings p. 75, 4

smoke is dispersed in the air, so evil thoughts are dispersed by the invocation of the Name of Christ[482].

We cannot rid ourselves of demonic thoughts by means of human thinking. We must abandon every thought, even if we are wise, and rest all our hope in God, saying "Lord, arrange the matter as you wish and as you know..."[483]. This passage is significant because in time of temptation many people attempt to confront it with human intelligence. However powerful intelligence is, it cannot be more powerful than the devil's thought. For in the struggle against a thought we are fighting against the devil and not against a simple thought.

Praying with watchfulness clears the mind of all images of evil thoughts, and so our mind is made conscious of both the devices of our enemies and the great benefit of prayer and watchfulness[484]. Through prayer the athlete of the spiritual life is clearly aware of the whole thought, makes a sober study of it, and in this way without having put the thought into action, is aware of its consequences. Therefore the ascetics who have practice in this spiritual contest, who do not allow the thought to enter them, usually know very well the life of the sin and the sinner without having their own personal experience.

If the enemy's seed is fire, hope in God through prayer is the water which puts out the fire[485]. Abba John the Dwarf said: "I sit in my cell and I am aware of evil thoughts coming against me, and when I have no more strength against them, I take refuge in God by prayer and I am saved from the enemy"[486].

An effective method of getting rid of thoughts is **to confess** them to an experienced spiritual father. St. John Cassian

482. Hesychios the Priest. Philok. 1, p. 179, 98
483. Abba Dorotheos. SC p. 514, 193
484. Hesychios the Priest. Philok. 1, p. 189, 154
485. Abba Poemen. Sayings. p. 158, 146
486. Ibid. p. 75, 12

says that "just as a snake which is brought from its dark hole into the light makes every effort to escape and hide itself, so the malicious thoughts that a person brings out into the open by sincere confession seek to depart from him"[487]. Nothing so harms a monk and brings such joy to the demons as hiding his thoughts from his spiritual father[488]. In this way his whole spiritual life is twisted and he becomes a plaything in the hands of the devil, who can do what he likes with him. Therefore St. John Cassian teaches that nothing leads so surely to salvation as confessing our private thoughts to the most discriminating of the fathers and being guided by them rather than by our own thoughts and judgement[489]. "He who conceals his thoughts remains unhealed"[490]. Therefore we must confess the persistent thought, bring it to our spiritual father who has responsibility for our salvation. "Any thought that tarries in you and engages you in warfare, reveal to your Abba, and he, with God's help, will heal you"[491]. When we speak of a persistent thought we mean one that does not go away in spite of our objection, scorn, and prayer, but continues to wage war against us, like the impassioned thought which is united with the passion.

St. John of the Ladder cites the case of a monk whom he met in a coenobium. He had a small book hanging in his belt and said that he wrote his thoughts in it each day and showed them all to his shepherd[492].

The discriminating shepherd can be illiterate according to the world, not knowing the wisdom of the world, but knowing God's wisdom. Abba Arsenios had the habit of going to ask about his thoughts to a discriminating father who neverthe-

---

487. Philok. 1, p. 103
488. Ibid.
489. Ibid. p. 106
490. Barsanuphios and John. Q. 317. ET p. 87
491. Ibid. Q 142. ET p. 58
492. Ladder. Step 4. CWS p. 105

less was crude, illiterate and uneducated. Another brother asked him: "How is it, Abba Arsenios, that you, with such a good Latin and Greek education, ask this peasant about your thoughts?" He replied: "I have indeed been taught Latin and Greek, but I do not know even the alphabet of this peasant"[493].

When a person has learnt to open himself to God through his spiritual father and to expose all his wounds created by thoughts, and the thoughts themselves, and at the same time listens to his advice, he is released from each one, he is inwardly at peace, and he knows what the peace of Christ means.

As we confess to our spiritual father we also ask for his **prayer** and **blessing**. St. John Chrysostom, referring to Christ's words to his Apostles when they were entering a house to give peace, says that often without anyone disturbing us we are at war in thought and are agitated, and cunning desires rise up in arms. This battle sends down the word of the saints, that is the saints' blessing, and this brings much calm within us. "At that utterance, every diabolical desire and unseemly thought slipped away from our soul"[494].

As we have emphasised in another place as well, we can rid ourselves of thoughts by **cultivating** the various **virtues**. Self-control and love rid us of impassioned thoughts[495]. By controlling anger and desire we quickly do away with evil thoughts[496]. Vigils also contribute a great deal: "The vigilant monk is a fisher of thoughts, and in the quiet of the night he can easily observe and catch them"[497].

The **reading** of God's law and the lives of the saints cut off thoughts. Therefore the words of the Apostles and Fathers as well as their lives have much power and give peace to the soul.

---

493. Sayings. p. 8, 6
494. Hom. on ITim. 5, 9, para. 14. PG 51, 334. NPNF vol. 13
495. St. Thalassios. Philok. 2, 308, 14
496. Ibid. 17
497. Ladder. Step 20. CWS p. 196

Another way is **to create good** thoughts. Indeed we have previously observed that we must cut off and cast away every thought, even if it is a good one, especially at the time of prayer. But at other times, particularly when we are at the beginning of the spiritual life, we can cultivate good thoughts. But again we need to be watchful not to cultivate fantasy through them, because in that way we would develop a demonic type of spirituality. "Cultivate good thoughts with care so that you find them again hereafter"[498]. Let us receive everything with a good thought. Even if everything is ugly, let us receive it with equanimity and then God will right the anomalies of things. "Accept with equanimity the intermingling of good and evil, and then God will resolve all inequality"[499]. Or yet let us transform the evil thoughts into good ones.

One of the best ways of curing and disposing of thoughts is to keep our nous in hell burning with the flames of the inferno. St. Silouan taught: "St. Makarios the Great, flying through space, never ceased humbling himself, and when devils, outdistanced, cried to him from afar that he had escaped them, he replied that he had not yet evaded them. He answered after this fashion because he was accustomed to stay his mind in hell, and thereby really did elude the devils.

"St. Poemen the Great, schooled by long experience of battle against devils, knowing that far the most dangerous and powerful enemy is pride, fought all his life to acquire humility, and so said to his disciples: 'Be assured, children, that where Satan is, there am I also'. But at the bottom of his heart, knowing how good and merciful is the Lord, he trusted that He would save him. To humble oneself in this wise is the best means of keeping one's mind pure from every passionate thought"[500].

---

498. Abba Dorotheos. CS p. 186
499. St. Mark the Ascetic. Philok. 1, p. 121, 159
500. Archim. Sophrony. Saint Silouan, p. 66

For a person to keep his mind in hell and for all his thoughts to be burnt by the flames of hell is a state which is imbued with repentance and especially with the great and ardent repentance which is a gift of the grace of Christ. If this is not present, at least a person should hold in remembrance the thought of impending death and his judgement in hell. This thought is enough to purify the nous and release the person from the tyranny of thoughts.

When a person is freed by this whole ascetic method from the tyranny of thoughts and both nous and heart are pure, then he is filled with the energy of the Holy Spirit and experiences the healing of his soul. The soul is freed from all its wounds and becomes a temple of the Holy Trinity. The person becomes a true priest of the grace of God and has a foretaste of the good things of the Kingdom of Heaven. This is the true, natural man, the man made divine by grace.

4. Orthodox Pathology

John the Evangelist, preparing to speak of the Lord's miraculous healing of the paralytic, gives us a description of the pool of Bethesda and the situation which prevailed there during the Lord's visit. Bethesda had five porches. "In these lay a great multitude of the sick, blind, lame, paralysed, waiting for the moving of the water" (Jn. 5, 3).

The Church too is a Pool, a spiritual Bethesda. All of us, its members, overcome by death and decay, corruptibility and mortality with all their consequences are waiting at this Pool, hoping for our spiritual healing.

St. John Chrysostom interprets the miracle performed by the Lord at Bethesda. He asks the question: "What manner of healing is this: what mystery is being intimated to us?" He answers that the pool portrays and typifies what is going to happen in the future, and this in fact is baptism. "He was on the point of giving baptism, which has much power and is a very great gift, baptism which cleanses of all sin and brings men to life, when they have been dead"[1].

Since baptism is the 'introductory' sacrament by which we enter the Church, we can extend the symbolism to say that the Church is the spiritual Bethesda – the spiritual sanatorium and Hospital. All Christians, having tasted God's love and charity towards mankind, at the same time sense our

---

1. PG 59, 203. Homily 36 on John. FC 33, p. 352

spiritual poverty. Because God's grace throws light on our inner condition, we see the strength of the passions in us and the law of sin in our members. That is why we feel ill. This feeling is the beginning of healing, or to express it better, it is the beginning of the vision of God, since repentance and inward grief are impossible in a carnal man. Only a sharer in God's grace experiences this inner reality.

Hospitals have special pathological clinics. And the Church, which is the spiritual hospital, the spiritual sanatorium, has its pathological clinic. We are not trying to create confusion about these terms, but we firmly believe that the study of passions is pathology. So here we shall take a longer look at the subject of passions. We shall define 'passion', go on to distinguish between passions, and then examine as analytically as we can the curing of the passions.

This account is necessary because it constitutes the Orthodox ethos. We are convinced that what one says about being Orthodox must include several basic elements. First one must refer to the fall of man from the divine life and the tragedy of the fallen state. Then one must speak of rebirth through holy baptism, and the continuation of rebirth which goes on in the Church. Teaching about rebirth is not Orthodox when it implies a momentary event which takes place through outward faith in Christ, because rebirth continues through our whole life, and there is no limit to perfection, it knows no bounds. We have the case of the Apostle Peter, who was granted to see the uncreated Light on Mt.Tabor. His eyes were transformed and thus they saw the glory of the Lord. Yet a few days later he denied Christ. Certainly that great moment of the Theophany led him to repentance and weeping. His fall showed itself to be great by contrast to the great vision. At any rate we observe here the fact that the power of the law of sin was so strong that it led to a fall even after the certainty of Christ's divinity. There is the mitigating circumstance that when the Apostle Peter saw the glory of the Lord it was before the Baptism which took place on the day of

Pentecost. The Apostle's nature had not yet been empowered by the energy of the Holy Spirit.

We see the same thing in the Apostle Paul as well. Although he felt his close communion with Christ, so that he could say: "It is no longer I who live, but Christ lives in me" (Gal. 2, 20), nevertheless he said, expressing all the pain of humanity: "I see another law in my members, warring against the law of my mind, and bringing me into captivity to the law of sin which is in my members. O wretched man that I am! Who will deliver me from this body of death?" (Rom. 7, 23-24).

In what follows we shall try to look at this law of sin, the "other law". We believe that this chapter which we have called pathology will be one of the most basic in this book. On a few points we shall try to be very analytical, listing all the passions as Christ, the Apostles and the Fathers present them, because we want to pinpoint the dreadful reality which is plaguing us and of which, unfortunately, we are most often unaware.

1. What the Passions are

'Passion' is derived from the verb 'pascho', 'to suffer' and indicates inner sickness. According to Philotheos of Sinai: "Passion, in the strict sense, they define as that which lurks impassionably in the soul over a long period"[2]. In what follows we shall see how a sin becomes a passion. Here we want to underline particularly the fact that when a sin is repeated often and lurks in our soul for a long time, it is called a passion. The Fathers go so far as to interpret the difference between passion and sin. Passion is "the movement which takes place in the soul" while sinful practice is "that which is manifested in the body"[3].

The Lord explained his teaching about the passions at

------

2. Philok. 3, p. 29, 35
3. Nicetas Stethatos. Practical chapters, Ch. 37

many points, and it is recorded in the Gospels. We underline just a few passages here because we are going to come back later. In response to the Pharisees' question: "Why do your disciples not walk according to the tradition of the elders but eat bread with unwashed hands?" the Lord directed attention to the inner man: "From within, out of the heart of man, come evil thoughts, fornication, theft, murder, adultery, coveting, wickedness, deceit, licentiousness, envy, slander, pride, foolishness. All these evil things come from within and they defile a man" (Mark 7, 21-23).

Interpreting the parable of the sower and especially referring to the seed which fell "among thorns", He said that the passions are those things which choke the seed and do not allow it to be fruitful. "As for what fell among the thorns, they are those who, hear, but as they go on their way they are choked by the cares and riches and pleasures of life, and their fruit does not mature" (Luk. 8, 14).

The Apostle Paul too knows that passions exist in the heart of man. Speaking of the condition before baptism, which is a carnal life, he writes: "While we were living in the flesh, our sinful passions, aroused by the law were at work in our members to bear fruit for death" (Rom. 7, 5). Describing the life of the heathen idolators, he writes: "For this reason God gave them up to dishonourable passions" (Rom. 1, 26).

Thus the passions lurk in our soul and create terrible problems in our whole being, as we shall see at many points in what follows. According to the teaching of St. Gregory Palamas, a person who loves wrongdoing hates his own soul, he tears apart and disables the image of God, that is, his soul, and "he experiences suffering similar to that of madmen who pitilessly cut their own flesh to pieces without feeling it". Like them he "unwittingly inflicts the most miserable sort of harm and rending upon his own innate beauty"[4]. Passion is a darkening and disabling and staining of the image, the beauty of God.

---

4. 150 Chapters, 40

In speaking about the passions we should point out more precisely what they are. Are they forces which enter our soul and which we should root out or are they natural powers of the soul which have been corrupted by sin and by our withdrawal from God? The whole biblico-patristic tradition believes the latter. Therefore in what follows we must examine the soul and its parts so that we can then see how these powers are corrupted.

St. Gregory Palamas teaches that as God is Nous, Word and Spirit, so also the soul has nous, word and spirit. The soul's spirit is "a certain motion of the nous which, however, involves a temporal extension in conjunction with our word and requires the same intervals and proceeds from incompletion to completion"[5]. According to this Athonite saint the threefold nature of the soul is nous, word and spirit; that of knowledge is noetic, intelligent and sensory and the trio of the nous, as turning towards itself and ascending towards God, is nous, knowledge and love[6].

Beyond these divisions St. Gregory Palamas, archbishop of Thessaloniki, also uses the division of the soul established at the time of the ancient Greek philosophers. Man's soul is one, although it has many powers[7]. It is divided into three parts: the intelligence, the appetitive power and the incensive power[8] appetitive and incensive aspects constitute the so-called passible part of the soul, and the word is the intelligence[9]. So as we go on to develop the subject of the passions, when we speak about the passible part of the soul which is defiled and must be cured, we should understand the incensive and appetitive parts. We may add to the teaching of

---

5. Ibid. 36
6. cf. ibid. p. 144ff and Amphilochiou Rantovits: The Mystery of the Holy Trinity according to St. Gregory Palamas, p. 55. In Gk.
7. EF 410, 3
8. St. Gregory Palamas, To Xeni, Gk. Philok. 4, p. 100
9. St. Maximus. Philok. 2, p. 89, 35

these two great Fathers of the Church that of St. Dorotheos, who, using a passage from St. Gregory the Theologian, writes that the soul is tripartite: "It has the appetitive, incensive and intelligent powers"[10].

These three powers should be turned towards God. That is their natural condition. According to St. Dorotheos, agreeing with Evagrius, "the intelligent soul works naturally when its appetitive part longs for virtue, the incensive part strives for it, and the intelligence devotes itself to the contemplation of beings"[11]. And St. Thalassios writes that the proper function of the soul's intelligent aspect is devotion to the knowledge of God, while that of its passible (appetitive and incensive) aspect is the pursuit of self-control and love[12]. Nicholas Cabasilas, referring to this theme, is in agreement with the preceding Fathers and says that human nature was created for the new man. We have received reason "in order that we may know Christ, our desire in order that we might hasten to Him. We have memory in order that we may carry Him in us", since Christ is the Archetype for men[13].

According to the above, man was not formed with passions as they function in our day in the man of flesh who does not have the operations of the Holy Spirit. The passions do not have essence or hypostasis. Just as darkness has no existence in essence but is the absence of light, so it is with passion. "It was by inclining away from the virtues through love of pleasure that the soul prepared the way for passions and gave them a firm place in itself"[14]. We can put this better by saying that the passions are a perversion of the powers of the soul. God did not form man with the passions of dishonour. As St. John of the Ladder says, "Evil or passion is not something natu-

10. Abba Dorotheos. CS p. 229. SC p. 478, 176
11. Ibid. CS p. 230. SC 480, 176
12. St. Thalassios. Philok. 2, p. 316, 52
13. Nicholas Cabasilas. The Life in Christ. Bk. 6, p. 190
14. Abba Dorotheos. CS p. 188

rally implanted in things. God is not the creator of passions. On the other hand, there are many natural virtues that have come to us from Him"[15]. The presence of virtues is the natural state of man, while the passions are the unnatural condition. We have altered and perverted the energies of the soul and steered them from their natural state to the unnatural state. According to St. John of the Ladder, God neither caused nor created evil. "We have taken natural attributes of our own and turned them into passions"[16]. The same saint gives several examples to make this clear. "The seed for childbearing" is natural in us, but we pervert it for fornication. The anger which God gave us against the serpent, to wage war against the devil, is natural, but we have used it against our neighbour. We have a natural urge to excel in virtue, but instead we compete in evil. Nature stirs within us the desire for glory, but that glory is of a heavenly kind, for the joy of heavenly blessing. It is natural for us to be arrogant – against the demons. Joy is ours by nature, but it should be joy on account of the Lord and for the sake of doing good to our neighbour. Nature has given us resentment, but that ought to be against the enemies of our souls. We have a natural desire for food, and not for profligacy[17].

For this reason the Fathers constantly emphasise the truth that the passions as we know them in the fallen state are an unnatural life, an unnatural impulse. "A culpable passion is an impulse of the soul that is contrary to nature"[18]. Explaining what this unnatural impulse of the soul is, St. Maximus calls it a "mindless love or mindless hatred for someone or for some sensible thing"[19]. At another point he writes that vice is a wrong use of our conceptual images of things, which leads

---

15. Step 26. CWS p. 238
16. Ibid. p. 251
17. Ibid. p. 251
18. St. Maximus. Philok. 2 p. 56, 35
19. Ibid. p. 67, 16

to misuse of the things themselves. Taking the example of marriage, he says that the right use of sexual intercourse is the begetting of children. A person who seeks in it only sensual pleasure "uses it wrongly, for he reckons as good what is not good. When such a man has intercourse with a woman, he misuses her". The same is true with regard to other things[20].

The intelligent part of the soul of fallen man is dominated by pride, the appetitive part of the soul chiefly by perversions of the flesh, and the incensive part by the passions of hatred, anger and rancour.

St. Maximus, who was concerned with the natural and unnatural life of the soul, analysed them exhaustively. The natural powers of the soul, he wrote, are intelligence, desire and the incensive power. The natural use of intelligence is "movement towards God in simplest seeking", that of desire is "direction towards God alone in longing", and that of the incensive power is a "struggle to attain God alone". That is to say, when a person lives naturally, he wants to know God completely, he desires only God, and he struggles to attain God, that is, to attain communion with God. The result of this natural impulse is love. A person united with God acquires the blessed state of love, since God is love. Holy Scripture says: "Love the Lord your God with all your heart, with all your soul, with all your mind, and with all your strength" (Mark 12, 30). When a person uses these three powers of his soul unnaturally, the result for intelligence is spiritual ignorance, for desire self-love, and for the incensive power tyranny. Thus the person becomes completely enslaved to the devil, and the soul's beauty is spoiled[21].

In another place St. Maximus analyses what misuse is. Misuse of the intelligent power is ignorance and stupidity. Misuse of the incensive and desiring powers is hatred and licen-

20. Ibid. p. 67, 17
21. Monk Artemiou Rantosavlievits: The Mystery of Salvation according to St. Maximus the Confessor. p. 130, note. (In Gk.)

tiousness. The proper use of these powers produces spiritual knowledge, moral judgement, love and self-restraint. Therefore nothing created by God is evil[22]. The fact that nothing natural is evil means that evil exists when the powers are distorted by us. St. Maximus also uses several examples. It is not foods that are evil, but gluttony, not the begetting of children, but unchastity, not material things but avarice, not esteem but self-esteem[23].

Misuse of the powers of the soul is sin, sickness. Vice, according to St. Dorotheos, is "a sickness of the soul depriving it of its own natural health, which is virtue"[24].

Thus we can speak of man's sickness which must be healed. For the impurity of the soul is that it is "not functioning according to nature" and this condition engenders impassioned thoughts in the nous. The natural state of man's soul, which is health par excellence, appears when in the face of provocations its passible aspects – that is, its incensive power and its desire – remain dispassionate[25]. And since the soul of man is uniform and has many powers, for this reason when one power of the soul sickens the rest of them also fall ill[26].

St. Gregory Palamas teaches that just as misuse of the knowledge of created things engenders 'the wisdom which has become folly', so also the misuse of the powers of the soul are what engenders "the terrible passions"[27].

That the passions are an unnatural impulse of the soul's powers, a turning of the passible and intelligent parts of the soul away from God towards created things, is shown by the fact that when a man is inwardly healed by the action of divine grace and his own struggle, then the passible powers of

---

22. Philok. 2. p. 83, 3
23. Philok. 2. p. 83, 4
24. SC p. 342, 106. cf.CS p. 166
25. Philok.2, p. 89, 35
26. Palamas. EF p. 410
27. Triads. 2, 2, 19. CWS p. 54

the soul are not suppressed, obliterated, but they turn towards God; they rush towards Him and attain knowledge and communion with Him. St. Gregory Palamas, referring to Barlaam, who maintained that pain and sorrow do not belong to prayer but that the passible powers, being evil, should be mortified during prayer, teaches that there are "blessed passions and common activities of body and soul which, far from nailing the spirit to the flesh, serve to draw the flesh to a dignity close to that of the spirit". These activities are spiritual, not moving from the body to the nous, but from the nous to the body[28]. Therefore when we try to obtain healing, we do not mortify the passions, but we redirect them, as we shall explain later. The tears, sorrow, repentance and pain, which are effective means for curing the soul, are the things which purify the passible and intelligent part of the soul.

In closing this section we want to stress mainly that the passions of the body are distorted energies of the soul. When the soul lacks love and self-control, the passions of the incensive and appetitive part of the soul are distorted. And these passions are aroused through the senses[29]. The passions of the carnal life, in the sense of the absence of the Holy Spirit, are an unnatural movement of the soul and are therefore its dying, death and sickness.

2. Types of Passions and their Development

Now that we have seen what the passions are, we are ready to look into how they are classified and how they develop. At the same time we shall undertake to list them, because we believe that this will help Christians who are fighting the good fight. If we are to be healed of passions we need to diagnose them.

---

28. Triads. 2, 2, 12. CWS p. 51
29. Maximus. Philok. 2, p. 59f, 65

The teaching about passions is found not only in the patristic writings but also in Holy Scripture. The Apostle Paul speaks of the flesh. It is well known that according to the Apostle, a carnal man is one who is deprived of the energies of the Holy Spirit. "The desires of the flesh are against the spirit and the desires of the spirit are against the flesh; for these are opposed to each other" (Gal. 5, 17). Then he defines the works of the flesh, which are the carnal passions: "The works of the flesh are plain: immorality, impurity, licentiousness, idolatry, sorcery, enmity, strife, jealousies, anger, selfishness, dissension, party spirit, envy, murders, drunkenness, carousing, and the like. I warn you, as I warned you before, that those who do such things will not inherit the kingdom of God" (Gal. 5, 19-21).

In his letter to the Romans the Apostle Paul lists the works of sin, the passions, which plague our entire existence. Referring to those who deserted God and worshipped idols, he writes: "And since they did not see fit to acknowledge God, God gave them up to a base mind and to improper conduct. They were filled with all manner of wickedness, evil, covetousness, malice. Full of envy, murder, strife, deceit, malignity, they are gossips, slanderers, haters of God, insolent, haughty boastful, inventors of evil, disobedient to parents, foolish, faithless, heartless, ruthless" (Rom. 1, 28-31).

He describes to his disciple Timothy the people's condition "in the last days". "For men will be lovers of self, lovers of money, proud, arrogant, abusive, disobedient to their parents, ungrateful, unholy, inhuman, implacable, slanderers, profligates, fierce, haters of good, treacherous, reckless, swollen with conceit, lovers of pleasure rather than lovers of God, holding the form of religion but denying the power of it" (2 Tim. 3, 1-5).

The three texts quoted show the whole situation of the man who is far from God. It is really a psychogram, a significant X-ray view of the soul of a man who is ruled by passions. But we shall go on to look at the analysis in the patristic works.

According to St. Maximus, the basic passion from which all the passions originate is self-love. A man is self-loving who loves himself excessively and idolises himself. When a person's attention is drawn away from God and he is not interested in uniting with Him and doing His will, then he necessarily turns towards himself, wanting to satisfy himself all the time. "Guard yourself from that mother of vices, self-love", says St. Maximus. And defining self-love, he says it is "mindless love for the body". It gives birth to the three first and "most general of the impassioned thoughts", which are gluttony, avarice and self-esteem. "All further vices are generated by these three"[30].

In another place, presenting the terrible consequences of self-love, he calls it the mother from which come many daughters. Talkativeness and gluttony cause intemperance. Avarice and self-esteem cause one to hate one's neighbour. Self-love, the mother of vices, is the cause of both these things[31].

In his writing 'To Thalassios' St. Maximus details the whole ancestry of self-love, which he arranges in two categories. In one category are the passions which lead to sensual pleasure and in the other those which keep pain away. In the first category he places the following passions: "gluttony, pride, self-esteem, being puffed up, avarice, tyranny, putting on airs, boastfulness, folly, frenzy, presumption, conceit, scorn, insult, impiety, frivolous talk, dissoluteness, licentiousness, ostentation, light-mindedness, stupidity, violence, mocking, chatter, unseasonable talk, indecent talk, and everything else of the sort". In the second category he places the following passions: "wrath, envy, hatred, enmity, rancour, abuse, backbiting, slander, sorrow, lack of trust, despair, disparagement of providence, listlessness, indifference, despondency, dejection, faint-heartedness, untimely mourning, tears, melancholy, lamentation, jealousy, envy, spite, and

---

30. Maximus. Philok. 2, p. 75, 59
31. Ibid. p. 84, 7

every other disposition that lacks any occasion for pleasure"[32].

St. Gregory Palamas creates another division. In the preceding section we emphasised that the soul is divided into three parts, the intelligent, incensive and desiring aspects. The first evil offspring of the appetitive part is love of possessions and the second is avarice. The offspring of the intelligent part of the soul is love of glory, and the characteristic mark of the incensive part of the soul is gluttony, from which comes "all uncleanness of the flesh"[33]. In other words, from self-love, which is the mistress and mother of all the passions, are born the three general passions, love of glory, avarice and self-indulgence. From these three great passions arise all the others which defile the soul and body of man.

St. Mark the Ascetic, endeavouring to evaluate the passions and to find the mothers which give birth to others, writes that there are three great giants, and when they have been overthrown and slain, all the other powers of the evil spirits are easily removed. These three giants are spiritual ignorance, which is the source of all evils, forgetfulness, its "close relation and helper", and laziness, which "weaves the dark shroud enveloping the soul in murk". Laziness, forgetfulness and ignorance "support and strengthen the other passions"[34].

This difference in the three Fathers is not an essential one. Self-love, forgetfulness, laziness and ignorance of God are the favourable climate in which all the passions of love of glory, self-indulgence and avarice develop. Each of the Fathers, according to his personal struggle and according to the topic which he wanted to emphasise, noted a different passion. The Fathers were not making a philosophy or analysing every soul when they listed these passions, but they were always speaking

32. Rantosavlievits: The Mystery of Salvation according to Maximus the Confessor. p. 131, note.1. (In Gk..)
33. St. Gregory Palamas. To Xeni. Gk. Philok. 4, p. 100 ff
34. St. Mark the Ascetic. Writings p. 28

from their personal experience. It must further be emphasised that self-love is very closely connected with ignorance,
forgetfulness and laziness, because turning one's attention to
oneself inevitably brings forgetfulness and ignorance of God,
resulting in the birth of all the other sins - passions.

According to St. John of Damascus, the soul has three parts:
the intelligent, incensive and appetitive aspects. The sins of
the intelligent aspect are unbelief, heresy, folly, blasphemy,
ingratitude, and "assent to sins originating in the soul's passible
aspect". The sins of the incensive aspect are heartlessness,
hatred, lack of compassion, rancour, envy, murder and "dwelling constantly on such things". The sins of the appetitive
aspect are gluttony, greed, drunkenness, unchastity, adultery, uncleanness, licentiousness, love of material things and
the desire for empty glory, gold, wealth and the pleasures of
the flesh. The same saint also lists the eight thoughts that
encompass all evil, which are naturally linked with the corresponding passions, since it is through thoughts that the sins
come into being which develop into passions. These eight
thoughts are those of gluttony, unchastity, avarice, anger,
dejection, listlessness, self-esteem and pride[35].

While the division of the passions which we have examined
so far is analogous to the division of the soul, we must now go
on to another division which we find in patristic teaching.
Here the passions are divided into those of the body and those
of the soul. The soul has its related passions, as the body has
the related passions of the flesh.

It is well known in patristic teaching that before the fall
man's soul was open to God and nourished by God's grace.
Certainly man would have to struggle to reach full communion and union with God, but even at that time he tasted the
grace of God. Thus the soul was nourished by uncreated grace
and the body was nourished by the "soul filled with grace".
The whole man tasted the gifts of God. Since the fall, the soul,

---

35. Philok.2, p. 337

separated from God, the real source of life, "seeks nourishment from the body. In this way the passions of the soul are born... The body for its part, not finding life in the soul, turns towards external things, and as is natural becomes enslaved to matter and imprisoned in the cycle of corruption. Thus the pleasure-loving bodily passions appear, whereby man struggles to draw life and joy from material things"[36]. This is the death of the body, and especially of the soul. If, however, through asceticism and the life in Christ we make the effort to turn our soul towards God in order to be nourished by Him, the body is then nourished by the "soul filled with grace" and thus the whole man is sanctified. We see this in the saints of the Church, in whom sometimes the bodily functions are suspended.

According to St. Maximus, some of the passions pertain to the body and others to the soul. The bodily passions are occasioned by the body, while those of the soul are occasioned by external objects[37]. We find the same distinction between passions in the teaching of Ilias the Presbyter, who says: "Bodily passions are one thing, passions of the soul another"[38].

St. John of Damascus undertakes to list the passions of the body and those of the soul. Those **of the soul** are forgetfulness, laziness and ignorance, by which the eye of the soul is darkened and the soul is then dominated by all the other passions. These are impiety, false teaching or every kind of heresy, blasphemy, wrath, anger, bitterness, irritability, inhumanity, rancour, back-biting, censoriousness, senseless dejection, fear, cowardice, quarrelsomeness, jealousy, envy, self-esteem, pride, hypocrisy, falsehood, unbelief, greed, love of material things, evil desire, attachment to worldly concerns, listlessness, faint-heartedness, ingratitude, grumbling, vanity, conceit, pomposity, boastfulness, love of power, love of popu-

36. P. Nela, Zoon theoumenon, p. 203-204, In Gk.
37. Philok.2, p. 59, 64
38. Philok.3, p. 63, 122

larity, deceit, shamelessness, insensibility, flattery, treachery, pretence, indecision, "assent to sins arising from the soul's passible aspect and dwelling on them continuously". Also wandering thoughts, self-love, the root and source of all evils which is avarice, and finally, malice and guile.

The passions **of the body**, according to St. John of Damascus, are gluttony, greed, over-indulgence, drunkenness, eating in secret, general softness of living, unchastity, adultery, licentiousness, uncleanness, incest, pederasty, bestiality, impure desires and every passion which is foul and unnatural, theft, sacrilege, robbery, murder, every kind of physical luxury and gratification of the whims of the flesh especially when the body is in good health. Further bodily passions are: consulting oracles, casting spells, watching for omens and portents, self-adornment, ostentation, foolish display, use of cosmetics, painting the face, wasting time, day-dreaming, trickery, impassioned misuse of the pleasures of this world. Further passions of the body are a life of bodily ease, "which by coarsening the nous makes it cloddish and brute-like and never lets it raise itself towards God and the practice of the virtues"[39].

St. Gregory of Sinai sums up the whole teaching of the Fathers about the passions of the body and those of the soul. He writes: "Passions have different names, but they are divided into those of the body and those of the soul. Bodily passions are subdivided into sorrowful and sinful; the sorrowful are again subdivided into those or sickness and those of punishment. Passions of the soul are divided into those of the incensive, appetitive and intelligent parts. The intelligent are subdivided into those of imagination and those of reason. All of them are either voluntary, through misuse, or involuntary, through necessity. The latter are so-called non-shameful passions, which the Fathers described as due to surroundings and natural characteristics (dispositions). Some passions are

---

39. Philok.2, p. 335

of the body, others are passions of the soul; some are passions of desire, others passions of the incensive part, yet others are passions of the intelligence, some of the nous and others of reasoning. All of these combine with one another in various ways and have an effect on one another: the bodily on the appetitive, those of the soul on the incensive, and again those of the intelligence on those of the nous and those of the nous on the passions of reason and memory"[40].

Despite the enumeration and division of the passions we must observe that the passions are not separated from one another in water-tight compartments. One is intimately connected with another, and in that way a person is completely defiled and deadened. Through the passions the soul becomes sick, the nous is deadened. Thus the person becomes an idolater and cannot inherit the kingdom of heaven. The Apostle Paul is clear and categorical: "Be sure of this, that no immoral or impure man, or one who is covetous (that is, an idolator), has any inheritance in the kingdom of Christ and of God" (Eph. 5, 5).

There is also another division of the passions. It is between monks and people in the world. Since the way of life of the monks who practise asceticism in monasteries differs from that of the people of the world, some passions dominate in one situation and others in another. St. John of the Ladder writes that in people who live in the world the root of all evils is avarice, but in monks it is gluttony[41]. To explain this he notes that some of the passions begin from within and are manifested in the body, while others come from outside into the interior of the soul. The former usually happens in monks, "because of the lack of stimulus from the outside", while the latter case is usually found in those living in the world[42]. Likewise the passions which appear during illness are different in monks and in people in the world. When people in the world are ill

---

40. Acrostics, 77. Writings. p. 50f
41. Ladder. Step 26. CWS p. 239
42. Ladder. Step 15. CWS p. 182

they suffer from the passions of gluttony and fornication. The monks, having their material support, find themselves plagued mainly by the demons of despondency and ingratitude[43]. Here we see that man does not always receive the same temptations. This depends on his spiritual condition, his way of life and other factors. The devil is resourceful and knows how to fight each person according to his condition.

We have previously pointed out that some of the passions are characterised as mothers and others as daughters: some passions give birth to other passions and some are offspring of others. St. John of the Ladder learned from holy men that gluttony is the mother of unchastity and self-esteem is the mother of listlessness. That is to say, when listlessness takes hold of us, we can be sure that the passion of self-esteem is at work. Likewise dejection and anger are daughters of these three. Self-esteem is the mother of pride. He was also taught that usually in mindless people there is no discretion and order, but rather disorder and confusion. Untimely jokes are born sometimes from unchastity, sometimes from self-esteem. Excessive sleep sometimes comes from an easy life, sometimes from fasting, sometimes from listlessness and sometimes from natural need. Garrulity sometimes is born from gluttony and sometimes from self-esteem. Listlessness is sometimes born from an easy life, sometimes from lack of fear of God. Blasphemy is properly the child of pride, but often it comes from readiness to condemn one's neighbour or the untimely envy of the demons. Hardheartedness sometimes comes from eating to satisfaction, and most often from insensitivity and attachment. Attachment, which is adhesion to anything sensory, comes from unchastity or avarice or self-esteem, as well as other things. Malice comes from conceit and from anger. Hypocrisy comes from independence and self-direction. And in general sensual pleasure and malice are generators of all the passions[44].

---

43. Ibid. Step 26. CWS p. 233
44. Ibid. Step 26. CWS p. 233

It is important at this point that we investigate how a sin develops into a passion. For the Fathers, experts on this inner struggle, are not satisfied simply with listing the passions, but they go on to record their causes and development. According to St. Thalassios, the passions are roused through these three things: "the memory, the body's temperament and the senses"[45]. A person who fixes his nous on sensory things, estranging himself from spiritual love and self-control and accepting the action of the demon, becomes an object of provocation. "It is when self-control and spiritual love are missing that the passions are roused by the senses"[46].

When the reins of the most sovereign senses are slackened, there is an uprising of the passions, "and the energy of the most servile passions is set in motion"[47]. When the irrationality of the senses is loosed from the chains of self-control, it creates the causes of the passions[48]. In fact, as we have observed before, when a man's nous dallies with some sensible thing, "it is clearly attached to it by some passion, such as desire, irritation, anger or rancour"[49]. Therefore the endeavour described by all the Fathers is not to let our nous be captured by any sensory thing or idea, because that is immediately followed by passion and disaster. The seeds of tragedy are sown in our soul by the capture of our nous.

Likewise, apart from the captivity of the nous, our desire plays an important role in creating passions. St. James, the Lord's brother, describes this condition. "Each person is tempted when he is lured and enticed by his own desire. Then desire when it has conceived gives birth to sin; and sin, when it is full-grown, brings forth death" (Jas. 1, 14f). When a brother asked Abba Sisoes "What shall I do about passions?"

---

45. Philok.2, p. 320f, 32
46. Philok.2, p. 321, 34
47. Gk. Philok. 3, p. 274, 6
48. Ibid.
49. St. Maximus. Philok. 2, p. 65, 2

the gerondas answered: "Each man is tempted when he is lured and enticed by his own desire"[50].

More analytically, the development of the passions is as follows. According to St. Maximus, first the memory brings some passion-free thought into the nous. And when this thought lingers, passion is set in motion. The next step is assent. Assent leads to committing the actual sin[51].

Hesychios the Priest sets forth the path which passion follows. The provocation comes first. Then follows our coupling follows with it when our own thoughts mingle with those of the devil. Then comes our assent, and after that "the concrete action – that is, the sin itself"[52]. And when the sin is repeated many times, a passion comes into being.

St. Gregory Palamas, in the Orthodox tradition of therapeutic treatment, writes that self-indulgence is the beginning of the bodily passions and a sickness of the soul. In these "the first to suffer is the nous" – that is to say, the nous is assailed first. It sets evil passions in motion. Through the senses it brings the imagination of sensory things into the soul and it is disposed towards these sins. The imprint of these images is mainly through the eyes...[53].

St. John of the Ladder describes analytically how this thought develops until it becomes a passion. Provocation, coupling, assent, captivity, struggle, and passion are all different things. Analysing them, he writes that **provocation** is a word or simple chance image which appears in the heart for the first time. This is not sinful. **Coupling** is communion with what has appeared either with or without passion. Still this state is sometimes not blameworthy. **Assent** is the delighted yielding of the soul to what it has encountered. This is bad or good according to the condition of the ascetic. **Captivity** is a

---

50. Sayings, p. 185, 44
51. St. Maximus. Philok. 2, p. 62, 84
52. Philok. 1, p. 170, 46
53. To Xeni. Gk. Philok. 4, p. 105

"forcible and unwilling abduction of the heart, a permanent lingering with what we have encountered". Captivity is judged differently, depending on whether it happens at the time of prayer or at some other time. **'Struggle'** means force equal to that which is leading the attack, that is, the soul's struggle and battle not to let sin be committed. This battle can earn a crown or punishment. Finally comes **passion**, which, as we have said, is something that "lies hidden in the soul for a long time" and from long habit has prevailed on the soul to surrender to it. This passion requires appropriate repentance or future punishment[54].

In addition to this description of how thought develops into passion, the Fathers also describe another development: how passions unfold with age. St. Gregory Palamas says that passions develop from early childhood in the following order. First come the passions of the appetitive part of the soul, that is, possessiveness and greed. Little children want to grasp things, and when they get somewhat older they want money. Later, "with the advance of age", the passions of the love of glory develop. Love of glory is seen in two forms. The first is worldly love of glory, which aims at "cosmetics and rich dress" and the second is that self-esteem which attacks the righteous and manifests itself in conceit and hypocrisy, through which the enemy contrives to scatter the soul's spiritual wealth. Finally, after possessiveness and love of glory, self-indulgence develops – that is, gluttony "from which comes every sort of uncleanness of the flesh". At the same time St. Gregory Palamas makes an interesting observation. Although self-indulgence "and natural impulses towards procreation mark babies at the breast", yet "they are not signs of a sick soul", the natural passions being blameless, since they were created by the good God "in order that through them we might walk in good works". Passion is evil "when we make provision for the flesh to fulfil its lusts". So to sum up, we point out that

---

54. Ladder. Step 15. CWS p. 182

according to St. Gregory, the passions of possessiveness and greed develop in babies, the passions of the love of glory develop in childhood, and later come the passions of self-indulgence[55].

It is true that the passions of both body and soul are hard to discern. This is because the demons who stir them are usually hidden and we cannot distinguish them. That is why a good therapist is needed, one who knows the hidden inner life and is a vessel of the Holy Spirit in order to discern and cure. This discernment is one of the great gifts of the grace of the Holy Spirit. St. John of the Ladder, referring to the example that often when we draw water from a well it can happen that we inadvertently also bring up a 'frog', connects this with the virtues. When we aquire virtues we can sometimes find ourselves involved with the vices which are imperceptibly interwoven with them. He offers several examples. Gluttony can be caught up with hospitality; unchastity with love; cunning with discernment; malice with sound judgement; duplicity, procrastination, slovenliness, stubbornness, wilfulness, and disobedience with meekness; refusal to learn with silence; conceit with joy; laziness with hope; censoriousness with love again; listlessness and sloth with stillness; acerbity with chastity; familiarity with humility[56]. It is clear from this that a great deal of watchfulness is needed in order to discover the passions. For we may think that we are being virtuous while we are really working for the devil, cultivating the passions. We must watch out for the frog, which is usually the passion of self-esteem. This passion defiles obedience to the commandments.

According to the same saint, the demon of avarice often simulates humility. And the demon of self-esteem or self-indulgence encourages the giving of alms[57]. Therefore we must,

---

55. To Xeni. Gk. Philok. 4, p. 100-105
56. Ladder. Step 26. CWS p. 237
57. Ladder. Step 26. CWS p. 239

above all, be watchful to discern the cunning of the demon even while we are cultivating the virtues. He mentions a case in which he had been overcome by the demon of laziness and was thinking of leaving his cell. But when several men came and praised him for leading the life of a hesychast, "my laziness gave way to self-esteem". And then he was amazed by the manner in which the demon of self-esteem stood up against all the other cunning spirits[58]. Likewise the demon of avarice fights very hard against those who are completely without possessions. When it fails to overcome them, it begins to tell them about the wretched conditions of the poor, thereby inducing them "to become concerned with material things"[59]. Another point mentioned by the Holy Fathers is the way in which we can detect the presence of passion. The discerning and dispassionate gerondas who will look at the impulses of our soul and correct us certainly has an important place. But beyond this we also have other ways of perceiving the presence and working of passions. It is a sign that a voluntary passion is working when a person is upset on being reproached or corrected for it. When he accepts calmly the reproach which comes, it is a sign that "he was defeated or unaware of it"[60]. In other words the reproach and the upset or calm show the existence of the passion and whether it is voluntary or not. "The foulest passions are hidden within our souls; they are brought to light only when we scrutinise our actions"[61].

In his effort to describe accurately what passion is, St. Maximus writes that a thing, a conceptual image and a passion are all different from one another. A man, woman, gold, and so forth are things; a conceptual image is "a passion-free thought of one of these things", a passion is "mindless affection or

---

58. Ladder. Step 27. CWS
59. Ibid. p. 249
60. Abba Dorotheos. CS p. 253. SC p. 530, 202, 18
61. St. Thalassios. Philok. 2, p. 320, 30

indiscriminate hatred for one of these same things"[62]. Abba
Dorotheos, distinguishing between sin and passion, writes
that passions are anger, self-esteem, self-indulgence, hatred,
evil desires and the like. Sins are the actions of the passions.
And so it is possible for a person to "have passions but not to
put them to work"[63]. From this passage we also understand
that it is possible to be full of passions without noticing it,
because we did not happen to commit any sins. This is why
complete healing by a discerning and experienced spiritual
counsellor is required.

In order to complete this section, we must summarise what
the terrible consequences of the passions are. We have already said in various connections that the passions deaden
our nous. We shall want to develop this theme further.

Resurgence of the passions "in an aged body and a consecrated soul" is a defilement of the soul[64].

Just as when a sparrow tied by the leg tries to fly "it is
pulled down to the earth", so also the nous, if it does not have
dispassion, "is held back by the passions and pulled down to
the earth"[65]. They attach the person to the earthly.

Reprehensible passions chain the nous, "binding it to sensible objects"[66].

The passions often defile the soul after a time, just as certain
foods which harm the body bring on illness after some time or
indeed after some days[67]. In any case it is apparent also from
this passage that the passions sicken the soul.

An impassioned person's soul is "a workshop of evil
thoughts". And such an evil soul brings forth a fund of evil[68].

62. Philok. 2, p. 89, 42
63. Abba Dorotheos. Ibid.
64. St. Mark the Ascetic. Gk. Philok. 1, p. 114, 77
65. Philok. 2, p. 63, 85
66. St. Thalassios. Philok. 2, p. 321, 41
67. Ladder. Step 15. CWS p. 178
68. St. Thalassios. Philok. 2, p. 323, 77

The nous is deadened by the passions and is impervious to advice. It will not even accept any spiritual correction[69].

"Every passion brings with it the seed of death".

The passions are hell. The impassioned soul is punished all the time by its own bad habit, always having the bitter memory and the painful mutterings of its passions burning and consuming it. This torment is a beginning, it is a small taste of another torment in those fearful places of suffering "where the bodies to be punished will receive and inflict such varied and terrible torment on the souls and not be destroyed, that unspeakable fire, the darkness..."[70].

The rewards for the toils of virtue are dispassion and spiritual knowledge, which are mediators of the kingdom of heaven, just as "passions and ignorance are mediators of eternal punishment"[71].

St. Gregory Palamas, interpreting the passage which tells how the demons came out of the demoniac and entered the swine which then fell into the sea, writes that "the swinish life symbolises" every evil passion because of its impurity. "But it is especially those who go around in a tunic soiled by the flesh who are swine"[72].

Thus finally the passions completely deaden the nous and effect our punishment. Spiritual healing is required for the nous to be freed and rejoice in God. We shall now turn to the subject of therapy.

3. Cure of the Passions

Now that we have become aware of the great destruction wrought in our whole existence by the passions, we must proceed to the subject of therapy. This is a fundamental part

---

69. St. Thalassios. Philok. 2, p. 327, 41
70. Abba Dorotheos. SC p. 386, 127. cf. CS p. 184
71. St. Maximus. Philok. 2, p. 71, 34
72. St. Gregory Palamas. Homily 50. EPE 11, p. 208. (In Gk.)

of the present chapter. Many of us realise that we are ill, we have a sense of being spiritually ill, but we are completely or partially ignorant of how to be cured. I think that Orthodoxy, being a therapeutic science, ought to be explaining these very topical matters. We are certain that one of the messages which the Orthodox Church should be offering to the contemporary stumbling world is the message of its sickness and, at the same time, of its healing. These matters will be our concern in what follows.

First we must clarify a few things. One is that to cure passions is mainly to transform them, as we have already described. Since the dispassionate passions, the natural, blameless passions, have been perverted, it is to be expected that with therapeutic treatment we shall change them. This is the curing of the passions. Abba Poemen said to Abba Isaac: "We were not taught to be slayers of the body but to be slayers of the passions"[73]. We must understand "slayers of the passions" in the sense of converting the passions. Another observation is that the Fathers offer a great deal of therapeutic treatment in their writings. Anyone reading St. Maximus's 'centuries' on love will see that they contain much therapeutic material. I must confess that when I wanted to read this work, I expected to find a few rules about love and a description of the value of love. But I noticed right away that St. Maximus gives more attention to the subject of thoughts, passions and the curing of passions. He attaches great importance to man's healing, because love for God and man is "born of dispassion". A heart which is ruled by passions is incapable of loving. A further observation is that when the Fathers speak of the healing of man they set forth the basic principles of it. That is to say, they have in view the universal man and they give various prescriptions or methods for therapy. We shall mention these in what follows, but we must emphasise that every person needs his own therapeutic method. This method is given by

---

73. Sayings, p. 162, 184

the discriminating and experienced therapist to anyone who comes and asks, with humility, obedience and a disposition for healing. Therefore we shall now set out the general rules of therapeutic treatment. Every individual must practise his own therapy under the spiritual guidance of contemporary 'living organisms'.

The cure of the sicknesses of our soul is absolutely **necessary**. We have already looked at this. We have pointed out the deformed state which the passions create in us. Many passages in Scripture refer to it.

The Apostle Paul gives the following advice to the Colossians: "Put to death therefore what is earthly in you: unchastity, uncleanness, passion, evil desire and greed, which is idolatry... But now put them all away: anger, wrath, malice, slander and foul talk from your mouth. Do not lie to one another, seeing that you have put off the old nature with its practices and have put on the new nature which is being renewed in knowledge after the image of its creator" (Col. 3, 5-10).

According to St. Maximus, the Apostle here was calling the will of the flesh 'earth'. 'Unchastity' is his word for the actual committing of sin. Actual committing of sin is assent which is acted on and becomes sin. 'Uncleanness' is how he designates assent to sin. 'Passion' is his term for impassioned thoughts. By 'evil desire' the Apostle means "the simple act of accepting the thought and the desire". 'Greed' is his name for "what generates and promotes passions". These 'earthly' things, which are part of the will of the flesh must be put to death[74]. When they are put to death – and later we shall see how – and transformed, that is, offered to God, then the old nature with its deeds and desires will be put off and the new nature put on. It will be in the image and likeness of God – a person.

In another letter the inspired Apostle gives the same instructions: "Immorality and all impurity or covetousness

---

74. Philok. 2, p. 62, 83

must not even be named among you, as is fitting among saints. Let there be no filthiness, nor silly talk, nor levity, which are not fitting; but instead let there be thanksgiving" (Eph. 5, 3f).

And in another letter he writes: "Let us have no self-conceit, no provoking of one another, no envy of one another" (Gal. 5, 26).

All these things show the necessity of therapy. The Christian as a dwelling place of the Holy Trinity must not be unclean, or rather, in order to become a temple of the Holy Spirit and for God to dwell within, the Christian must previously have been purified spiritually, and after becoming a temple of the Holy Spirit, he must keep it pure.

This also shows the **goal** of therapy. We are not struggling simply to become good people, adjusted to society. The aim of therapeutic treatment is not to make people sociable and to be an anthropocentric exercise, but it is to guide them to communion with God, and for this vision of God not to be a fire that will consume them but a light which will illuminate them. The Fathers are clearly aware or this aim of therapeutic treatment, but they also know the aims which different people set. St. Maximus says that some people abstain from passions "because of human fear", others through self-control, and others are delivered from passions "by divine providence"[75]. Abba Dorotheos makes the point by saying that one must not wish release from passion "in order to escape its torment, but because one truly hates it, as it is said: "I hated them with perfect hatred"[76]. The saints realise that some people wish to be released from passions because they cause so much pain. But this is not the true aim of Orthodox therapeutic treatment. The basic aim is to attain communion with God. We do know very well that there are different spiritual ages and conditions within the Church. Some, as the Fathers

75. Ibid. p. 68, 23
76. Abba Dorotheos. SC p. 530, 202, 16. cf. CS p. 252f, 16

teach, keep the word of God through fear of hell, others to gain Paradise and others do it out of love for Christ. The first are slaves, the second are salaried workers, and the third are children of God. We accept these spiritual ages, but we emphasise that we are struggling to reach the third category. Continual healing even of the aim of the treatment is required.

It must be pointed out that healing of the passions is not the work of man alone or of God alone. The two must work together. This is the synergy of God and man. Everything in our Church is theandric. At first the grace of Christ must be given. The purification of man, which is healing, takes place by the energy of Christ that is offered through the whole spiritual life which the Christian lives within the Orthodox Church. In his epistles the Apostle Paul often stresses this fact. The man of flesh has in him the energy of the passions. But when he receives the grace of Christ, he is freed from this old world, the world of sin. "While we were living in the flesh, our sinful passions, aroused by the law, were at work in our members to bear fruit for death. But now we are discharged from the law, dead to that which held us captive, so that we serve not under the old written code but in the new life of the Spirit" (Rom. 7, 5f).

Only the people of Christ, those who live in Christ, are released from the flesh and the lust of the flesh, which constitute the world of sin: "And those who belong to Christ Jesus have crucified the flesh with its passions and desire. If we live by the Spirit, let us also walk by the Spirit" (Gal. 5, 25f). When a person walks by the Spirit, that is when he has the grace of the Holy Trinity, he is healed inwardly: "I say, walk by the Spirit, and do not gratify the desires of the flesh. ...If you are led by the Spirit you are not under the law" (Gal. 5, 16-18). And we are well aware that, as we indicated before, the works of the flesh are all the passions (v. Gal. 5, 19-21).

To wage war against sin and passion, "to struggle, yes, to continue to fight, to inflict blows" is our own work, but to "uproot" the passions, to transform them in an essential way, is the work of God. Just as man cannot see without eyes and speak without a tongue or hear without ears or walk without feet or work without hands, so he cannot "be saved without Jesus nor enter into the kingdom of heaven"[77]. For the soul can contradict sin, but without God it cannot conquer or uproot evil[78].

The sense of the love of God, which is communion with the grace of God, and our own love towards God, which is a fruit of the Holy Spirit, are the things which transform and cure the passions. To mortify the passible part of the soul does not mean that we enclose it "idle and motionless in ourselves", but that we turn it from its connection with evil "to love for God"[79]. But this change to love for God does not happen without a life of love. In any case when a person is ablaze with love for God, which is a divine inspiration, his whole inner world is transformed, it is warmed by divine grace and sanctified. "When love of God dominates the nous, it frees it from its bonds, persuading it to rise above not only sensible things but even this transitory life"[80]. These things show that healing of the passions takes place when divine grace, God's love, is at work. This divine grace is offered through the holy sacraments. Likewise we want to underline the fact that the divine Eucharist and Communion of the Body and Blood of Christ is an effective help in a person's effort to purify his soul. Holy Communion is a medicine of immortality.

But in addition to the power of Christ, which plays a very important role, the human will must also cooperate. If this does not happen, it is almost impossible for a person to overcome passions, to overcome the demons substantially, since

---

77. St. Makarios. Homily 3, 4, CWS p. 48
78. Ibid.
79. St. Gregory Palamas. Triads. 2, 2, 23
80. St. Maximus. Philok. 2, 65, 3

"he who has conquered the passions wounds the demons"[81], and "a person will banish the demon of the passion which he has mastered"[82]. In what follows we shall try to look at this cooperation of the human will.

Self-knowledge is needed first of all. It is very important; for us to be aware of our spiritual condition. Ignorance of our illness makes us permanently incurable. John the Evangelist writes: "If we say that we have no sin, we deceive ourselves, and the truth is not in us" (1 Jn. 1,8).

Peter of Damascus, specifying the eight spiritual contemplations, of which the first seven are of this age and the eighth is of the age to come, regards knowledge as the second: "knowledge of our own faults and of God's bounty"[83]. That is to say, the knowledge of our own faults and of God's bounty is theoria.

Since pride is interwoven with courage, "we must be ever on guard against yielding to the mere thought that we have achieved any sort of good"[84]. The Fathers know from the great spiritual experience which they hand down, that the symptoms of passions are not easy to diagnose with accuracy, since we are sick and they have united with our nature. Therefore the Fathers advise us to seek out our passions assiduously. "Watch out continually for signs of the passions and you will discover that there are many within you"[85]. Regarding every passion and every virtue, especially the passions, we must "scrutinise ourselves unceasingly to see where we are, at the beginning, middle or end"[86]. It is essential that this should be done, because the spiritual life is a continuous journey and healing is endless. We are constantly purifying ourselves in order to attain communion with God. This is indispensable,

---

81. Ladder. Step 26. CWS p. 248
82. Sayings. p. 168, 1
83. Philok. 3, p. 108
84. Ladder. Step 26. CWS p. 252
85. Ibid.
86. Ibid. CWS p. 239

because stagnation and self-sufficiency are constantly lurking on our spiritual way.

Self-knowledge is indispensable also because there are three conditions in man: "that of activating passion, that of holding it back, and that of uprooting it"[87]. This is to say, it is not enough to use various therapeutic means to stop the working of a passion, but we must transform it into love for God and men. In order to have good self-knowledge we need outward stillness. We must put a stop to the actual committing of sin. As long as the senses are functioning carnally, self-knowledge is impossible. "Hence one must watch over the nous in the presence of things and must discern for which of them it manifests a passion"[88].

Knowledge of our passions is very closely connected with **repentance** and **confession**. The first stage of repentance is knowledge of our sins, the sense of our soul's illnesses. The expression of repentance is to confess our error. We are speaking here of holy confession.

It must be said that in the biblical and patristic texts there are two forms of confession. The first is the noetic confession which we make in prayer to God and the second is the confession we make to our spiritual physician, who is also our therapist. St. John of the Ladder defines compunction as "an eternal torment of the conscience which brings about the cooling of the fire of the heart through noetic confession"[89]. Noetic confession produces compunction, and compunction gives consolation to the heart of man. Beyond that, confession is unrestrained repentance and it takes place in an atmosphere of repentance. It is the heart's grief, which produces "forgetfulness of nature". "Confession is a forgetfulness of nature since because of this a man forgot to eat his bread"[90].

---

87. Abba Dorotheos. CS p. 167. SC p. 346, 108
88. Philok. 2, p. 95f, 78
89. Ladder. Step 7. CWS p. 136
90. Ibid.

According to St. Diadochos of Photike, we must offer to the Lord at once a strict confession even of our involuntary failings and not stop until our "conscience is assured through tears of love that we have been forgiven"[91]. Furthermore the saint exhorts us to be very watchful lest our conscience "deceive itself into believing that the confession which it has made to God is adequate"[92]. He says this because when we pray to God and confess our sins, we often do it inadequately, and thus we live in the satisfaction that we have made our confession. This is self-deception, so we need to be in constant readiness, for if we do not confess as we should, we shall be seized with an ill-defined fear at the hour of our death[93].

Confession to God through prayer does not take the place of our confession of sins to our spiritual father, nor does confession to the spiritual therapist take the place of confession through prayer. It is essential that the two types of confession be linked together. At any rate after confession through prayer it is necessary also to go to the spiritual father. God has given them the right to forgive sins: "Receive the Holy Spirit. If you forgive the sins of any, they are forgiven; if you retain the sins of any, they are retained" (Jn. 20, 22f). From this passage it is clear "how great is the honour which the Holy Spirit has bestowed upon priests"[94]. According to St. John Chrysostom, the priests living on earth "have been entrusted with the stewardship of heavenly things", since "what priests do on earth, God ratifies above. The Master confirms the decisions of his slaves"[95]. Therefore we need to have recourse to spiritual physicians for our healing. "Above all let us make our confession to our good judge, and to him alone". Yet if the good judge commands us to confess before

---

91. St. Diadochos of Photike. Philok.1, p. 295
92. Ibid.
93. Ibid.
94. St. John Chrysostom. On the Priesthood. III, 4. p. 71
95. Ibid. p. 71f

all the people, we must do it, for the basic principle is that wounds which are made known are healed. "Wounds shown in public will not grow worse, but will be healed"[96]. Certainly in order for healing to succeed, a good physician is essential. All of the confessors are able to perform the sacrament of confession, but they cannot all heal, as some lack spiritual priesthood, as we said in another chapter.

"If the diagnosis of bodily illnesses is inaccurate, and in very few cases certain, this is much more so with spiritual illnesses". "The diagnosis of souls is far more inaccurate". The passions of the soul are "harder to understand"[97]. When a priest finds it impossible to heal, we must have recourse to another priest, for "without a doctor, few are cured"[98].

The value of confession has also been pointed out by many contemporary psychiatrists. It is fundamental that a person should be open, not closed within himself. In the language of the Church we say that when a person knows how to open himself to God through the confessor, he can avoid many psychic illnesses, and insanity as well. We feel the value of confession in practice. An existing sin tires us physically as well. We even experience bodily illness. When we decide to make a confession, the healing stage begins. Soul and body are flooded with calm. But of course it is necessary to go on to make the real confession.

Since the devil knows the value of confession, he does his best to press us not to confess or to do it as if someone else had committed the sins, or else to ascribe the responsibility to others[99]. However, it takes spiritual courage for a person to reveal his wound to a spiritual physician. St. John of the Ladder advises: "Lay bare your wound to the healer". And along with the revelation of the illness, take all the blame on

---

96. Ladder. Step 4. CWS p. 93
97. Nicetas Stethatos. Natural chapters, Ch. 11
98. Ladder. Step 4. CWS p. 109
99. Ibid. p. 108

yourself, saying humbly: "This is my wound, Father, this is my injury. It happened because of my negligence and not from any other cause. No one is to blame for this, no man, spirit or body or anything else. It is all through my negligence"[100]. One should not be ashamed, or rather one should overcome the shame of sin and of laying it bare. In revealing our inner wounds to our spiritual director, we should look and behave and think like a condemned person. And indeed St. John advises: "If you can, shed tears on the feet of your judge and healer as though he were Christ"[101]. The same saint affirms that he has seen men confessing who showed such a humble disposition and confessed with such tearful eyes and cries of despair that they softened the harshness of the judge and "turned his rage to mercy"[102].

It is natural to feel shame when one has to confess one's wound, but one should overcome it. "Do not conceal your sins"[103]. Immediately after confessing, laying bare, there comes an inner calm. It is reported that a zealous monk mastered by a blasphemous thought dissolved his flesh by fasting and vigils and yet did not feel any help. When he decided to confess this thought to the spiritual physician and wrote it on a piece of paper, he was healed at once. "And the monk assured me that even before he had left the cell of this old man his infirmity was gone"[104]. This demonstrates the truth that confession is not a human endeavour, but it works by the power of God. The soul is healed by divine grace. Neither fasting nor vigil is very helpful unless it is linked with confession.

Usually spiritual physicians receive attacks from those confessing when they do not make their confession with

---

100. Ibid.
101. Ibid. p. 109
102. Ibid. p. 108
103. Ibid. Step 22. CWS p. 205
104. Ibid. Step 23. CWS p. 213

humility and self-knowledge. A spiritual operation takes place with confession and therefore the patient resists. But the advice of the Fathers to him is clear. "Do not be angry with a person who unwittingly operates on you like a surgeon. Look rather at the abomination he has removed and, blaming yourself, bless him because by the grace of God he has been of such service to you"[105]. Confession extracts all the loathsomeness of our soul and this must move us, on the one hand to compassion for ourself, and on the other hand to gratitude towards the spiritual physician. At least whoever rejects criticism shows the existence of passion, while anyone who accepts criticism "is free of this fetter"[106].

We must again emphasise that repentance linked with holy confession heals one's wound. Repentance, which is inspired by the Comforter, burns up the heart, and where there is mourning all the wounds are healed. A person in this state possesses the great treasure of virginity. Nicetas Stethatos advises: "Do not say to yourself: 'It is no longer possible for me to regain the purity of virginity because in various ways I have fallen into defilement and bodily passion'". Even if a person has lost his virginity, he can acquire it anew through the tears of a second baptism which is repentance. Therefore the same holy Father continues: "for where the pains of repentance are overcome by mortification and warmth of soul, and rivers of tears flow from compunction, all of sin's defences fall, every fire of passion is extinguished, heavenly rebirth takes place through the coming of the Comforter, and once more the soul becomes a palace of purity and virginity"[107].

A man's rebirth cannot happen without submission to spiritual fathers who will heal him in Christ: "If a person does not submit to a spiritual father" in imitation of Christ, who submitted to His Father unto death on the cross, it also means

---

105. Ilias the Presbyter. Philok.3, p. 37, 31
106. Ladder. Step 23. CWS p. 208
107. Natural chapters. Ch. 50

that "he will not be reborn"[108]. For this rebirth "comes about through submission to spiritual fathers"[109].

But often the wretched passions of the soul are not healed immediately after confession. A great struggle and much asceticism are required for the soul to be freed from its passions. Essentially it is not formal confession, perhaps made under great psychological pressures, which brings forgiveness of sins, but freedom from passions. A person who has not been freed from passions by the grace of Christ "has not yet received forgiveness"[110]. Just as someone who has been ill for many years cannot acquire instant health, so it is not possible to overcome passions – not even one of them – "in a quick moment"[111]. Time and especially ascetic life are needed, because "passions performed in practice are also healed with practice"[112]. So "constraint and self-control, labours and spiritual struggles" offer dispassion[113].

In what follows we shall attempt to describe the healing of the three parts of the soul, the passions of body and soul, what things precede and what things follow. We shall describe here just the **general** methods of healing the soul.

In another section we emphasised that St. Gregory Palamas, dividing the soul into three parts, the intelligent, the incensive and the appetitive, says that when a man withdraws from God, every power of his soul becomes sick, and the entire soul as well. So healing is needed. Healing lies in spiritual poverty, which the Lord blessed. "Let us too be 'poor in spirit' after humbling ourselves, suffering in the flesh and having no possessions", so that we may inherit the kingdom of heaven[114]. With humility we will heal our intelligence, in which the

---

108. Ibid. Ch. 54
109. Ibid. Ch. 53
110. St. Thalassios. Philok.2, p. 312, 101
111. Ladder. Summary of Step 26. CWS p. 259
112. Nicetas Stethatos. Practical chapters, Ch. 34
113. Ibid.
114. To Xeni. Gk. Philok. 4, p. 106

passions of ambition rage. We will heal our appetitive part, where the passions of love of possessions and avarice rage, by shedding all possessions; and we will heal our incensive part, in which the carnal passions rage, by asceticism and self-control. It is very characteristic that St. Gregory includes solitude and noetic hesychia among the methods of curing the passions of ambition. "Solitude and remaining in one's cell are an excellent help in the curing of these passions"[115]. And the carnal passions are cured in no other way than through suffering of the body, and prayer coming from a humbled heart, which is to be 'poor in spirit'"[116].

The life of triple poverty gives birth to godly mourning, which is connected with the appropriate supplication. Mourning engenders tears. The value of mourning for purifying a man's nous is very great. Bodily poverty breaks the heart. "Heartbreak is also brought about by the triple restraint of sleep, food and bodily ease. The soul, freed of evil and bitterness through this crushing, receives spiritual joy in their place"[117]. Self-reproach, which plays a great role in man's spiritual life, is born of this humility and bodily mourning.

Material poverty expressed in non-possession, joined with poverty in spirit, purifies the nous. According to St. Gregory Palamas, when the nous is freed from the senses and rises above the flood of noise of earthly things and turns to itself, then it sees "the horrible mask which it has acquired through wandering in worldly things" and hastens to wash it away with mourning[118]. In this way the nous attains purity and enjoys peace from thoughts. When the nous tastes the goodness of the Holy Spirit, "grace begins, as it were, to paint the likeness on the image"[119]. Then the man becomes a person,

---

115. Ibid. p. 103
116. Ibid. p. 105
117. Ibid. p. 108
118. Ibid. p. 109
119. Ibid. p. 111

since experiencing what it is to be in the likeness of God makes us persons. At first mourning is painful, for it is linked with fear of God, but it is very beneficial. With the passage of time, love for God is engendered, and the likeness with it. And when one lives grief deeply, "it brings as fruit the sweet and holy consolation of the goodness of the Comforter"[120]. The beginning of godly mourning is "like trying to obtain betrothal with God". Since betrothal with God seems impossible, the lovers of God beat their breasts and pray. The end of mourning is "perfect, pure nuptial union" of the soul with God[121].

Therefore, according to St. Gregory Palamas, the healing of the tripartite soul is attained through the corresponding tripartite poverty. Poverty begets mourning, which finds many expressions before it leads the person to communion with God. Mourning is a purgative of the nous and the heart.

St. John of Damascus too, as we have seen, divides the soul into three powers, the intelligent, incensive and appetitive aspects. The therapy and cure of the intelligent aspect is through "unwavering faith in God and in true, undeviating and orthodox teachings, through the continual study of the inspired utterances of the Spirit, through pure and ceaseless prayer, and through the offering of thanks to God". The cure and therapy of the incensive aspect of the soul is "deep sympathy for one's fellow men, love, gentleness, brotherly affection, compassion, forbearance and kindness". And the therapy and cure of the appetitive aspect is "fasting, self-control, hardship, a total shedding of possessions and their distribution to the poor, desire for the imperishable blessings held in store, longing for the kingdom of God, and aspiration for divine sonship"[122].

St. John of the Ladder's formulation is concise: "Let us arm ourselves with the Holy Trinity against the three by the

---

120. Ibid. p. 114
121. Ibid.
122. Philok. 2, p. 337

three", that is, in alliance with the Holy Trinity let us arm ourselves against the three: self-indulgence, avarice, and love of glory, by these three: self-control, love and humility[123].

We have mentioned that the Fathers call the incensive and appetitive aspects 'passible'. Thus the soul has an intelligent and a passible part. The intelligent part is purified by spiritual reading and prayer, the passible part by love and self-control[124].

St. Mark the Ascetic, as we have observed, regards the passions of forgetfulness, ignorance and laziness as the three great giants. He exhorts us to heal forgetfulness "by mindfulness of God", to expel the destructive darkness of ignorance "through the light of spiritual knowledge" and to drive out laziness "through true ardour for all that is good"[125].

There is also the distinction between passions of the soul and those of the body. These passions are healed by corresponding spiritual practices. Bodily appetites and leapings of the flesh are stopped by self-control, fasting and spiritual struggles. Inflammations of the soul and "swellings of the heart are cooled by reading Holy Scripture and humbled by constant prayer. And all of these are calmed by the oil of compunction"[126].

In their asceticism of healing the Fathers also set out the order in which the warfare against the passions should proceed. According to Nicetas Stethatos, the basic passions are self-indulgence, avarice and love of glory, which correspond to the three aspects of the soul. As there are three general passions, so there are three ways of fighting against them: the initial, intermediate and final ones. "The beginner who has entered the struggle for piety" fights against the spirit of self-indulgence. He crushes the flesh by fasting,

123. Ladder. Step 26. CWS p. 234
124. St. Thalassios. Philok.2, p. 317, 84
125. Philok. 1, p. 159
126. Nicetas Stethatos. Natural chapters, Ch. 68

sleeping on the ground, vigil and prayers at night. He over-whelms the soul by remembrance of the punishments of hell and by the thought of death. One who is in the intermediate struggle, that is, when he has been cleansed from the pas-sions of self-indulgence, "takes up arms against the spirit of ungodly avarice". And "he who has passed through the inter-mediate with contemplation and dispassion", who has entered the darkness of theology, fights against the spirit of love of glory[127]. So self-indulgence is tackled first, then avarice and finally love of glory. This is the order of therapy.

So far we have listed the therapeutic means which we should use to heal the three different powers of the soul, we have spoken of the bodily and psychical passions, the three great giants among the passions, and so forth. Now we must examine the **general therapeutic** methods which apply to **all the passions**.

First of all, one should not be agitated in this spiritual struggle. Agitation is very harmful to the struggling soul. When a passion crowds in on us, we must not be upset: "Allowing ourselves to be disturbed by these experiences is sheer ignorance and pride because we are not recognising our own condition and are running away from labour". We must be patient, wrestle and call on God[128].

Next, it is essential not to have great confidence in our-selves, but to turn to God. "Being passionate, we absolutely must not trust our own heart; for a crooked ruler makes even straight things crooked"[129].

Another method is to fight the passions while they are still small. While the offence is still small, "pluck it up before it spreads and covers the field". If a person is negligent when a fault seems slight, he will later "find it an inhuman master". A man who fights against a passion from the start "will soon

---

127. Ibid. Practical chapters, Ch. 40-42
128. Abba Dorotheos. SC p. 406f, 141. CS p. 194f
129. Ibid. SC p. 526, 202, 2. CS p. 251, 2

subdue it"[130]. For obviously it is one thing "to uproot a small plant and another to uproot a large tree"[131]. In the beginning cutting out passions is easy, and only a small effort is needed, while if they grow large, if much time elapses, then "they require more labour"[132]. The younger they are, the easier is the struggle against them.

We must cut off the provocations and causes which evoke the passions. We have already described how a thought develops into a passion. When we watch our thoughts and reject the proposal of the evil one, we avoid engendering and kindling passions. He who repels the provocation "cuts off at once everything that comes after"[133]. When our nous dallies with a sensual object, passions are naturally born or kindled. It is necessary to become detached from the thing by which the nous has been captivated. Unless the nous becomes detached from this thing, "it will not be able to free itself from the passion affecting it"[134]. In this spiritual contest we must draw away from vile desires and acts "and show that we are leaving them for good"[135].

It is the common patristic teaching to cut off the causes and impulses of sin. God, the Physician of souls and bodies does not call on us to give up "associations with people", but to cut off the evil causes in ourselves"[136]. "He who hates the passions gets rid of their causes"[137]. If he opposes the thought, "the passion grows weak and becomes powerless to fight and torment him" and so, "little by little, struggling and helped by God, he prevails over the passion itself"[138]. To summarise the

---

130. St. Isaac the Syrian. Ascetical Homilies, 5, p. 43
131. Abba Dorotheos. SC p. 360, 114. CS p. 173
132. Ibid. SC p. 360, 115. CS p. 174
133. St. John of Damascus. Philok.2, p. 338
134. St. Maximus. Philok.2, p. 65, 2
135. St. Gregory Palamas. Triads. 2, 2, 24
136. St. Cassian of Rome. Philok. 1, p. 84
137. St. Mark the Ascetic. Philok.1, p. 135, 119
138. Abba Dorotheos. SC p. 510, 190. EF p. 177, 109. cf. CS p. 243

subject of cutting off the causes of passions and impulses, we can say that the general advice of the Fathers is: "any time a passion attacks you, cut it away at once"[139].

In order to diminish the passions we need to put up a hard struggle, and then spiritual vigilance is needed "lest they increase once more". Again, fight to acquire the virtues and then be vigilant in order to keep them[140]. So all of our efforts will be between warfare and vigilance.

The struggle is great. It is not an easy thing to transform oneself, to cleanse oneself from passions and fill oneself with virtues. For the purification of man is negative and positive. According to the Fathers, spiritual warfare is carried on by keeping the commandments of Christ, and we know that when a person struggles to subject his body to his soul and his soul to God, the virtues of body and soul are produced. In fallen man the body is nourished by matter, material things, and the soul is nourished by the body. Now the opposite should come about. We must get rid of the unnatural state. Our soul must learn to take nourishment from the grace of God, and the body to be fed by the "grace-filled" soul, and then our organism will come into balance. We achieve this by endeavouring to acquire virtues such as humility, love, fasting, asceticism, prayer, obedience, and so forth. At this point we would like to point out some of the virtues which are essential for our transformation.

The pursuit of a life of love banishes all the passions: "Strive to love every man equally, and you will simultaneously expel all the passions"[141].

Unceasing prayer, "unceasingly calling on the Name of God is a medicine destructive not only of all the passions, but also of this conduct". And just as a doctor places a dressing on the patient's wound and it works without the patient's knowing

---

139. Sayings, p. 182, 22
140. St. Maximus. Philok.2, p. 66, 11
141. St. Thalassios. Philok.2, p. 315, 39

how, so also calling on the Name of God "removes the passions without our knowing how and why"[142].

St. John of the Ladder says that the remedy for all the passions is humility. "Those who possess that virtue have won the whole battle"[143]. The prophet king David (in Psalm 104), referring to the beasts of the forest, says, "When the sun arises, they gather together and lie down in their dens". And St. John of the Ladder interprets this, saying that when the sun rises in our soul "through the darkness of humility", then "the wild beasts gather where they belong, in sensual hearts and not in ours"[144]. The sun of righteousness rises through humility, and all the wild beasts of the passions are put to flight.

Yoking the powers of the soul with the virtues will free us from the tyranny of the passions[145].

Subordination to the spiritual father, coupled with self-control, subordinates the wild beasts of the passions[146].

The Christian struggles "to restrain his senses by frugality and his nous by the single-word Jesus prayer", and "thus detached from the passions he will find himself caught up to the Lord during prayer"[147].

"If you want to be free of all the passions, practise self-control, love and prayer"[148]. There are certain actions which stop the movement of the passions and do not allow them to grow, and there are other actions which subdue them and make them diminish. For instance, where desire is concerned, fasting, labour and vigil do not allow passion to grow, while withdrawal, theoria, prayer and intense longing for God subdue it and make it disappear. With regard to anger, forbearance, freedom from rancour, and gentleness, for example, all arrest it

---

142. Barsanuphius and John. Q.324. In Gk.
143. Ladder. Step 26. CWS p. 236
144. Ibid. p. 252
145. St. Thalassios. Philok.2, p. 310, 65
146. Sayings. p. 7, 36
147. Ilias the Presbyter. Philok.3. p. 57, 75
148. St. Thalassios. Philok.2, p. 312, 93

and prevent it from growing, while love, acts of charity, kindness and compassion make it diminish[149]. He who has ge-
nuinely renounced worldly things, and lovingly and sincerely
serves his neighbour, "is soon set free from every passion and
made a partaker of God's love and knowledge"[150].

Watchfulness, rebuttal and prayer drive away the provocation of temptation and everything remains inactive, that is,
the provocation does not reach assent and passion: "If the
nous is attentive and watchful and at once repulses the provocation by counter-attacking and gainsaying it and invoking
the Lord Jesus, its consequences remain inoperative"[151].

God has bestowed upon man two great gifts of grace by
which he may be saved and "may be delivered from all the
passions of the old man: humility and obedience"[152].

The word of God too is a helpful means of purification and
release from passions. The Apostle Paul, in speaking of the
spiritual armour which every Christian must have, refers to
the word of God. "And take the sword of the Spirit, which is
the word of God" (Eph. 6, 17). We need to have the words of
God continually before our eyes. "Devote yourself ceaselessly
to the words of God: application to them destroys the passions"[153]. In another place St. Thalassios tells us to strive to
fulfil the commandments "so that we may be freed from the
passions"[154]. The commandments of God refer to the tripartite soul. The commandments of Christ "legislate for the
tripartite soul and seem to make it healthy through what
they enjoin. They do not merely seem to make it healthy, but
they actually have this effect"[155]. Then St. Philotheos mentions several examples to make it clear. With regard to the

---

149. St. Maximus. Philok.2, p. 73, 47
150. Ibid. p. 55, 27
151. Hesychios the Priest. Philok.1, p. 170, 46
152. Barsanuphius and John. ET Q.550, p. 119
153. St. Thalassios. Philok. 2, p. 326, 18
154. Ibid. p. 313, 13
155. Philotheos. Philok. 3, p. 21, 16

incensive aspect he refers to the commandment "Whoever is angry with his brother without good cause will be brought to judgement" (Matt. 5, 22), with regard to the appetitive aspect the commandment "Whoever looks at a woman with lust has already committed adultery with her in his heart" (Matt. 5, 28) and with regard to the intelligence the commandment "He who does not renounce everything and follow Me is not worthy of Me" (cf. Matt. 10, 37f). According to St. Philotheos, Christ legislates for the tripartite soul through the commandments. But the devil fights against the tripartite soul, and hence he fights the commandments of Christ[156]. If Christ's commandments are fulfilled, we are cleansed of our passions, which are the bad dispositions "of our inner man"[157].

We have previously emphasised that mourning, repentance and confession are among the most effective weapons against the passions. "Those who are clouded by wine are often washed with water, but those clouded by passion are washed with tears"[158].

The various trials and temptations in our life, that is, "involuntary causes" also are a supplement to repentance. The virus of evil is great and requires the purifying fire of repentance through tears. For we are cleansed from the defilements of sin either through the voluntary sufferings of asceticism or through involuntary trials. When the voluntary sufferings of repentance precede, then involuntary ones, that is, great trials do not follow. God has arranged so that if voluntary asceticism does not effect purification, then involuntary causes "more sharply activate our restoration towards the original beauty"[159]. This means that many trials which come into our life are there because we have not willingly repented. Taking up the cross of repentance voluntarily and willingly results in

---

156. Ibid. p. 22f
157. Abba Dorotheos. SC p. 154, 6. cf CS p. 80
158. Ladder. Step 26. CWS p. 253
159. Nicetas Stethatos. Natural chapters. Ch. 9

our avoiding the involuntary and unwilled cross of temptations and trials.

Another great weapon against passions is hesychia, mainly stillness of the nous, about which we shall speak in another chapter. The Apostle Paul gives assurance that "No one engaged in warfare entangles himself in the affairs of this life" (2 Tim. 2,4). And St. Mark the Ascetic comments that he who wants to conquer the passions by involvement in worldly things is like one who wants to put out a fire with straw[160]. Certainly the subject of hesychia and withdrawal is great and very delicate. Withdrawal is not good for everyone. For if one has a passion hidden in his soul he cannot be healed in the desert, since there is no object which would evoke the passion. St. John of the Ladder says that when a man sick with a passion in his soul attempts the solitary life he is like one who has jumped from the ship into the sea and thinks that he will reach shore on a plank[161].

The advice of the Fathers about hesychia is not contradictory. Hesychia is "abiding in God" and purity of the nous. This is called noetic hesychia. The effort to minimise stimulations of the senses and to devote oneself to prayer helps towards freedom from passions. But when a person without special preparation and the special blessing of a discerning spiritual director flees from men and goes off to the desert, he may not be cured. For the desert conceals the passions of a man who goes there without the necessary preparations instead of curing them[162].

So far we have spoken of various means for curing passions in general. Now we wish also to present several particular therapeutic methods which cure **particular** passions.

According to St. John Cassian of Rome, there are eight evil thoughts: gluttony, unchastity, avarice, anger, dejection, list-

---

160. Philok. 1, p. 117, 107
161. Ladder. Step 27. CWS p. 262
162. Philok. 1, p. 85

lessness, self-esteem and pride. How are these eight thoughts, which correspond to the eight passions, to be healed?

Gluttony is cured by control of the stomach "to avoid overeating and the filling of our bellies", by "a day's fast" and "not to be led astray by the pleasures of the palate"[163].

Unchastity is cured by guarding the heart "from base thoughts". It is cured by contrition of heart and "intense prayer to God, frequent meditation on the Scriptures, toil and manual labour". "Humility of soul helps more than anything else"[164].

Avarice is cured by renunciation and poverty, as the Scriptures and the Fathers teach[165].

Anger, which blinds the eyes of the heart, is cured by forbearance towards our fellow men. Inner peace, which is the opposite of anger, "is not achieved through the patience which others show towards us, but through our own long-suffering towards our neighbour". It is not enough to avoid anger towards men, but "also towards animals and even inanimate objects". Likewise it is cured by restraining not only "the outward expression of anger, but also angry thoughts". We are not only to control our tongue in time of temptation, but "to purify our heart from rancour and not harbour malicious thoughts against our brethren". The final cure is to "realise that we must not become angry for any reason whatsoever, whether just or unjust"[166].

Dejection is cured by a warfare which should be directed "against the passions within". We must struggle "against the demon of dejection which casts the soul into despair. We must drive him from our heart". Let us cultivate only the sorrow "which goes with repentance for sin and is accompanied by hope in God". That is, dejection is expelled and cured when, by the grace of God and our own courage, we turn it into

---

163. Ibid. p. 73f
164. Ibid. p. 75
165. Ibid. p. 81f
166. Ibid. p. 83ff

spiritual sorrow, the sorrow of repentance. This godly sorrow prepares us and makes us obedient and eager for every good work, "accessible, humble, gentle, forbearing and patient in enduring all the suffering or tribulation God may send us"[167].

Listlessness is not cured in any other way than "through prayer, through avoiding useless speech, through the study of the Holy Scriptures, and through patience in the face of temptation". Physical work is also needed. The holy fathers of Egypt "do not allow monks to be without work at any time". They not only work for their own requirements, "but from their labour they also minister to their guests, to the poor and to those in prison, believing that such charity is a holy sacrifice acceptable to God"[168].

Self-esteem is multiform and subtle. It requires great attention. One must use every method to overcome "this multiform beast". One should not do anything with a view to being praised by other people and, "always rejecting the thoughts of self-praise that enter one's heart, regard oneself as nothing before God"[169].

Finally, pride is a struggle "most sinister, fiercer than all that have been discussed up till now". It is cured through humility, which is achieved through faith and fear of God, gentleness and the shedding of all possessions. It is by means of these that we attain perfect love[170].

But the enemy of our salvation, the devil, is ingenious. Therefore the Christian who is struggling in this fight must himself be ingenious. The shrewdness in a man shows in the ways which he employs to deceive the devil. In the patristic writings we find many "clever" cases in which the devil is evaded and the soul is healed.

---

167. Ibid. p. 87f
168. Ibid. p. 89ff
169. Ibid. p. 91f
170. Ibid. p. 92f

The passions usually tend to come back[171]. When it seems that they have been healed or have fled, they come back more strongly after a while. Christ's words about the unclean spirit are well known: "When an unclean spirit goes out of a man, he goes through dry places, seeking rest, and finds none. Then he says, 'I will return to my house from which I came'. And when he comes he finds it empty, swept and put in order. Then he goes and takes with him seven other spirits more wicked than himself, and they enter and dwell there; and the last state of that man is worse than the first" (Matt. 12, 43-45). The saints are aware of this and they take all necessary measures.

In what follows we would like to set forth a **few methods** and suggestions of the Fathers.

We should mainly fight against the dominant passion, "for until this particular vice has been wiped out it will be useless for us to have mastered other passions"[172].

When we are fighting two passions at the same time, we should prefer to submit to the milder one in order not to be conquered by the stronger one. St. John of the Ladder offers two examples. Sometimes when we are at prayer, brothers may happen to come. Then we must do one of two things, either not receive the brothers or stop praying, for the sake of the brothers. We should prefer to let the prayer stop because "love is greater than prayer". Another time, the saint says, he was in a city and while sitting at table he was afflicted by thoughts of gluttony and vainglory; he preferred to be conquered by vainglory (that is to be temperate and to be praised as one who fasts) because he was more afraid of gluttony: "Knowing and fearing the outcome of gluttony (lust) he decided to give in to vainglory"[173].

Abba Joseph teaches that sometimes it is preferable to let

---

171. Ladder. Step 3. CWS p. 86
172. Ibid. Step 15. CWS p. 176
173. Ibid. Step. 26. CWS p. 238f

the passions come into us and fight them there, and sometimes to cut them off right from the start. Therefore he answered one brother who asked him about this matter: "Let them come, and fight with them", saying that this was preferable. But to another brother who asked the same question, whether he should let the passions approach or cut them off, he answered: "Do not let the passions come in at all, but straightaway cut them off"[174]. This shows that the spiritual therapist is the one who will assign to us the appropriate kind of struggle and battle, as well as the method, because each person is different and each case is unique.

St. John of the Ladder mentions ways in which one can conquer the demons. These ways seem extreme, and it must be noted that not everyone can apply them, but only "he who has conquered the passions". In other words, the pure in heart have many means for wounding the demons.

A brother who had suffered disgrace was not at all troubled by it, but was prayerful in his heart. However, he then began to remonstrate and lament about the dishonours which he had undergone so that with a feigned passion he hid his dispassion.

Another brother pretended to be eager for the position of father superior when in fact he had no wish at all for it.

Another brother who was distinguished for his chastity went into a brothel "for what appeared as a determination to commit sin" and enticed the harlot to take up the ascetic life.

Another brother was given a bunch of grapes. And after the brother who brought them had left, the hermit ate them, seeming to stuff them in, but in fact taking no pleasure in them, and in this way he "fooled the demons into imagining that he was a glutton".

Such things were done by the so-called 'fools in Christ' in order to deceive the devil and to benefit the brothers in various ways. But this requires a particular purity, a partic-

---

174. Sayings p. 87, 3

ular blessing and grace from God. Therefore St. John of the Ladder, in view of these circumstances, writes that people who use this method should be very watchful, for "in their efforts to fool the demons they may fool themselves"[175].

After a hard struggle, by the grace of God a man can heal his passions, the pains of his soul, and become a king. The athlete of the spiritual struggle experiences such gifts, so he can repeat the words of Abba Joseph: "I am a king today, for I reign over the passions"[176]. He enjoys the life of Christ then, for "he who has put his passions to death and overcome ignorance goes from life to life"[177].

But as long as we are in this life and bear corruptibility and mortality we have to fight continuously. Therefore even when a man has overcome "almost all the passions", there remain two demons to fight the man of God. One of them troubles the soul "by diverting it from its great love of God into a misplaced zeal, so that it does not want any other soul to be more pleasing to God than itself". That is to say, this demon pushes the soul into an untimely zeal to reach perfection and for no other soul to be more pleasing to God than itself. The other demon, with God's permission, "inflames the body with sexual lust". The Lord allows this temptation to one who is doing well in a multitude of virtues "so that the ascetic will regard himself as lower than those living in the world" and in this way through humility and compunction will win his salvation. We should fight the first of these temptations with much humility and love, and the second with self-control, freedom from anger, and intense meditation on death[178]. God allows us throughout our life to be fought by the devil in order to make us humble.

A brother said to Abba Poemen, "My body is getting sick,

---

175. Ladder. Step. 26. CWS p. 248
176. Sayings. p. 88, 10
177. St. Thalassios. Philok. 2, p. 328, 53
178. St. Diadochos. Philok. 1, p. 294, 99

and yet my passions are not getting weaker"[179]. Despite these things, in his effort to be purified a man experiences the blessed state of dispassion. So we come now to study the blessed life of dispassion.

4. Dispassion

We shall endeavour to make our study of dispassion fairly brief, because what has been said before also shows us the way to attain this blessed state.

The **value** of dispassion for the spiritual life is very great. The man who has attained it has come close to God and united with Him. Communion with God shows that there is dispassion. Dispassion, according to the teaching of the Fathers, is "health of the soul"[180]. If the passions are the soul's sickness, dispassion is the soul's state of health. Dispassion is "resurrection of the soul prior to that of the body"[181]. A man is dispassionate when he has purified his flesh from all corruption, has lifted his nous above everything created, and has made it master of all the senses; when he keeps his soul in the presence of the Lord[182]. Thus dispassion is the entrance to the promised land[183]. The Spirit sheds its light on him who has approached the borders of dispassion and ascended, in proportion to his purity, from the beauty of created things to the Maker[184]. In other words, dispassion has great value and is extolled by the Fathers, for it is liberation of the nous. If the passions enslave and capture the nous, dispassion frees it and leads it towards the spiritual knowledge of beings and of God. "Dispassion stimulates the nous to attain a spiritual

---

179. Sayings. p. 159, 161
180. St. Thalassios. Philok. 2, p. 313, 2
181. Ladder. Step 29. CWS p. 282
182. Ibid.
183. Ilias the Presbyter. Philok. 3, p. 49, 14
184. Nicetas Stethatos. Practical chapters, Ch. 90

knowledge of created beings"[185]. Hence it leads to spiritual knowledge[186]. A result of this spiritual knowledge is that one acquires the great gift of discrimination. A man in grace can distinguish evil from good, the created energies from the uncreated ones, the satanic energies from those of God. "Dispassion engenders discrimination"[187].

Our contemporaries speak a great deal about common ownership and poverty. But the error of most of them is that they limit poverty to material goods and forget that it is something more than these things. When a man's nous is freed from everything created and ceases to be a slave to created things and lifts itself up towards God, then he experiences real poverty. This real poverty of spirit is obtained by the dispassionate man: "Spiritual poverty is complete dispassion; when the nous has reached this state it abandons all worldly things"[188].

But we must define **what dispassion is**. From ancient times the Stoic philosophers spoke of dispassion as mortification of the passible soul. We have emphasised that the passible part of the soul consists of the incensive and appetitive aspects. When these have been mortified, according to the ancient interpretation, then we have dispassion. However, when the Fathers speak of dispassion, they do not mean mortification of the passible part of the soul, but its transformation. Since it is through the fall of man that our soul's powers are in an unnatural state, it is through dispassion, that is, freedom from passions, that our soul is in the natural state.

According to the teaching of the Fathers, dispassion is a state in which the soul does not yield to any evil impulses;

---

185. St. Thalassios. Philok.2, p. 326, 20
186. St. Maximus. Philok.2, p. 107, 58
187. Ibid. p. 69, 25
188. St. Thalassios. Philok. 2, p. 318, 90

and this is impossible without God's mercy[189]. According to
St. Maximus, "dispassion is a peaceful condition of the soul in
which the soul is not easily moved to evil"[190]. This implies
that dispassion means that one does not suffer with the
conceptual images of things[191]. That is to say, the soul is free
of thoughts which are moved by the senses and by things
themselves. Just as in early times the bush burned with fire
but was not consumed, so also in the dispassionate man,
"however ponderous or fevered his body may be", yet the heat
of his body "does not trouble or harm him, either physically or
in his nous". For in this case "the voice of the Lord holds back
the flames of nature"[192]. Thus a dispassionate person has a
free nous and is not troubled by any earthly thing or by the
heat of his body. Certainly this freedom of the nous from all
impulses of the flesh and conceptual images of things is
inconceivable to those who live not in a state of dispassion but
by the energies of the passions. For men of God, however,
what the world calls natural is unnatural and they experience as natural what is called supernatural. St. Symeon
the New Theologian, confronted by accusations that it is
impossible for men to live in such supranatural states, to live
in freedom of the flesh, wrote that he who is not dispassionate
does not know what dispassion is, "and cannot believe that
anyone on earth could possess it"[193]. And this is natural in a
way, "for when a man judges the affairs of his fellows for good
or evil, he can do so only on the basis of his personal condition"[194]. Each one judges according to the content of life and
the way in which he lives. Anyway it is certain for those who
have experience, that the characteristic sign of a dispassionate

189. Ibid. p. 309, 40
190. Philok. 2, p. 56, 36
191. Ibid. p. 89, 38
192. St. John of Karpathos. Philok. 1, p. 298, 3
193. CS 41, p. 58
194. CS 41, p. 58

person is "to remain calm and fearless in all things", since one has received from God "the strength to do anything"[195].

All this is to underline the truth that dispassion is an entirely natural state; it is the transformation of the passible part and its return to natural life. This was the subject of a great discussion in the fourteenth century between St. Gregory Palamas and the philosopher Barlaam. The latter, condemning the type of prayer practised by the hesychasts then and now, insisted that dispassion is mortification of the passible part. But St. Gregory, having personal experience of the matter and expressing the whole experience of the Church, refuted this view. "But we, oh philosopher, were taught that impassibility does not consist in mortifying the passionate part of the soul, but in removing it from evil to good, and directing its energies to divine things, turning it away from evil things towards good things[196]. An impassible man is one who "is marked by the virtues, as men of passion are marked by evil pleasures". Men of passion subject their reason to the passions, while the impassible man subjects the passible part of the soul, that is the incensive and appetitive parts, "to the faculties of knowledge, judgement and reason in the soul"[197]. With the intelligent part of the soul, through the knowledge of created things, spiritually understood, he will gain knowledge of God, and with the passible part he will practise "the corresponding virtues: with the appetitive part he will embrace love and with the incensive part he will practise patience"[198]. Thus dispassion is the transformation of the passible part, its subjection to the nous, which is by nature appointed to rule, so that one may ever tend towards God, as is right, "by the uninterrupted remembrance of Him". Then one will "come to possess a divine disposition and cause the

195. Peter of Damascus. Philok. 3, p. 147
196. St. Gregory Palamas. Triads. 2, 2, 19. CWS p. 54
197. Ibid.
198. Ibid.

soul to progress towards the highest state of all, the love of
God"[199]. So we understand that the passible part is not mortified, but possesses great power and life. In another place St.
Gregory teaches that to crucify the flesh "with its passions
and desires" does not mean to mortify each energy of the body
and each power of the soul, that is to say, to commit suicide,
but to withdraw from vile appetites and practices "and to
demonstrate irrevocably this flight from them", that is, never
to return to them, and so to become men of spiritual desires
and go forward courageously, after the prototype of Lot, who
departed from Sodom. In summary we can say that according
to St. Gregory Palamas, those who are dispassionate do not
mortify the passible part of their soul but "keep it alive and
acting for the best"[200].

Thus dispassion is linked with love and is life, movement.
According to St. John of the Ladder, just as light, fire and
flame "join to fashion one activity", the same is true of love,
dispassion and adoption. "Love, dispassion and adoption are
distinguished by name, and name only"[201]. Dispassion is
closely connected with love and adoption: it is life and communion with God.

Certainly when we say 'dispassion' it does not mean that
the person is not under attack by the devil. The enemy of our
life continues to pester even the dispassionate man; for he
even tempted the Lord in the desert with the three well-
known temptations. But dispassion is "to remain undefeated
when the demons attack"[202].

There are many **stages or degrees** of dispassion which we
wish to mention in presenting the teaching of the Fathers.

St. Maximus sets out four degrees of dispassion. The first
type of dispassion is observed in beginners and is "complete

199. Ibid. p. 54f
200. Ibid. 2, 2, 24
201. Ladder. Step 30. CWS p. 287
202. St. Diadochos of Photike. Philok. 1, p. 294, 98

abstention from the actual committing of sin". In this stage the man does not commit the acts outwardly. The second dispassion, which occurs in the virtuous is the complete rejection in the mind of all assent to evil thoughts. The third dispassion, which is complete quiescence of passionate desire, is found in the deified, and the fourth is the complete purging even of passion-free images, in those who are perfect[203]. It seems from this passage that according to the degree of a man's purity, the corresponding dispassion is manifested.

St. Symeon the New Theologian divides dispassion into two categories. One is the dispassion of the soul and the other is that of the body. "The first can even sanctify the body by its own brilliance and the radiance of the Spirit, but that of the body alone without that of the soul cannot be of any benefit to the man who has it"[204]. Yet even if a person practises every practical virtue, he should not assume that he has attained dispassion[205].

St. John of the Ladder, who is in the tradition of the Church, writes that one man is dispassionate and another is more dispassionate than he. The one will loathe evil while the other will have "the blessing of an inexhaustible store of virtues"[206]. So it appears here too that dispassion is not only a negative work, but also positive. It is the acquisition of the virtues, which is a fruit of the Holy Spirit.

Nicetas Stethatos divides dispassion into two parts. The first comes to the contestants after they have completed practical philosophy, that is, after the contest proper, when the passions are deadened and the impulses of the flesh remain inactive and the powers of the soul are moving towards the natural. The second and more perfect dispassion comes to them with inspiration after the beginning of natural theoria.

203. Philok. 2, p. 222, 51
204. CS 41, p. 58
205. St. Theognostos. Philok. 2, p. 365, 29
206. Ladder. Step 29. CWS p. 283

This perfect dispassion, which "is raised from spiritual still-ness of thoughts to a peaceful state of the nous, makes the nous very clear-sighted and foreseeing". The nous of the dis-passionate person becomes very perceptive of divine matters, of the visions and revelations of the mysteries of God, and very foreseeing of human matters, when it sees people at a distance who are about to come to him[207].

The Fathers generally advise giving great attention to the subject of dispassion, because it is possible not to be disturbed by the passions when the objects which rouse them are ab-sent, but once those objects are present, the passions distract the nous. This is partial dispassion[208]. Dispassion has degrees, and a person who is struggling to attain it must never stop, but struggle continually, because perfection has no end. In general it must be emphasised that remission of sins is one thing and dispassion is another. St. John of the Ladder writes: "Many have been speedily forgiven their sins. But no one has rapidly acquired dispassion, for this requires much time and longing, and God"[209]. That is why in another place we stressed the fact that confession alone is not enough, but the soul needs to be healed, that is, we must acquire partial or even complete dispassion.

From these things it seems clear that there are several elements which **distinguish true** from **false** dispassion. St. John of the Ladder, an expert on the inner life of the soul and one who had the gift of discernment, writes that the passions and the demons flee from the soul for a limited time or per-manently. But few people know the ways and causes of the withdrawal. The first way is that the passions are made to disappear by divine fire. Divine grace, as fire, burns up the passions and purifies the soul. The second is that the demons draw away in order to make us careless, so that suddenly

---

207. Practical chapters. Ch. 89
208. St. Maximus. Philok. 2, p. 106, 53
209. Ladder. Step 26 summary. CWS p. 259

they can attack and seize the soul. Thirdly, the demons withdraw when the soul has become accustomed to the passions,
"when it has become its own betrayer and enemy". It is rather
like what happens to infants "weaned from the mother's
breast, who suck their fingers because the habit has taken
hold of them". And finally, another dispassion comes "from
great simplicity and innocence"[210].

Further, the difference between true and false dispassion
appears in the attitude we have towards people. Dispassion is
connected with love, and therefore usually our attitude
towards our brothers manifests true or false dispassion. He
who "cannot overlook a friend's fault when some trial occurs"
does not have dispassion. For when the passions in the soul
are disturbed, they blind the mind, "preventing it from perceiving the light of truth". Nor can they discriminate between
better and worse[211]. Changeless dispassion in its highest
form is found only in those who have attained perfect love and
"have been lifted above sensory things through unceasing
contemplation and have transcended the body through humility"[212]. A person who has come close to the threshold of dispassion has simple esteem for all men, "always thinks well of
everyone and sees them all as holy and pure and has right
judgement about divine and human things". The nous of a
dispassionate person is freed from all the material things of the
world "and is wholly absorbed in the spiritual things of God.
He sees the divine beauty and in a way worthy of God prefers
to frequent the divine places of the blessed glory of God, in
speechless silence and joy. With all his senses transformed,
he associates with men immaterially, like an angel in a material body"[213]. And when a dispassionate man speaks of the sins
of a brother he does it for one of two reasons, either to correct

210. Ibid. Step 26. CWS p. 238
211. St. Maximus. Philok. 2, p. 112, 92
212. St. Theognostos. Philok. 2, p. 365, 29
213. Nicetas Stethatos. Practical chapters. Ch. 90

him or to benefit another. But if someone reports the sins of a brother "to abuse him or ridicule him", he will not escape being abandoned by God and will fall into the same or another sin and, "censured and reproached by other men, will be put to shame"[214].

Perfect dispassion is present when a person remains unmoved by both the object and the memory of it. "Virtue when habitual kills the passions, but when it is neglected they come to life again"[215]. Therefore a person who is sometimes disturbed by the passions and at other times calm and at rest is not dispassionate, but rather he is dispassionate who "enjoys dispassion continually and, even when the passions are still present within him, he remains unaffected by the things that provoke them"[216].

Another sign of the existence of perfect dispassion in a man is when during prayer no conceptual image of anything worldly disturbs his nous[217].

St. John of the Ladder says that many of the proud who think that they are dispassionate "find out how poor they really are only after they die"[218].

This distinction between true and false dispassion brings us to the point of examining what are the **true** characteristics of real dispassion.

True discrimination is a mark of dispassion[219].

It has previously been emphasised that a sign distinguishing true from false dispassion is love. Now we wish to carry the distinction still further. According to St. Maximus, "for him who is perfect in love and has reached the summit of dispassion there is no difference between his own and another's

---

214. St. Maximus. Philok. 2, p. 95, 73
215. Ibid. p. 106, 54
216. St. Theognostos. Philok. 2, p. 364, 25
217. St. Maximus. Philok. 2, p. 63, 88
218. Ladder. Step 23. CWS p. 210
219. St. Thalassios. Philok. 2, p. 309, 43

things or between Christians and unbelievers, or between slave and free, or even between male and female". Having in view the single nature of man, "he looks on all in the same way and shows the same disposition to all"[220]. Again St. Maximus says that since God is by nature good and dispassionate and loves all men equally, "He glorifies the virtuous man because in his will he is united to God, and in His goodness He is merciful to the sinner; by chastising him in this life He brings him back to the path of virtue". He who loves does the same. He loves the virtuous man because of his nature and his good intention; he loves the sinner too because of his nature and through compassion[221]. Likewise a dispassionate man is one who harbours no rancour against someone who has injured or slandered him[222]. The dispassionate man loves all people, "and does not distinguish the godly from the ungodly"[223]. And furthermore, the dispassionate man suffers and prays for his neighbour. "Do not say that a dispassionate man cannot suffer affliction; for even if he does not suffer on his own account, he is under a liability to do so for his neighbour"[224].

Likewise a person who is running towards dispassion and towards God "considers lost any day on which he is not reviled"[225]. That is to say, he not only is not upset by the dishonours and insults of men, but he is upset when he is not criticised. This shows his heart's purity from passions, even hidden ones.

In general the dispassionate man is filled with the gifts of the Holy Spirit: he is a tree full of splendid fruits, the fruits of the Holy Spirit, the virtues. When the Fathers refer to the virtues, they do not regard them as autonomous ethical acts

---

220. St. Maximus. Philok. 2. p. 70, 30
221. Ibid. p. 55, 25
222. Ibid. p. 105, 42
223. Nicetas Stethatos. Natural chapters. Ch. 44
224. St. Mark the Ascetic. Philok. 1, p. 136, 132
225. Ladder. Step 4, CWS p. 120

but as ontological. That is, the virtues are not good deeds or abstract values, but person, though naturally not impersonated in the sense of being self-existent. Love is communion with real love, which is Christ. Peace is not an abstract value, but Christ Himself. The same is true of righteousness, and so forth. Inasmuch as the dispassionate person has communion with Christ, it is natural that the virtues of Christ become his as well. We do not wish to dwell on the subject of the virtues. We only say that just as there are passions of the body and of the soul, so there are virtues of the soul and of the body. And just as there are stages and degrees of passions, so there are stages and degrees of virtues. And just as there are mothers and daughters of passions, so there are mothers and daughters of virtues. But we do not think that it is necessary to list them here. We refer the reader to the following Fathers: for the virtues of body and soul we refer to St. John of Damascus[226]. And for the virtues which correspond to the three spiritual ages – beginners, intermediate and advanced – we refer to St. John of the Ladder[227].

When a person is not troubled by any passion, if his heart yearns more and more for God, if he does not fear death but regards it as sleep, then he has attained the pledge of his salvation "and, rejoicing with inexpressible joy, he carries the kingdom of heaven within him"[228].

A person does not receive the grace of dispassion in a casual way. Intensive effort and a great struggle are required. Therefore we are now going to see how dispassion comes about. Indeed what we said in the preceding section about the struggle to cure the passions shows the way to acquire dispassion. Here we want to go over in brief the paths leading to the land of promise, that is, the land of dispassion. We will necessarily have to be concise, citing patristic passages.

---

226. St. John of Damascus. Philok. 2, p. 334
227. Ladder. Step 26. CWS p. 232
228. St. Theognostos. Philok. 2, p. 361, 12

"Humility arises out of obedience, and from humility itself comes dispassion"[229]. The humility which arises from obedience brings about dispassion. If a man proceeds by another path than this he cannot find what he desires[230]. Dispassion is not achieved without love[231]. Since there are degrees of love and since there is interpenetration of virtues, because the spiritual life is unified and organically bound together, therefore the life of love brings dispassion, and dispassion is closely connected with love. Love and self-control "keep the nous dispassionate in the face of things and the conceptual images we derive from them"[232]. Dispassion is "the reward of self-control"[233]. Fasting, vigils and prayer help greatly in the development of dispassion: "Judicious fasting and vigils, together with meditation and prayer, quickly lead to the threshold of dispassion", provided that the soul is also in possession of humility, full of tears, and burning with love for God[234]. A rather dry and not irregular diet, joined with charity, "leads the monk rapidly to the threshold of impassibility"[235]. When a person works with patience, with self-control in all things and constant entreaty and at the same time keeps the ground he has won, with self-reproach and the utmost humility, he will "then in good time receive the grace of dispassion"[236]. St. John of the Ladder says that dispassion attained through stillness of the body does not remain unshakeable "whenever the world impinges on it", whereas "dispassion achieved through obedience is genuine and is everywhere unshakeable"[237]. The state of purity which comes from

---

229. Ladder. Step 4. CWS p. 109
230. St. Theognostos. Philok. 2, 364, 25
231. Ibid. 367, 36
232. St. Maximus. Philok. 2, p. 89, 39
233. Ibid. p. 69, 25
234. Nicetas Stethatos. Natural chapters. Ch. 79
235. Abba Evagrios. Sayings. p. 54, 6
236. St. Theognostos. Philok. 2 p. 365f, 30
237. Ladder. Step 15. CWS p. 176

doing God's commandments begets dispassion[238]. This shows that the keeping of God's commandments has great value. "The keeping of God's commandments generates dispassion"[239].

But through bodily exercise alone, without faith, men cannot enter "into the resting-place of dispassion and the perfection of spiritual knowledge"[240]. St. Theognostos also says clearly that when a person attains practical virtue, he cannot approach dispassion "unless spiritual contemplation confers on his nous illuminative knowledge and the understanding of created beings"[241]. This passage is very important. For today too there are men who say that we can arrive at dispassion through practical virtue. St. Theognostos does not accept this. It must necessarily be accompanied by spiritual contemplation, repentance and prayer, especially 'noetic prayer'.

Godly sorrow is an important help for achieving dispassion. According to St. John of the Ladder, "For many people, mourning prepared the way for blessed dispassion. It worked over, ploughed, and got rid of what was sinful"[242]. So mourning is a way of life. It cleanses the soul, purifies the nous and makes it capable of receiving the divine consolations. This mourning is linked with repentance, and true repentance with hatred of self. The Lord spoke of hating our life in connection with following Christ and gaining the kingdom of heaven. "He who loves his life will lose it and he who hates his life in this world will keep it for eternal life" (Jn. 12, 25), and "If anyone comes to me and does not hate his father and mother, ...yes, and his own life also, he cannot be my disciple" (Lk. 14, 26). St. Gregory Palamas writes that those who live in the world should force themselves to use the things of this world in conformity with the commandments of Christ. Such forcing,

---

238. St. Maximus. Philok. 2, p. 112, 91
239. St. Thalassios. Philok. 2, p. 314, 25
240. Nicetas Stethatos. Gnostic chapters. Ch. 71
241. Philok. 2, p. 369, 46
242. Ladder. Step 7. CWS p. 143

prolonged by habit, makes it easy for us to accept God's commandments and transforms our changeable disposition into a fixed state. This condition brings about a steady hatred "towards evil states and dispositions of soul", and the hatred produces dispassion[243]. So the hatred of our evil and twisted self becomes a source of dispassion. And when man possesses dispassion, then sin does not master him and he rests in freedom and in the law of the Spirit[244].

When we see that there are some outstanding people in the spiritual life who have a few faults and small passions, we should not be scandalised, for God in His providence often leaves some vestiges of passions so that they will blame themselves and obtain a wealth of humility that no one can plunder[245].

This is the great treasure of dispassion. It is connected with all the virtues and the spiritual life. Therefore we must **pray** to acquire blessed dispassion. St. John of the Ladder urges all of us who are swept by passion to pray "ceaselessly to the Lord, for all the dispassionate have advanced from passion to dispassion"[246]. Indeed we should not seek this dispassion with pride and egoism in order to have great and supranatural gifts. For it is possible that a man should seek such a gift and be given it by the devil in order to delude him with vanity. Therefore St. Theognostos urges: "Do not ask for dispassion, for you are unworthy of such a gift; but ask persistently for salvation, and with it you will receive dispassion as well"[247].

In spite of our prayer and intense struggle, it is possible that God may not permit us to be rid of one passion, so that we may taste dispassion in part or altogether. This happens either because we asked it of God prematurely or unworthily

---

243. St. Gregory Palamas. Triads. 2, 2, 20. CWS p. 55
244. Nicetas Stethatos. Gnostic chapters. Ch. 75
245. Ladder. Step 26. CWS p. 239
246. Ibid. Step 28. CCWS p. 277
247. Philok. 2, p. 366, 32

or vaingloriously or because if granted it would lead to conceit or we would become negligent or careless as a result. So we should not be grieved "if for a while the Lord seems to allow our requests to go unheard". God would be delighted to make us dispassionate "in one moment", but His providence is for our sake, as we have said before[248]. Besides, in the history of the Church we have cases in which men who had dispassion asked God to take this blessing away from them so that they could fight against the enemy. After St. Ephrem had conquered all the passions of soul and body by the grace of Christ, "he asked that the gift might be taken away from him" so that he would not fall into idleness and be condemned because he no longer had to fight the enemy[249].

Partial or complete dispassion demonstrates the healing of the soul. The soul attains health. The nous which was mortified by the passions revives, is raised up. "Blessed dispassion raises the poor nous from earth to heaven, raises the beggar from the dunghill of passion. And love, all praise to it, makes him sit with princes, that is with holy angels, and with the princes of the Lord's people"[250].

248. Ladder. Step 26. CWS p. 237
249. Peter of Damascus. Philok. 3, p. 152
250. Ladder. Step 29. CWS p. 285

5. Hesychia as a Method of Healing

One of the fundamental methods of curing the soul is still-ness in the full sense of the word. I believe that we have already made this clear. Contemporary man is seeking heal-ing for his life, especially for his inner condition, precisely because he is over-strained. Therefore one of the messages which Orthodoxy can offer to the contemporary weary, dis-couraged and floundering world is the message of silence. I think that the Orthodox tradition has a great deal to offer in this area. So in what follows I shall try to explain further the value of hesychia and hesychasm for the healing of the soul, nous, heart, and intelligence. We have the impression that hesychia and hesychasm are among the most basic medicines for gaining inner health. And since lack of silence is what creates the problems, the pressure, anxiety and insecurity, as well as the psychological, psychical, and physical illnesses, we shall try to look at their cause, which is anti-hesychasm. The anti-hesychastic desert wind that is blowing and burning everything is prevalent everywhere and is the dominant cause of the abnormal situation. So we shall look at hesychia as a method of healing the soul, and anti-hesychasm as a cause of psychic and physical illness.

1. Hesychia (Stillness)

Before defining hesychia, or stillness, let us look at its great value for the healing of the soul.

The Holy Fathers who lived the whole breadth of the Orthodox tradition have stressed the great importance of Orthodox hesychia. St Gregory the Theologian regarded hesychia as essential for attaining communion with God. "It is necessary to be still in order to have clear converse with God and gradually bring the nous back from its wanderings"[1]. With stillness a man purifies his senses and his heart. So he knows God, and this knowledge of God is his salvation.

St. Thalassios, who fully adheres to this line, declares: "Hesychia and prayer are the greatest weapons of virtue, for they purify the nous and confer on it spiritual insight"[2]. Through hesychia man's nous is purified and becomes an acceptable instrument for seeing God. Indeed as we know from patristic teaching, nous is different from intelligence. When the nous is hidden by the passions it ceases to behold the mysteries of God (it is dead), whereas when it is freed from passions it becomes clear-sighted and sees God as light, and this light is the life of man. As we have said, this purification of the nous comes about through hesychia.

It is well known to those engaged in studying the works of the Fathers and to those trying to live this life of quiet, that there is hesychia of the body and hesychia of the soul. The former refers to outward things and the latter to the inward. Hesychia of the body usually refers to the hesychastic posture and the effort to minimise external representations, the images received and brought to the soul by the senses. Hesychia of the soul means that the nous attains the capacity and the power not to accept any temptation to delusion. In this state man's nous, possessed of watchfulness and compunction, is centred in the heart. The nous (energy) is concentrated in the place of the heart (essence), uniting with it, thus attaining a partial or greater knowledge of God.

Stillness of the body is a limiting of the body. "The begin-

---

1. PG 95, 1245c
2. Philok. 2, p. 311, 67

ning of hesychia is godly rest"[3]. The intermediate stage is that of "illuminating power and vision; and the end is ecstasy or rapture of the nous towards God"[4]. St. John of the Ladder, referring to outward, bodily stillness, writes: "The lover of stillness keeps his mouth shut"[5].

But it is not only those called neptic Fathers who mention and describe the holy atmosphere of hesychia, it is also those known as "social". Actually in the Orthodox tradition there is no direct opposition between theoria and praxis, nor between the neptic and social Fathers. The neptics are eminently social and those in community are unimaginably neptic.

I would like to refer to St. Basil the Great as an example of holy hesychia. In a letter to his friend St. Gregory he writes about hesychia as the beginning of purity of soul, and about hesychia of the body, that is, restriction of the tongue, sight, hearing and words. For example, he says: "The very beginning of the soul's purgation is tranquillity, in which the tongue is not given to discussing the affairs of men, nor the eyes to contemplating rosy cheeks or comely bodies, nor the ears to lowering the tone of the soul by listening to songs whose sole object is to amuse, or to words spoken by wits and buffoons - a practice which above all things tends to relax the tone of the soul".

This expresses the state of quietude which the holy Father enjoyed in the desert when he was trying to acquire knowledge of God in the university of the desert after the time he spent in human schools acquiring human knowledge. As a result, this luminary of Caesarea provides us with a classic passage which shows that he had an excellent knowledge of the life of hesychia. He writes: "When the mind is not dissipated upon extraneous things, nor diffused over the world about us through the senses, it withdraws within itself, and

---

3. St. Gregory of Sinai. Acrostics, 111. Writings, p. 61
4. Ibid.
5. Ladder. Step 11. CWS p. 159

of its own accord ascends to the vision of God. Then when it is illuminated without and within by that glory, it becomes forgetful even of its own nature. No longer able to drag the soul down to thought of sustenance or to concern for the body's covering, but enjoying leisure from earthly cares, it transfers all its interest to the acquisition of the eternal goods..."[6].

Hesychia of the body is helpful for attaining inner stillness of the soul. It appears from the patristic teaching that the former, even if not entirely necessary, is nevertheless very much needed in the godly life. "Stillness of the body is the knowledge and management of one's feelings and perceptions"[7]. In another place where St. John of the Ladder speaks of this hesychia, he is thinking especially of "solitary abodes"[8].

Certainly, as we said before, the desert, and in general hesychia of the body, is helpful for attaining inner spiritual hesychia. But the Fathers understood hesychasm "neither as living like a recluse nor as distancing oneself in the desert, but as uninterrupted dwelling in God"[9]. Although the desert has great value in that it helps to limit the images and representations coming from the world outside, yet it is not made an absolute. Nicetas Stethatos is characteristic on this point. He points out that virtue is not limited to a particular place and that man's aim is "to restore the powers of the soul and concentrate the general virtues at one point in action according to nature". Saying that these things do not come from outside but "they have been provided us from creation", he concludes: "The desert is unnecessary if we come into the Kingdom of Heaven without it, through repentance and keeping all the commandments of God"[10]. It is very characteristic that Nicetas, formulating the problem spoken of by many who say

---

6. St. Basil the Great. FC vol. 13, p. 7. Letter 2
7. Ladder. Step 27. CWS p. 261f
8. Ibid. Step 21. CWS p. 199
9. Archim.Sophrony. Saint Silouan. p. 140
10. Practical chapters. Ch. 72

that it is impossible to attain the habit of virtue "without withdrawal and flight into the desert", writes: "I was surprised that which knows no limits was thought by them to be in a limited place"[11].

In any case the desert and hesychia of the body in general helps one to acquire hesychia of the spirit, the holy content of which we are now going to describe.

St. John of the Ladder, writing compactly in his remarkable work, says that **stillness of the soul** is "accurate knowledge and management of one's thoughts". "Stillness of the soul is a science of thoughts and an inviolable mind. Brave and determined thinking is a friend of stillness. It keeps constant vigil at the doors of the heart, and kills or repels the thoughts that come"[12].

St. Symeon the New Theologian, speaking of inner stillness and describing its holy atmosphere, says: "Hesychia is an undisturbed state of the nous, calmness of a free and rejoicing soul, a heart's untroubled and unwavering foundation, vision of light, knowledge of the mysteries of God, a word of wisdom, depth of conceptual images of God, rapture of the nous, pure converse with God, a vigilant eye, inner prayer, union with God and contact and complete deification, and painless repose in great ascetic labours"[13].

Other Fathers too speak of this holy state of the soul, since life in Christ is a common experience of all the saints. According to St. Gregory of Sinai, "Hesychia means cutting off all thoughts except the most divine which come from the Spirit, lest in accepting the former as good, we lose what is greater"[14].

This rejection of conceptual images is part of man's attempt to purify the intelligent part of his soul. The athlete of the spiritual life struggles to drive away the thoughts which

---

11. Ibid.
12. Ladder. Step 27. CWS p. 262
13. SC 51, p. 115
14. Acrostics, 9. Writings, p. 90

the evil one sows with the sole purpose of breaking up the inner unity of the powers of the soul and making a man's heart sick. It is a fact that Orthodoxy is a therapeutic science. As we read the works of the holy Fathers who refer to these subjects, we see clearly that Christianity cures the sick soul, and among the means of healing, first place belongs to guarding the nous, repelling intrusive thoughts and trying to slay them before they can enter the gate of the heart.

"What is hesychia, other than keeping one's heart away from giving and taking and pleasing people, and such doings? When the Lord told the scribe about the man who fell among thieves and asked him who was his neighbour, he said: 'He who showed mercy on him'. Again, He said 'I desire mercy and not sacrifice'. If you simply have mercy, it is more than sacrifice. Incline your heart to mercy; for the pretext of hesychia leads to haughtiness before a person has gained himself and become faultless: then hesychia is that he has borne the cross. If you are compassionate you find help. If you restrain yourself as if to avoid going beyond the measure, learn this, that you have lost even what you have: go neither in nor out, but straight ahead, being aware of the Lord's will, because the days are evil"[15].

That hesychia is, above all, guarding the nous, watching one's thoughts, is expressed by St. Thalassios: "Seal your senses with stillness and sit in judgement upon the thoughts that attack your heart"[16].

St. Gregory Palamas, however, is the chief defender of hesychia, as we shall see further on. By the grace of Christ he struggled to safeguard this method of purifying the heart and thoughts, which is an indispensable prerequisite for knowledge of God and communion with Him. In his sermon on the Presentation of the Virgin he speaks of the hesychastic life. It is characteristic that this Athonite saint, speaking from ex-

---

15. Barsanuphius and John. Q. 314. In Gk.
16. Philok. 2, p. 308, 22

perience, sees the Virgin Mary as the model of noetic hesychia, since she entered into communion with the Holy Trinity
in the Holy of Holies in stillness. He writes that we cannot
reach God and commune with Him unless we are purified and
unless we abandon sensory things and the senses, and unless
we rise above thoughts and reasonings and human knowledge and all thought. This is just what the Virgin did. Seeking this communion with God, "the Virgin finds holy hesychia
her guide: silencing the mind, the world standing still, things
below forgotten, sharing of the secrets above, laying aside conceptual images for what is better. This practice in reality is a
true entering into theoria or vision of God - or to put it better,
the only example of a truly healthy soul". Then St. Gregory
describes the virtues as medicines for the ills of the soul, for
the passions; but theoria, he says, is "the fruit of recovery,
whose end and form is deifying". The soul, in other words, is
healed through virtues, but when healed it is united with God
through theoria, to which the way of silence leads. "Through
this (theoria) a man is deified, not through reflecting on
words or visible things, but taught by silence"[17].

By this method of Orthodox hesychia and teaching we are
healed, being "released from the things below and turning
towards God". With constant entreaties and prayers "we somehow touch that untouchable and blessed essence. And thus
those who have been purified in heart through holy hesychia,
after being ineffably permeated by the light which is above
sense and nous, see God within themselves as in a mirror"[18].

The main points in this sermon are that by the Orthodox
method, which is essentially a method of noetic hesychia, we
purify our heart and our nous, and in this way we are united
with God. This is the only method of contact with God and
communion with Him.

The holy Fathers call this the soul's peace and Sabbath

17. St. Gregory Palamas. Homily 51. EPE vol.11, p. 328
18. Ibid.

rest. Man's nous, purified by the method and training of holy stillness, keeps the Sabbath, rests in God. St. Gregory Palamas, speaking of the divine rest, God's rest when He "rested from all his labours", and of Christ's rest at the descent of His soul with its divinity into Hell and the sojourn of His body with its divinity in the tomb, writes that we too should pursue this divine rest, that is, we should concentrate our nous with persevering attention and unceasing prayer. This divine Sabbath rest is noetic hesychia. "If you withdraw your nous from every thought, even good ones, and turn wholly towards yourself with persevering attention and unceasing prayer, you too will come into the divine rest and attain the blessing of the seven beatitudes, seeing yourself, and through yourself being lifted up to the vision of God"[19]. It is noteworthy that the saint says these things in a talk to the flock of his diocese of Thessalonica. This means that all, at different depths, can attain the experience of divine rest. I believe that this is the teaching which has been lost in our time.

From what we have said about noetic hesychia one can see why the person who practises this is called a hesychast. A hesychast is one who follows the way of stillness, which in reality is the way of the Orthodox tradition. Its aim is to lead us to God and unite us with Him. We may recall St. John of the Ladder: "Strange as it may seem, the hesychast is a man who fights to keep his incorporeal self shut up in the house of the body... A hesychast is like an angel on earth. With paper of love and letters of zeal, he has freed his prayer from sloth and carelessness... A hesychast is one who cries out: 'O God, my heart is ready'. He says: 'I sleep, but my heart is awake'"[20].

Indeed, as has already been pointed out, hesychasm is the most suitable method for self-concentration and the ascent of the soul to God and communion with Him. It is very necessary for communion with God. St. Gregory Palamas, after

19. St. Gregory Palamas. Homily 17, 10. EPE 9, p. 498
20. Ladder. Step 27. CWS p. 262f

explaining at length that man's nous (energy) should be turned to the heart and that it is in the heart, which is the "reservoir of intelligence and the first intelligent organ of the body", "the reservoir of thoughts", that the grace of God is found, writes: "Can you not see, then, how essential it is that those who have determined to pay attention to themselves in inner quiet should gather together the nous and enclose it in the body, especially in that 'body' most interior to the body, which we call the heart?"[21].

But we must emphasise and properly underline that training in hesychia is not simply a human attempt to bring the nous back to itself, and its union with the heart is not just a technical method. This training in hesychia is inspired and guided by the Holy Spirit and is expressed in repentance and sorrow. It is not simply an artificial method, which in some depth and breadth can also be found in anthropocentric systems. "The hesychasm of the Orthodox monk springs organically from deep repentance and his longing to keep the commandments of Christ. It is not the artificial application to spiritual life of Areopagitic theology. The theological teaching in the 'areopagitics' does not gainsay the results of mental quiet, and in this sense approaches and even falls in with hesychasm. But there is this essential difference: the Orthodox ascetic does not arrive at mental quiet through the abstract philosophy of apophatic theology but by repentance and struggle against the 'law of sin' (Rom. 7, 23) acting in human nature"[22].

All the Fathers make this connection between **noetic hesychia** and **repentance**. St. Gregory of Sinai writes: "Without the practice of constant weeping, it is impossible to bear the boiling cauldron of stillness." He who weeps about the things which precede and follow death will have patience and humility, which are the two foundation stones of hesychia. Without

---

21. St. Gregory Palamas. Triads. 1, 2, 3. CWS p. 43
22. Archim. Sophrony. Saint Silouan. p. 178

repentance and these two foundations a hesychast will have "conceit and negligence"[23].

Therefore the method of training in hesychia – and this must be strongly emphasised – is connected with repentance, tears, sorrow, compunction. Without these it is false and therefore not helpful. For the aim of hesychia is purification of the heart and nous. This is not conceivable without tears and mourning. Hence, for the athlete of noetic hesychia, tears are a **way** of life. Through concentrating his nous in his heart he becomes capable of seeing his wretchedness, and at once his eyes, and his heart itself, shed tears of repentance. As repentance grows, he is purified and acquires knowledge of God.

But hesychia is also closely connected with **keeping the commandments of Christ**. The greatest weapons of anyone striving to lead a life of inner stillness with patience are "self-control, love, attentiveness and spiritual reading"[24]. According to St. Gregory of Sinai, anyone who practises hesychasm must have as a foundation the virtues of "silence, self-control, vigils, humility and patience". Likewise he should have three activities pleasing to God: "psalmody, prayer and reading, and work with his hands"[25]. In another connection the same saint emphasises that "the first requirements of hesychia are to have faith and patience, and with one's whole heart, strength and power, to love and to hope"[26]. In another place again he emphasises other virtues such as self-control, silence and self-reproach, "that is, humility. For these support and protect one another; prayer is born of them and grows for ever"[27]. Of course one must also give attention to food, exercising all restraint so that the nous will not be dulled by food: "one who practices hesychia must always be in need, not

---

23. Acrostics, 108. Writings, p. 60
24. St. Thalassios. Philok. 2, p. 313, 11
25. Acrostics, 99. Writings, p. 57
26. Acrostics, 103. Writings, p. 58
27. St. Gregory of Sinai. Writings, p. 83

satiated. For with a heavy stomach and a mind dulled in this way one cannot pray with purity and firmness". Sleep comes from much food, and innumerable dreams fill the mind[28].

These things show that the hesychastic way of life presupposes keeping Christ's commandments, since this gives birth to virtues. So too the virtues are not independent of stillness, but neither is stillness independent of keeping God's commandments, His "ordinances".

On the contrary, not keeping the commandments and having passions do not constitute Orthodox hesychia, and if hesychia begins to appear, it is devoured, it disappears. "Nothing has a greater power of disturbing the state of stillness and of depriving it of God's help than the following passions: presumptuousness, gluttony, talkativeness and vain cares, arrogance, and the mistress of all passions - conceit"[29].

All these things show that holy noetic hesychia is necessary for keeping the soul pure from passions and for communion with God. It is not a luxury in one's life, it is not a training for only a few people, not a method only for monks to adopt, but it is for everyone. It is indispensable for attaining contemplation of God and for deification, which is man's goal. However there are differing degrees of noetic hesychia.

Many times in the Gospels the Lord is seen teaching about purifying the heart from passions, about inner prayer, liberation from the power of thoughts, and so forth. He Himself demonstrated to His disciples the value of the desert. It helps a person to conquer the enemy. Thus the Apostles included many so-called neptic topics in their teaching.

This is not the place for developing all these themes. We simply wish to mention a few.

It is well known that after His baptism, the Lord "was led up by the Spirit into the wilderness to be tempted by the devil" (Matt. 4, 1). It was there in the wilderness that he

---

28. Gk. Philok.4, p. 84
29. St. Gregory of Sinai. Acrostics, 104. Writings, p. 59

conquered the devil, who put to him the three well known temptations. Many times we find the Lord withdrawing into the wilderness in order to rest, but also in this way to teach His disciples the value of the desert. "He departed from there by boat to a deserted place by himself" (Matt. 14, 13). And after the miracle of multiplying the five loaves, "when He had sent the multitudes away, He went up on a mountain by himself to pray: and when evening had come, He was alone there" (Matt. 14, 23).

It is very significant that when the disciples gathered "and told Him all things, both what they had done and what they had taught", the Lord said to them: "Come aside by your-selves to a deserted place and rest awhile" (Mark 6, 30-31).

The Lord spent whole nights in prayer. Luke the Evangelist has preserved the information: "He went out to the mountain to pray, and continued all night in prayer to God" (Lk. 6, 12).

And in His teaching Christ emphasised the value of noetic hesychia and release from the passions that are in us.

Teaching the way of true prayer, He said: "when you pray, go into your room, and when you have shut your door, pray to your Father who is in the secret place..." (Matt. 6, 6). Interpreting this exhortation of the Lord, St. Gregory Palamas writes: "...the closet of the soul is the body; our doors are the five bodily senses. The soul enters its closet when the mind does not wander hither and thither, roaming among things and affairs of the world, but stays within, in our heart. Our senses become closed and remain closed when we do not let them be attached to external sensory things, and in this way our nous remains free from every worldly attachment, and by secret mental prayer unites with God its Father. 'And your Father who sees in secret will reward you openly,' adds the Lord. God who knows all secret things, sees spiritual prayer and rewards it openly with great gifts. For that prayer is true and perfect which fills the soul with divine grace and spiritual gifts. As chrism perfumes the jar the more strongly the tighter it is closed, so prayer, the more fast it is imprisoned in the heart, abounds the more in divine grace"[30].

The Lord said to His disciples who were sleeping in the Garden of Gethsemane: "Watch and pray, lest you enter into temptation" (Matt. 26, 41).

He further advised us to keep our nous, and especially our heart, pure from passions and various thoughts: "When Jesus perceived their thoughts, he answered and said to them, 'Why are you reasoning in your hearts?' (Lk. 5, 22)". Accusing the Scribes and Pharisees, He said: "Blind Pharisee, first cleanse the inside of the cup and dish, that the outside of them may be clean also" (Matt. 23, 26).

The Apostles' letters also point to the great value of the wilderness, noetic hesychia, inner purification and watchfulness. Here too I would like to recall a few relevant passages.

After turning to Christ, the Apostle Paul journeyed into the Arabian desert, and there he repented of his previous behaviour (Gal. 1, 17).

The Apostle, who knew this inner stillness of the nous, gave much advice to his disciples. Sensing that Christians who have been united with Christ have the nous of Christ, he wrote: "But we have the nous of Christ" (1 Cor. 2, 16). In another place he exhorts: "Put to death your members which are on the earth" (Col. 3, 5). By the grace of God the Apostle saw the inner law in his members warring against the law of his nous (Rom. 7, 23).

In the Apostle's teaching, importance is given to watchfulness, that is, spiritual vigilance not to let one's nous be captured by an external evil power: "Therefore let us not sleep as others do, but let us watch and be sober... let us who are of the day be sober..." (1 Thess. 5, 6-8). He exhorts the Apostle Timothy: "But you be watchful in all things" (2 Tim. 4, 5).

And on the subject of prayer he is clear. Prayer should go on unceasingly in the hearts of Christians. "Continue earnestly in

---

30. EF p. 413f. Gk. Philok. 5, p. 111

prayer, being vigilant in it with thanksgiving" (Col. 4, 2). "Pray without ceasing" (1 Thess. 5, 17).

The Apostle Peter gives the same commandments, thus showing that the members of the Church have a common life. "Be sober, be vigilant; because your adversary the devil walks about like a roaring lion, seeking whom he may devour" (1 Pet. 5, 8).

All these things show that practically all Christians can attain stillness and thereby also vision of God. On this point too the Fathers are absolute and expressive.

Peter of Damascus writes: "For **all men** need this devotion and stillness, total or partial, and without it, it is impossible to attain any humility and spiritual knowledge"[31].

In this teaching of Peter of Damascus we need to note the words "all men need this devotion and stillness". If this is supposed to be the case with all men, it is much more so with monks. It is inconceivable that there should be a monk who does not devote time to participating in godly hesychia. We say this because there have always been different ideas in a few circles, especially among those who, if they come upon monks struggling to achieve this godly "hesychia", call them deluded. For this reason we shall take the opportunity to say a number of other things in the next section. The other point which must be emphasised is that "without it, it is impossible to attain any humility and spiritual knowledge". It is the only method and the only way of knowing God, as we mentioned previously, according to the teaching of St. Gregory Palamas.

Some people maintain that hesychia in the way described by the Fathers is inaction, not action. In reality the opposite is the case. **Hesychia is very great action** in invisibility and silence. The person is in repose and stillness in order to speak with God, in order to allow himself his freedom and to receive God Himself. And if we consider the fact that the greatest problems which torment us are psychical and internal, and if

---

31. Philok. 3, p. 194

we think that most illnesses (psychological and physical) originate from the elaboration of thoughts, that is, from impurity of the nous and the heart, we can understand the great value of noetic hesychia. So it is action and life. Hesychia offers the indispensable conditions for loving one's brothers dispassionately, for acquiring selfless and dispassionate love. "He who is not attracted by worldly things cherishes stillness. He who loves nothing merely human loves all men" (St. Maximus the Confessor)[32]. How can one have selfless love, which is one of the aims of the spiritual life, when one is possessed by passions?

So the hesychastic life is a life of intense activity, but a genuine and good activity. "The stillness of the saints should not be regarded as indolence, but as a form of intense activity. Moreover God is revealed in a similar way in his relations with men. The movement of God towards men is not only a movement of manifestation, but also a movement of revelation. It is not only revelation of a word but also an expression of stillness. That is why man, in order to come nearer to God, is not satisfied only to receive His revealed energies but must also advance towards receiving in silence the mystery of His unknowing. It is not enough to hear His word, but one must also advance towards the unhearing of His stillness. This second part leads to perfection, and so the first is presupposed. In fact, as St. Ignatius the Godbearer observed, only 'he who has truly acquired the word of Jesus can also hear His stillness, so as to be perfect'. So then the movement of man towards God should not be only a movement of action, but also a movement of hiddenness; it should not only be a witness of confession, but also a witness of silence and stillness"[33].

Therefore the Fathers speak of "fruiting stillness". When rightly practiced it offers great help to a person, it reshapes his personality, renews his being, unites it with God. Then

---

32. Philok. 2, p. 89, 37
33. G. Mantzarides. Palamika. p. 15. In Gk.

his social relationships are set right as well. When a man acquires love for God he also acquires love for mankind.

2. Hesychasm

So far we have explained as best we could what hesychia is, what are its characteristics and how indispensable it is for our spiritual life. It is recommended by all the Fathers as the best method of purification and returning to God. Moreover, as we have pointed out, Orthodoxy is a therapeutic science which aims to cure man's illnesses. This should never be overlooked, because to do so would be to destroy the whole essence and content of Christianity. Purification, a necessary precondition for deification, is attained through the method of Orthodox devotion in which hesychia has a very important place.

This whole method and its way of life is called hesychasm. That is to say, the person struggling in an atmosphere of stillness is called a hesychast, and this way of living in stillness is called hesychasm. We certainly know hesychasm as a theological movement of the fourteenth century, mainly represented by St. Gregory Palamas, which uses a particular psychosomatic method and seeks, with the help of divine grace, to unite the nous with the heart and so to live in communion with God. St. Gregory maintained that this goes on in the body as well. That is to say, the body too can acquire experience of the life of God. Barlaam, on the contrary, without knowing this method, became its opponent, with the result that he was condemned by the Church and finally removed from the Orthodox sphere. The hesychastic conflict, as it was called, ended with the Councils which took place in Constantinople in 1341, 1346 and 1351. The last Council, which "justified" St. Gregory Palamas, proponent of the hesychastic life, is considered to be Ecumenical: "We think that the Council of Constantinople in the time of Saint Gregory Palamas in 1351, judging at least on the basis of its great theological work, can be and deserves to be counted among the Ecumenical Councils of the Orthodox Church, to which it is in no way inferior as to the soteriological significance of its theology. This Council constitutes the proof of the continuing conciliarity of the Orthodox Church and of the living experience and theology concerning salvation in Christ"[34].

However, this hesychastic movement did not make its first appearance in the fourteenth century but has existed since the first centuries in the life of Church. We find hesychia in Holy Scripture, in the first Fathers of the Church. We have already mentioned examples of Fathers from all the centuries of the history of the Church. We mentioned St. Ignatius the Godbearer, St. Basil the Great, St. Gregory the Theologian. St. Maximus the Confessor, St. Thalassios, St. John of the Ladder, St. Symeon the New Theologian and St. Gregory Palamas. St. Gregory Palamas was not the introducer of hesychasm, but its exponent, the one who lived and expressed this whole holy journey of the soul. So hesychasm constitutes the authentic form of the Christian life.

However, we also use the term hesychasm to characterise the method used to concentrate the nous in the heart. This is a very large subject and I would like simply to point to a few topics.

In the effort to be purified, a man's nous "stands prayerfully in the heart", constantly repeating the single-word Jesus prayer. It is not busied with many words. It unceasingly recalls the Name of Jesus Christ. At the same time the nous watches to see that thoughts do not enter the door of the heart. So, as St. Maximus the Confessor says, watchfulness is linked with the prayer.

"But the nous can still more deeply penetrate into the heart when, by divine impulse, it so unites with the heart as to be divested of all images and concepts, while the heart is closed against every foreign element. Then the soul penetrates into the 'darkness' of a quite especial nature, and is subsequently

---

34. Athanasius Gievtits. Christ Beginning and End. p. 195. In Gk.

deemed worthy of standing ineffably before God with a pure nous"[35].

Many methods are used for attaining this concentration and the return of the wandering nous to the heart. It is essential that the method we use should be combined with repentance because otherwise it degenerates into a mechanical method.

In his sermon for the Sunday of the Publican and the Pharisee St. Gregory Palamas presents the prayer of the Publican, the way in which he prays, as the type of the hesychast's prayer. He refers to the Gospel: "The tax collector, standing afar off, would not so much as raise his eyes to heaven, but beat his breast, saying: 'God be merciful to me a sinner'" (Lk. 18, 13). Interpreting this passage, St. Gregory says that the word used here for 'standing' shows the long continuation of the standing, together with the persistence of the supplication and the penitential words. The Publican said "God be merciful to me a sinner". Nothing more. "Neither intending nor considering anything else, he was paying attention only to himself and God, rotating his prayer on itself, multiplying only the simple entreaty which is the most efficacious type of prayer." One sees here the value of the simple prayer "Lord Jesus Christ, Son of God, have mercy on me." The hesychast, like the Publican, thinks about absolutely nothing, but concentrates his nous on the words of the prayer. St. Gregory Palamas interprets Christ's words that the Publican 'would not so much as raise his eyes to heaven' by referring to the figure of the hesychast: "This standing was at the same time both standing and submission, and signified not only a lowly servant, but also one condemned." By this manner and figure the Publican showed "right condemnation and self-reproach, for he regarded himself as unworthy of both heaven and the earthly temple". The fact that he beat his breast also shows the participation of his body in the pain and sorrow of his

35. Archim. Sophrony. Saint Silouan. p. 145

soul. "Beating his breast, out of extreme compunction, and thus presenting himself as worthy of punishment, groaning with deep mourning, and bowing his head like one condemned, he called himself a sinner and with faith begged for mercy"[36].

It seems clear here that the parable of the Publican and the Pharisee was used by Christ, and also by St. Gregory Palamas, interpreting the parable 'hesychastically', to present stillness and prayer as the best way to receive mercy from God. It is the most perfect prayer. It is prayer of a single word, it contains deep penitence, the body participates in the prayer since it too will receive the grace of God, and the prayer has an atmosphere of self-reproach and just condemnation.

Because the heretic Barlaam derided the hesychasts of his time for using a particular bowing of the head and body to achieve concentration of the nous and a uniform development of the powers of the soul, St. Gregory referred to the case of the prophet Elijah, who prayed to God with his head between his knees: "And this Elijah, perfect in vision of God, with his head on his knees, thus assiduously collecting his nous to himself and God, relieved the many years' drought"[37]. Then St. Gregory recommended a way of concentrating the nous: "...for the eye not to turn here and there, but somehow, resting on the right breast or the navel, to send the power of the nous which was scattered through looking outward, back into the heart, through the body's being in that position..."[38].

Referring to this subject of how to pray, St. Gregory of Sinai recommends: "In the morning, sitting on a low stool, force your nous to descend from your head to your heart and hold it there; bending painfully, and with your chest, shoulders and neck very sore, cry out ceaselessly in your soul and spirit: 'Lord Jesus Christ, have mercy on me'". He also says we should restrain the breath in order to concentrate the nous. "Re-

---

36. St. Gregory Palamas. Homily 2, 13f. EPE vol.9, p. 62ff. In Gk.
37. Letter to Barlaam, 49. Syggrammata I, p. 288. In Gk.
38. Ibid. 50

strain the inhaling of breath so that you do not breathe unhindered, for air in motion, going up from the heart, darkens the nous and ventilates the reason, taking the nous away from the heart"[39].

There are other patristic witnesses on this subject[40].

In another place too St. Gregory of Sinai describes the method of prayer which concentrates the nous and is called hesychasm. "Sometimes, most often, because it is tiring, sit on a stool; sometimes again, more seldom, temporarily lie outstretched for some relaxation. Your sitting should be in patience, 'persisting in prayer'. Do not give in to faint-heartedness because of the laborious effort, but labour in your heart and drive your body, seeking the Lord in your heart. Compel yourself by every means to do this work. For 'behold', said the Prophet, 'pangs have taken hold of me like the pangs of a woman in labour'. But bending from below and gathering your nous in your heart, if it has indeed been opened, call on the Lord Jesus for help. Even if your shoulders are weary and your head is often in pain, persevere in these things with diligence and love, seeking the Lord in your heart. For 'the kingdom of heaven suffers violence, and the violent take it by force'. With these words the Lord showed us how truly to persevere in these labours. For patience and perseverance in everything generate labours of both body and soul"[41].

We must emphasise the fact that the value of noetic hesychia, unceasing prayer, repetition of the single-word Jesus prayer, the special way of concentrating the nous and uniting it with the heart, the standing of the body during prayer and the confining of the senses, the teaching that the grace of God is uncreated and that a person can receive it in his heart, that the light of Tabor is higher than human knowledge and not "inferior to thought", all of which define what is called hesy-

---

39. Gk. Philok. 4, p. 71f
40. Ibid. p. 72, 3
41. Ibid. p. 80

chasm, have been "justified" by the Council of Constantinople and consequently one who speaks against these things is no longer within the Orthodox tradition and at any rate creates preconditions for being cut off from its life.

3. Anti-hesychasm

Since we have already seen briefly what hesychia is and what hesychasm is and that hesychasm has been confirmed by a Synod which can rightly be called Ecumenical, let us take a brief look at the anti-hesychastic method for knowing God and the anti-hesychastic way of life, which unfortunately prevail in our time and which show that these are evil days.

"Hesychia has always met with antagonism, especially in the West. Lacking the necessary experience, its opponents argue in the abstract and go so far as to see in the practice something mechanical, some spiritual technique leading to vision of the Divine"[42].

Unfortunately this life of the West has also influenced Greece itself, so that we have a serious distortion of the Orthodox tradition. To be sure, many people assert that we have been changed by the Western spirit, and they have mainly located this change at various other points, such as habits and customs. I believe, however, that the greatest change has taken place in the matter of hesychia and hesychasm. Hesychia is regarded as an antiquated method, as a life of inactivity, and not suited to our day, which is an age of action. Unfortunately these conceptions prevail even among people who wish to live in the Orthodox tradition. Our time is a time of action. "The contemporary world is not a world of recollection and stillness but one of action and struggle"[43]. In an age like ours, which is hedonistic and self-gratifying, hesychasm cannot find an echo. It is happening as St. John of the Ladder

---

42. Archim. Sophrony. Saint Silouan. p. 143
43. G. Mantzarides. Palamika. p. 25. (In Gk.)

said: "A fish turns swiftly from the hook. The passionate soul turns from solitude"[44]. A pleasure-loving age is very anti-hesychastic. A nun said to me that in our time a "hot anti-hesychastic wind" is blowing which is burning everything. And I think that this judgement is absolutely true. This is the contemporary reality. The atmosphere prevailing today is rather the atmosphere of Barlaam and not that of St. Gregory Palamas.

Today theology is being developed through the elaboration of logic. It has become simply a logical system. I would characterise it as philosophical. It is a history of theology. It is not a fruit of hesychia and participation in God. This is why many errors and many differences in theological thoughts and views have appeared. Today most of us do not live theology as a therapeutic science, as I said before. We do not recognise the way of Orthodox devotion. If we read the Philokalia, where the most representative texts relating to the method of theology are concentrated, we see that most of them speak of how to cure passions. They do not make analyses, nor are they content with presenting the higher states, but at the same time they describe the ways we must employ in order to be cured of passions. I believe that it is a fundamental shortcoming of contemporary theology that it has not taken enough interest in the Philokalia. Perhaps a special chair should be established for introducing asceticism and hesychasm, based on the texts of the Philokalia.

Beyond these things, there is need of personal experience of the method of Orthodox theology as described in the patristic texts.

What Archimandrite Sophrony says is very characteristic in showing the difference between conjectural theology and that which takes place in God: "Unless the heart be cleansed it is impossible to attain real contemplation. Only a heart purified of passion is capable of that peculiar awe and wonder before God which stills the nous into joyful silence.

---

44. Ladder. Step 15. CWS p. 176, 45

"The theologian thinker aims at theoria by one means, the monk ascetic by another. The main object of the monk is to achieve the stillness of prayer in the heart, with the nous free from reflections, keeping quiet watch like a sentry to make sure that nothing enters into the heart from without. Where this state of sacred silence exists, heart and nous feed on the Name of Christ and His commandments. They live as one, controlling all happenings within, not by logical investigation but intuitively, by a specific spiritual sense.

"So soon as the nous unites with the heart it can see every movement in the realm of the subconscious. (Here we use this term from contemporary scientific psychology in a conventional way.) While the nous dwells in the heart it perceives the images and thoughts around it proceeding from the realm of cosmic being which attempt to seize heart and nous. The attack of intrusive thoughts is fierce. To weaken their onset the monk is constrained the livelong day not to admit a single passionate consideration, not to allow himself a predilection of any kind. His constant aim is to reduce the number of outside impressions to its very minimum. Otherwise at the time of inner noetic prayer all the impressions of the day will crowd unrestrained into his heart, causing the greatest disturbance.

"The monk's purpose is to achieve continual vigilance of the nous in the heart; and when, after long years of such striving – which is the most difficult of all ascetic feats, harder than any other – the heart becomes more sensitive, while the nous, from much weeping, receives strength to thrust off the slightest hint of a passionate thought, then one's prayerful state can continue uninterrupted, and the feeling of God, present and active, becomes powerful and plain"[45].

Orthodox theology needs to be imbued with this hesychastic method in order to be really Orthodox and not academic. Efforts are being made in this area. But the problem remains

45. Archim. Sophrony. Saint Silouan. p. 139

essentially a problem. Does contemporary theology speak of tears and mourning, self-reproach and humility? Does it regard as a way of knowing God "to make the nous and the world stand still, forget things below... lay aside meanings for what is better?" Does it presuppose that for us to attain communion with God, "we should abandon everything sensory along with sensation, rising high above thoughts and reasonings and all knowledge and **thought itself,** wholly surrendered to the energy of spiritual sensation, which Solomon called a sense of the divine, and reaching the unknowing above knowledge, that is, above every form of the much talked-of philosophy..."[46]?

I believe that on the contrary, contemporary theology is conjectural, rationalistic. It is based on the 'wealth' which is reason. What Archimandrite Sophrony says is characteristic: "One other kind of imagination about which we wish to speak, is the attempt of intelligence to penetrate the mystery of being and apprehend the Divine world. Such endeavours inevitably involve the imagination, to which many are inclined to give the high-flown label, divine inspiration. The ascetic, devoting himself to active inner silence and pure prayer, resolutely combats this 'creative' impulse within himself because he sees in it a 'processus' contrary to the true order of being, with man 'creating' God in his own image and likeness"[47].

Archimandrite Sophrony also writes: "The theologian who is an intellectual constructs his system as an architect builds a palace or a church. Empirical and metaphysical concepts are the material he uses, and he is more concerned with the magnificence and logical symmetry of his ideal edifice than that it should conform to the actual order of things.

"Strange as it may seem, many great men have been unable to withstand this, in effect, artless temptation, the hidden cause of which is pride.

---

46. St. Gregory Palamas. Homily 53. EPE vol. 11, p. 326ff. In Gk.
47. Archim. Sophrony. Saint Silouan. p. 155

"One becomes attached to the fruits of one's intelligence as a mother to her child. The intellectual loves his creation as himself, identifies with it, shuts himself up with it. When this happens no human intervention can help him - if he will not renounce what he believes to be riches, he will never attain to pure prayer and true theoria"[48].

This is Barlaamite theology and not Palamite-Orthodox theology.

Likewise today there is a prejudice against the Jesus prayer and the way it is said. Certainly we must say that we have a flowering of prayer, of efforts to publish the works of the Fathers and writings about prayer, but at the same time one observes that people are ignorant of these things and are unable to approach the life of prayer. Most of the reading is done in order to be in fashion. Or again we find that 'spiritual' men are ridiculing the hesychastic life, or worse, preventing people under their guidance from engaging in these things. The view that "these things are not for us", and so forth, is heard repeatedly. Many think that for people to take several minutes in the morning and several minutes in the evening to say an improvised prayer or read a few services with suitable passages is enough. What is more, even the holy atmosphere of hesychia, that is, compunction, self-reproach and mourning, are regarded as unsuitable for the laity, in contrast to what the Fathers say, as we have shown.

Worst of all is the fact that this 'worldly' attitude, the anti-hesychastic life, is even dominating the monks, it has crept even into the monasteries, which were supposed to be "schools dedicated to God", to be the medical schools where medical science would be taught. An attitude of mind prevails that we must know about those things but they are not for us! I have personal knowledge that "prominent" monks who have responsibility for Orthodox guidance of young monks charac-

---

48. Ibid. p. 160f

terise all the subjects related to the hesychastic life as 'fables', as not worth speaking about, as cases of delusion!!!

This is really sad. "Hesychia has from the beginning been a characteristic mark of Orthodox monastic life. Orthodox monasticism is also hesychasm at the same time"[49].

Fortunately, now at last we can see an attempt to return to the Fathers. And by this we mean an attempt to live the life of the Fathers, **mainly the hesychastic life**. There are many young people disenchanted with the contemporary climate of struggle and anguish, of action without stillness and mission without silence, who are turning more towards the hesychastic life and are being nourished by it. Many people with such desires are coming to monasticism and are continuing to live by the springs of the holy Fathers, that is the Orthodox tradition. Even in the world, centres of living in stillness are being created.

This life should be developed and increased in the cities too. This is how I see the organisation of Church and parish life. Thus we will come to understand that the Church is a place where souls are healed, but also a place of theophany. Within purification there comes knowledge of God, vision of God. Perhaps each person should to the best of his ability cultivate the Jesus prayer, which can be the teacher for his whole spiritual life. It will teach us when to speak and when to be silent, when to interrupt prayer in order to help our brother and when to continue it, when we have sinned and when we have God's blessing. Likewise we must struggle to keep and preserve a pure nous.

St. Thalassios' exhortation should become a rule of life: "Enclose your senses in the citadel of hesychia so that they do not involve the nous in their desires"[50].

The words of St. Gregory the Theologian which we quoted

---

49. G. Mantzarides. Tradition and Renewal in the Theology of Gregory Palamas. p. 9. In Gk.

50. Philok. 2, p. 313, 10

at the beginning should be regarded as a basic aim of life: "It is necessary to keep silence in order to come into pure contact with God and to minimise any delusion of the soul"[51].

We must be well aware that this hesychia is "indeed the **true** and **unerring mode** of life in God, **as handed down to us by the Fathers**", according to the Fathers Kallistos and Ignatios Xanthopoulos.

I would like to end these thoughts about hesychia with the teaching of Kallistos and Ignatios of Xanthopoulos: "This way, this spiritual life in God, this sacred practice of true Christians is the true, unerring and genuine secret life in Christ. Sweetest Jesus, the God-Man, laid this path and gave it His mysterious guidance; the divine Apostles trod it, as well as those who came after them. From the very beginning, from the first coming of Christ on earth up to our time, our glorious teachers who followed Him, shining like lamps in the world with the radiance of their life-bearing words and wonderful deeds, have transmitted to one another right up till today this good seed, this sacred drink, this holy germ, this inviolate token, this grace and power from above, this precious pearl, this divine inheritance of the Fathers, this treasure buried in the field, this betrothal of the Spirit, this kingly symbol, this springing water of life, this divine fire, this precious salt, this gift, this seal, this light, and so on. This inheritance will continue to be so transmitted from generation to generation, even after our time up to the very second coming of Christ. For true is the promise of Him Who said: 'I am with you always, even unto the end of the world. Amen'"[52].

---

51. PG 95, 1245C
52. Writings. p. 267f, 97

6. Orthodox Epistemology

The subject of epistemology belongs to this book, and it forms the final chapter, as it is closely connected with the cure of man's soul. Previous chapters have shown that the fall, sickness and death of a man are precisely the death of his soul, nous, heart and reason, under the influence of evil thoughts. The fall is mainly the fall of the nous. When the soul, nous and heart are cured, one attains knowledge of God. Indeed it is not only when they are cured that one acquires knowledge of God, but also as far as they are cured. When they are cured as completely as possible, one attains a knowledge of God that is not in words about God, but knowing God Himself. In other words, it is in the cured heart that God is revealed and offers knowledge of Himself. Thus it is clear that Orthodox epistemology is closely related to the therapy of the soul. Knowledge of God is increased as healing increases, and a pure knowledge of God is given to that person who has been purified and cured.

In order to see this more clearly, we may concentrate on the teachings of two Fathers of the Church: St. Isaac the Syrian and St. Gregory Palamas. We shall look first at the three degrees of knowledge according to St. Isaac the Syrian and then at knowledge of God according to St. Gregory Palamas.

The three degrees of knowledge
according to St. Isaac the Syrian

St. Isaac the Syrian develops the theme of the three degrees of knowledge in chapters fifty-two and fifty-three of his Ascetical Homilies.

He begins by contrasting knowledge and faith. Human knowledge is marked by the fact that it has no authority to do anything "without investigation and examination", but it must investigate whether that which it desires is possible (p. 254). In human knowledge there is a great deal of intelligence, and it is mainly fallen intelligence which is at work, having overstepped its natural limits; that is to say, it is an intelligence which dominates the nous as well. Faith, however, has different limits, and herein seems to lie its great difference from human knowledge, as well as its great value. St. Isaac says that when we use the word 'faith' we do not mean the handing down of the dogmatic truths about the Persons of the Holy Trinity and about Christ's becoming man and about the assumption of human nature by the Second Person of the Trinity, "although this faith is also very lofty", but the main meaning of what we call faith is "that light which by grace dawns in the soul and fortifies the heart by the testimony of the mind, making it undoubting through the assurance of hope". This spiritual faith does not learn the mysteries by aural tradition, "but with spiritual eyes it beholds the mysteries concealed in the soul, and the secret and divine riches that are hidden away from the eyes of the sons of the flesh, but are unveiled by the spirit to those who abide at Christ's table through their study of His laws" (p. 262). That is to say that while human knowledge is acquired through activity of the intelligence and through human research, divine knowledge is acquired through faith. This faith is mainly that which dawns in the soul from the light of grace, and through this power one learns all the mysteries which are hidden from the eyes of the carnal men of this age. So "faith is more subtle than knowledge, just as knowledge is more subtle than palpable things" (p. 262). Faith, which is divine knowledge, is more subtle than human knowledge.

St. Isaac explains the difference between human knowledge and faith. Human knowledge cannot learn without examination, while faith "requires a mode of thinking that is single, limpidly pure and simple, far removed from any deviousness or invention of methods... The home of faith is a childlike thought and a simple heart" (254). While human knowledge has intelligence at its centre, faith has the simple and guileless heart. Human knowledge "keeps within the boundaries of nature" while faith "makes its journey above nature" (254). That is to say, human knowledge is a purely natural condition, working within natural limits, while faith is a supranatural condition. Likewise human knowledge is unable to do anything without matter; it moves in a material world, while faith has authority, after the likeness of God, to make a new creation (p. 254). Human knowledge does not dare nor wish to overstep the boundaries of nature, while faith "transgresses them with authority" (p. 255). This is demonstrated by the lives of all the saints who, by the power of faith "have entered into flames and bridled the burning power of the fire, walking unharmed through the midst of it, and they have trodden upon the back of the sea as upon dry land" (p. 255). And all these things which faith does are above nature and contrary to the ways of human knowledge. Human knowledge "keeps within the limits of nature", while faith "passes above nature" (p. 255). Human knowledge always seeks means "to safeguard those who have acquired it", that is, it always takes protective measures and seeks to protect man by human means. But faith leaves it entirely to God. "The man who prays in faith never employs, or is engaged in, ways and means" (p. 255). Human knowledge does not begin a piece of work without having examined how it will end, while faith says: "All things are possible to him that believes. For to God nothing is impossible" (p. 256).

It is true, according to St. Isaac, that human knowledge is not faulty, but faith is higher (p. 256). Knowledge is perfected by faith, since "knowledge is a step whereby a man can climb up to the lofty height of faith" (p. 257). When faith comes, what is in part is abolished. Then "it is by our faith that we learn those things that cannot be comprehended by the investigation and power of knowledge" (p. 257). All the works of righteousness which are the virtues, that is, fasting, alms, vigil, holiness and all the "rest of such works performed with the body" and all those which are performed in the soul, that is, love for one's neighbor, humility of heart, forgiving "those who have sinned", recollection of good things, investigation of the mysteries concealed in the Scriptures, the mind's occupation with good works, the bridling of the soul's passions, and the rest of such virtues, "all these require knowledge". Knowledge "guards them and teaches their order". And all these things are steps by which the soul ascends "to the more lofty height of faith". However, "faith's way of life is more exalted than virtue's labour, and it is not labour but perfect rest, consolation, and is accomplished in the heart and within the soul" (p. 256-7).

All these things indicate that, according to the teaching of St. Isaac and the other holy Fathers, faith is higher than human knowledge, higher even than knowledge acquired through the practice of virtue. For faith is a charismatic condition, communion with God; it is "the heart's understanding and vision"; it is the life which develops in the soul with the coming of the light of divine grace. In the next section, in the teaching of St. Gregory Palamas, we shall look at this knowledge of God, which is really "communion in being", man's communion and union with God. Thus it is a knowledge higher than any human knowledge, even than knowledge acquired through the practice of virtues, for with it we find Christ Himself, who is hidden in the depths of the commandments.

St. Isaac the Syrian speaks of three kinds of knowledge.

Let us examine how they differ, for I think that this will show us how the Orthodox tradition differs from the human cultural tradition, how divine knowledge differs from human knowledge.

There are three conceivable ways in which knowledge ascends and descends. These ways are body, soul and spirit (p. 258). Indeed when the Fathers speak of body, soul and spirit they do not mean the three parts of man, but by the word 'spirit' they mean the gift of grace, that divine grace with which man is blessed. Without the grace of God a man is said to be a man of soul or flesh, while with the presence of grace he is called spiritual. While the nature of knowledge is one, it is refined and changes its modes according to these intelligible and sensible realms (p. 258). Thus just as there are three sentient and intelligible modes: body, soul and spirit, so there are three kinds of knowledge related to them. According to the kind of knowledge which a man possesses, he shows his spiritual progress and his spiritual condition. Moreover, the kind of knowledge which someone has is an indication of his purification and healing. One whose soul is unhealthy has bodily knowledge, while one who is being healed has soul knowledge, and one who has been healed has spiritual knowledge. The latter knows the mysteries of the Spirit, which are unknown and incomprehensible to the man of flesh.

The first knowledge is acquired by constant study and diligence in learning, the second knowledge comes from a pure and good manner of life and from the mind's faith, and the third knowledge "is allotted to faith alone. For by faith knowledge is abolished, works come to an end, and the employment of the senses becomes superfluous" (p. 264).

Let us look more analytically, on the basis of St. Isaac's teaching, at these three kinds of knowledge which indicate the sickness or health of a man's soul.

First, bodily knowledge. Some characteristic elements of human knowledge which are connected with the desires of the flesh are wealth, vainglory, adornment, bodily rest, and

assiduity in rational wisdom, such as is suitable for the governance of the world and which devises the novelties of inven-
tions and arts and sciences (p. 258). This knowledge is opposed to faith, as we have explained before, because it thinks
that "all things are by its own providence" (p. 258). Wisdom
and knowledge of things of this world without the other two
kinds of knowledge are useless and create many problems for
man. This knowledge is shallow and rude, for it is "naked of
all concern for God" (p. 258). Its concern is only for this world,
and because it is controlled by the body, "it introduces into
the mind an irrational impotence" (p. 258).

Most men of our time, unhealed in soul, possess this knowledge and cultivate it continually. The whole of contemporary
civilisation, which creates many anomalies of soul and body,
is in this state. Hence this one-sidedness of knowledge
creates many problems. Here is how St. Isaac describes them.
The man of this bodily knowledge is a prey to faint-heartedness, sorrow, despair, fear of the demons, trepidation before
men, the rumour of thieves and the report of murders, anxiety
over illnesses, concern over want and the lack of necessities,
fear of death, fear of sufferings, of wild beasts and of other
similar things that make up the sea of the present life (p.
258). The man who possesses this human and bodily knowledge does not know how to abandon himself to God's mercy
but tries in his own ways to solve the various problems. But
when he cannot give solutions, for different reasons, then he
"strives with men as though they hindered and opposed" this
knowledge (p. 258). He comes to blows with men because they
hinder the possession of the goods of bodily knowledge.

This bodily knowledge, worldly care, completely eradicates
love. It makes one examine other people's small sins and
errors and their causes, and their weaknesses, it makes one
dogmatise and oppose the words of others, become sly in all
one's doings and devise ways to dishonour people. This
knowledge contains presumption and pride (p. 259).

We see clearly that bodily knowledge is characteristic of

contemporary civilisation. With prophetic insight St. Isaac presents the causes and pursuits of this carnal man, describes his struggle and anguish, and also presents the frightful results of this bodily knowledge. Disturbance of personal relationships, lack of love, obstinacy and cunning in all actions are the things which define the contemporary man who is sick in soul, far from God.

The second knowledge, that **of the soul**. When a man renounces the first, bodily, fleshly knowledge and turns to the desires and conversations of the soul, then all the good deeds of the soul's knowledge follow. These are fasting, prayer, mercy, reading of the Scriptures, the modes of virtue, battle with the passions, and so forth (p. 258). All these deeds are made perfect by the Holy Spirit. They do not happen by the power of man but by the working together of man and the Holy Spirit. There are stages in the acquisition of knowledge. The second degree of knowledge is made perfect "when it has laid the foundation of its action on seclusion from men, reading the Scriptures, and prayer" (p. 260). That is to say, the possessor of this knowledge of the soul lives in stillness, with all that implies, as we described in the preceding chapter. He prays to God unceasingly and studies the Scriptures in this holy atmosphere of stillness in order to nourish his soul, not in order to learn the words of God out of curiosity. This category includes those people who are being cured of psychic ulcers and the wounds of their soul. This cure offers a knowledge which can be called the preliminary stage and anteroom of that other, spiritual knowledge, which the coming of the grace of God will provide in the heart of man.

The **third, spiritual knowledge**. When man's knowledge is raised above worldly concerns and begins to see inwardly "what is hidden from the eyes" and when it scorns the things "from which the perverseness of the passions arises" and stretches itself upward in its desire for the promises of the age to come and in its searching into hidden mysteries, "then faith itself swallows up knowledge, converts it, and begets it anew, so that it becomes wholly and completely spirit" (p. 261).

Then it can fly to the places of the bodiless angels; it knows the spiritual mysteries, the governings of the spiritual and the corporeal. That is to say, it knows the inner principles of beings. Then the inner senses awaken and the soul receives the resurrection which gives assurance of the future resurrection of men. St. Isaac, who possessed this spiritual knowledge which is the life of faith, wrote: "Then it can soar in the realms of the bodiless and touch the depths of the unfathomable sea, musing upon the wondrous and divine workings of God's governance of intelligible and corporeal creatures. It searches out spiritual mysteries that are perceived by the simple and subtle nous. Then the inner senses awaken for spiritual doing, according to the order that will be in the immortal and incorruptible life. For even from now it has received, as it were in a mystery, the intelligible resurrection as a true witness of the universal renewal of all things" (p. 261).

This knowledge was possessed by all the saints of God, such as Moses, David, Isaiah, the Apostle Peter, the Apostle Paul and all the saints who were accounted worthy of this perfect knowledge, "to the degree possible for human nature" (p. 259). In reality this knowledge comes from vision of God and of the uncreated light, from divine revelations or, as St. Isaac puts it, "by diverse contemplations and divine revelations, by the lofty vision of spiritual things and by ineffable mysteries..." (p. 259). Then knowledge is swallowed up by these visions of God and the person feels that he is dust and ashes (p. 259). He acquires the blessed state of humility and simplicity. Thus spiritual knowledge, that is, knowledge of God, is the fruit of theoria. It is received by the person who has progressed from carnal knowledge to that of the soul and thence to spiritual knowledge.

Briefly one can say that the first knowledge "renders the soul cold to works that go in pursuit of God". The second knowledge warms the soul to the swift course "on the level of faith". The third knowledge is rest from labour, "which is the type of the age to come, for the soul takes delight solely in the mind's meditation upon the mysteries of the good things to come" (p. 262).

This teaching of St. Isaac is very relevant to the subject which we are treating, for the following reason. In the beginning of the book we mentioned that the members of the Church are not divided into good and bad or moral and immoral, making human ethics the criterion, but into the sick in soul, those being cured, and those cured. Precisely these three categories correspond to the three degrees of knowledge. Those whose soul is sick are people of bodily, worldly knowledge, those being cured are the ones who in different degrees are acquiring the soul's wisdom and knowledge, and those cured are the saints of God, who possess spiritual knowledge, true knowledge of God. Most people of our time, who are sick in soul because they know nothing of the nous and the heart, are in the first bodily, fleshly knowledge. Others belong to the second knowledge, because they are struggling to be cured by means of the whole ascetic method available in the Orthodox Church. And the saints, who exist even today, belong to the third knowledge, since they have been cured of their sicknesses and so have acquired knowledge of God.

Knowledge of God according to St. Gregory Palamas

Now that we have explained the teaching of St. Isaac the Syrian about the three degrees of knowledge, we can go on to look at knowledge of God according to the Athonite saint Gregory Palamas. When a person rises from bodily knowledge to the soul's knowledge and from that to spiritual knowledge, then he sees God and possesses knowledge of God, which is his salvation. Knowledge of God, as will be explained further on, is not intellectual, but existential. That is, one's whole being is filled with this knowledge of God. But in order to attain it, one's heart must have been purified, that is, the soul, nous and heart must have been healed. "Blessed are the pure in heart, for they shall see God" (Matt. 5,8).

Let us look at things more analytically.

As I have indicated, Barlaam insisted that knowledge of God depends not on vision of God but on one's understanding. He said that we can acquire knowledge of God through philosophy, and therefore he considered the prophets and apostles who saw the uncreated light, to be below the philosophers. He called the uncreated light sensory, created, and "inferior to our understanding". However, St. Gregory Palamas, a bearer of the Tradition and a man of revelation, supported the opposite view. In his theology he presented the teaching of the Church that uncreated light, that is, the vision of God, is not simply a symbolic vision, nor sensory and created, nor inferior to understanding, but it is deification. Through deification man is deemed worthy of seeing God. And this deification is not an abstract state, but a union of man with God. That is to say, the man who beholds the uncreated light sees it because he is united with God. He sees it with his inner eyes, and also with his bodily eyes, which, however, have been altered by God's action. Consequently theoria is union with God. And this union is knowledge of God. At this time one is granted knowledge of God, which is above human knowledge and above the senses.

St. Gregory explains this whole theology in places throughout his writings. But since it is not our intention in this chapter to make a systematic exposition of his whole teaching about the knowledge of God, we shall limit ourselves to analysing the central point in it as it is presented in his basic work 'On the Holy Hesychasts', known as the Triads. Again we must add that we shall not present the whole teaching as it is set out in that book, but only the central points. After each quotation we shall give the reference.

Here is a characteristic passage in which he briefly presents this teaching: "One who has cleared his soul of all connection with things of this world, who has detached himself from everything by keeping the commandments and by the dispassion that this brings, and who has passed beyond all cognitive activity through continuous, sincere and immaterial prayer, and who has been abundantly illuminated by the inaccessible light in an inconceivable union, he alone, becoming light, contemplating by the light and beholding the light, in the vision and enjoyment of this light recognises truly that God is transcendently radiant and beyond comprehension; he glorifies God not only beyond his nous's human power of understanding, for many created things are beyond that, but even beyond that marvelous union which is the only means by which the nous is united with what is beyond intelligible things, 'imitating divinely the supracelestial nouses'" (2, 3, 57).

We find the central teaching of St. Gregory in this passage. In order to attain vision of the uncreated light, a person must cut off every connection between the soul and what is below, detach himself from everything by keeping Christ's commandments and through the dispassion which comes from that, he must transcend all cognitive activity "through continuous and sincere and immaterial prayer". Therefore he must have been healed already, through keeping Christ's commandments and through freeing his soul from all sinful connection with created things. He is illuminated by the inaccessible light "abundantly through an inconceivable union". He sees God through union. Thus he becomes light and sees by the light. Seeing the uncreated light, he recognises God and acquires knowledge of Him, because now "he recognises truly that God is above nature and beyond comprehension".

St. Gregory also develops this teaching at other places in the Triads.

The vision of God, theoria of the uncreated light, is not a sensory vision but a deification of man. Speaking of Moses' vision of God "face-to-face and not in enigmas", he recalls the passage in St. Maximus the Confessor that says: "Deification is an enhypostatic and direct illumination which has no beginning but appears in those worthy as something exceeding their comprehension. It is indeed a mystical union with God, beyond nous and reason in the age when creatures will no longer know corruption" (3, 1, 28; CWS p. 84). So the vision of the uncreated light is man's deification. He sees God through deification and not through cultivating intelligence. The vision of uncreated light is called a deifying gift. It is not a gift of created human nature, but of the Holy Spirit. "Thus the deifying gift of the Spirit is a mysterious light which transforms into light those who receive its wealth. He not only fills them with eternal light but also grants them knowledge and life appropriate to God" (3, 1, 35; CWS p. 90). Thus the vision of God is not external but comes through deification (2, 3, 25).

This deification is union and communion with God. According to St. Gregory, "Vision of the uncreated light is not simply abstraction and negation, it is a union and a divinisation which occurs mystically and ineffably by the grace of God, after the stripping away of everything from here below which imprints itself on the nous, or rather after the cessation of all noetic activity; it is something which goes beyond abstraction" (1, 3, 17; CWS p. 34f). The contemplation of uncreated light is "by the divinising communion of the Spirit" (1, 3, 5; CWS p. 33). "So the contemplation of this light is a union, even though it does not endure in the imperfect: but is the union with this light other than a vision?" (2, 3, 36; CWS p. 65)

St. Gregory speaks of ecstasy. But this ecstasy, in patristic teaching, has nothing to do with the ecstasy of Pythia and the other religions. Ecstasy comes when, in prayer, the nous abandons every connection with created things: first "with everything evil and bad, then with neutral things" (2, 3, 35; CWS p. 65). Ecstasy is mainly withdrawal from the opinion of the world and the flesh. With sincere prayer the nous "abandons all created things" (2, 3, 35; CWS p. 65). This ecstasy is higher than abstract theology, that is, than rational theology, and it belongs only to those who have attained dispassion. But it is not yet union. That is to say, the ecstasy which is unceasing prayer of the nous, in which one's nous has continuous remembrance of God and has no relation with the 'world of sin' is not yet union with God. This union comes about when the Paraclete "illuminates from on high the man who attains in prayer the stage which is superior to the highest natural possibilities and who is awaiting the promise of the Father, and by His revelation ravishes him to the contemplation of the light" (2, 3, 35; CWS p. 65). Illumination by God is what shows His union with man.

Vision, deification and union with God are the things which offer man existential knowledge of God. Then man possesses real knowledge of God. The deifying gift of the Holy Spirit, which is a mysterious light, transforms into divine light those who have attained it and not only fills them with eternal light, "but also grants them a knowledge and a life appropriate to God" (3, 1, 35; CWS p. 89). In this state a person possesses knowledge of God. In reply to Barlaam's teaching that God is known by the greatest contemplators, the philosophers, and that knowledge of God transmitted "by noetic illumination... is by no means true" (2, 3, 78), St. Gregory Palamas declares: "God makes Himself known not only through all that is but also through what is not, through transcendence, that is, through uncreated things, and also through an eternal light that transcends all beings". This knowledge, he says, is offered today as a kind of pledge to those who are worthy of it and which "illuminates them unendingly in the unending age". That is just why the saints' vision of God is true, "and he who calls it false has strayed from the divine knowledge of God" (2, 3, 78). Thus anyone who ignores and disregards the vision of God, which offers true knowledge, is in reality ignorant of God.

These things show that the vision of God, deification, union and knowledge of God are closely bound together. They cannot be understood apart from one another. Breaking this unity takes man further away from knowledge of God. The basis of Orthodox epistemology is illumination and God's revelation within the purified heart of man.

As we have seen, knowledge of God is beyond human knowledge. Vision of the uncreated light surpasses all epistemological activity and is "beyond sight and knowledge" (2, 3, 50). Since vision of the uncreated light is offered to the hearts of the faithful and perfect, that is why "it is superior to the light of knowledge" (2, 3, 18; CWS p. 63). And not only is it superior to the light of human knowledge "from Hellenic studies", but also the light of this theoria differs from "the light that comes from the Holy Scriptures", since the light of the Scriptures may be compared to "a lamp that shines in an obscure place, whereas vision of the uncreated light resembles the morning star which shines in the day, that is to say, the sun" (2, 3, 18; CWS p. 63). The grace of deification thus transcends nature, virtue and human knowledge (3, 1, 27).

The vision of the uncreated light and the knowledge that comes from this are not an unfolding of the rational power, they are not perfection of rational nature, as Barlaam asserted, but they are superior to reason. They are knowledge offered by God to the pure in heart. Anyone who asserts that the deifying gift is a development of the rational nature puts himself in opposition to Christ's Gospel. If contemplation were a natural gift, then all people should be gods, one less and another more. But "the deified saints transcend nature", they are engendered by God, God gave them power to become "children of God" (3, 1, 30; CWS p. 85).

The vision of the uncreated light, which offers knowledge of God to man, is sensory and suprasensory. The bodily eyes are reshaped, so they see the uncreated light, "this mysterious light, inaccessible, immaterial, uncreated, deifying, eternal", this "radiance of the Divine Nature, this glory of the divinity, this beauty of the heavenly kingdom" (3, 1, 22; CWS p. 80). St. Gregory Palamas asks: "Do you see that light is inaccessible to senses which are not transformed by the Spirit?" (2, 3, 22). St. Maximus, whose teaching is cited by St. Gregory, says that the Apostles saw the uncreated Light "by a transformation of the activity of their senses, produced in them by the Spirit" (2, 3, 22).

Vision of the uncreated Light and the knowledge which comes from it transcend not only nature and human knowledge, but virtue as well. Virtue and the imitation of God prepare us for the divine union, but the mysterious union itself is effected by grace (3, 1, 27; CWS p. 83).

Thus deification, which is the goal of the spiritual life, is a manifestation of God to the pure heart of man. This vision of the uncreated Light is what creates spiritual delight in the soul. For, according to St. Gregory, evidence of that light is that the soul ceases to give itself over to wrong pleasures and passions, and that it acquires peace and quietening of thoughts, and rest and spiritual joy, contempt for human glory, humility joined with secret rejoicing, hatred of the world, love of heavenly things, or rather love of the God of Heaven alone, and a vision of uncreated light even if one's eyes should be covered or plucked out (3, 1, 36; CWS p. 90).

From what has been said it is clear that the end of man's cure is vision of the uncreated light. But since in this chapter we are speaking about theoria, we may also look at St. Gregory Palamas' teaching that there are many degrees of theoria. He says that this theoria has a beginning, and the things that follow on from this beginning differ in degrees of darkness or clarity, but there is never an end, for its progress, like that of the rapture in revelation, is infinite. Illumination is one thing and continuous vision of light is another, and still another is the vision of things in that light whereby even things far off are accessible to the eyes, and the future is shown as already existing (2, 3, 35; CWS p. 65). So there are degrees of theoria, and with it, degrees of knowledge.

At this point we may also look at the teaching of St. Peter of Damascus about the eight stages of theoria (Philokalia 3,108). The first seven belong to this age, while the eighth belongs to the age to come. The first theoria is knowledge of the trials and tribulations of this life. The second is "knowledge of our own faults and of God's bounty". The third is knowledge of the terrible things before and after death. The fourth is deep understanding of the life led by our Lord Jesus in this world and of His disciples and the other saints, that is to say, the words and actions of the martyrs and the holy Fathers. The fifth is knowledge of the nature and flux of things. The sixth is theoria of created beings, or knowledge and understanding of God's visible creation. The seventh is understanding of God's spiritual creation, that is to say, of the angels. The eighth is knowledge concerning God, or what we call 'theology'.

Consequently theoria has many stages and degrees, and many must come before vision of the uncreated light, which is "the beauty of the age to come", "the food of the heavens". Among the degrees of theoria are remembrance of death, which is a gift from God, unceasing prayer, the inspiration to keep Christ's commandments fully, knowledge of our spiritual poverty, that is to say, understanding of our sins and passions, and the repentance following it. All these things come about through the operation of divine grace. Certainly perfect theoria is vision of the uncreated light, which itself is differentiated into vision and continuous vision, as St. Gregory Palamas says (3, 1, 30).

So the purification which takes place by the grace of God creates the necessary preconditions for attaining that theoria which is communion with God, deification of man, and knowledge of God. The ascetic method of the Church leads to this point. It is not based on human criteria and it does not aim to make the person 'nice and good', but to heal him perfectly and for him to achieve communion with God. As long as a man is far from communion and union with God, he has not yet attained his salvation. The spiritually trained person who sees the uncreated light is said, in the language of the Fathers, to be 'deified'. This expression is used by St. Dionysios the Areopagite, St. John of Damascus, and repeatedly, as we have seen, by St. Gregory Palamas (3, 1, 30; CWS p. 85f).

The healing of the soul, nous and heart leads a person to the vision of God and makes him know the divine life. This knowledge is man's salvation.

We must pray fervently for God to grant us to reach this knowledge of God. The exhortation is clear:

"Come, let us ascend into the mountain of the Lord,
even to the house of our God,
and behold the glory of His transfiguration,
glory of the Only-begotten of the Father.
Let us receive light from His light,
and with uplifted spirits
let us for ever sing the praises of the consubstantial
Trinity".

Here we rise and sing:

"Thou wast transfigured upon the mountain, O Christ our God, showing Thy glory to Thy disciples as far as they were able to bear it. At the intercessions of the Mother of God, make Thine everlasting light shine forth also upon us sinners, O Giver of light, glory to Thee."

(Feast of the Transfiguration, Festal Menaion p. 475-477)

356 *Prayers*

Prayers

a) In quest of a spiritual healer

"O Lord, who desirest not the death of a sinner but that he should turn and live, Thou who didst come down to earth in order to restore life to those lying dead through sin and in order to make them worthy of seeing Thee the true light as far as that is possible to man, send me a man who knows Thee, so that in serving him and subjecting myself to him with all my strength, as to Thee, and in doing Thy will in his, I may please Thee the only true God, and so that even I, a sinner, may be worthy of Thy Kingdom".

St. Symeon the New Theologian
(SC 129, 186-188)

b) For knowledge of God and love for Him

"Make me worthy, O Lord, to know and love Thee, not with knowledge from the exercise of a scattered nous; but make me worthy of that knowledge whereby, beholding Thee, the nous glorifies Thy nature, in divine vision which robs the mind of awareness of the world. Account me worthy to be lifted above my will's wandering eye which begets imaginings, and to behold Thee in the constraint of the Cross's bond, in the second part of the crucifixion of the nous, which willingly ceases from its conceptual imagings to abide in Thy continuous vision that surpasses nature. Implant in my heart an increase of Thy love, that it may be drawn back from this world by fervent love for Thee. Awake in me understanding of Thy humility, wherewith Thou didst sojourn in the world in the covering of flesh which Thou didst bear from our members by the mediation of the Holy Virgin, that with this continual and unfailing recollection I may accept the humility of my nature with delight.

St. Isaac the Syria
Hom. 36 (Gk.), Hom. 16 (Eng.)

Index of persons

Agathon, Abba 235

Ammon, Abba 147

Anthony the Great, St. 53, 115

Arsenios, St. 184, 238

Barlaam 43, 143, 195, 209, 326, 252, 298

Barsanuphios, St. 191, 222, 233

Basil the Great, St. 61, 136 143

Cabasilas, Nicholas 75, 234

Cassian of Rome, St. 222, 237, 238, 289

Chrysostom, St. John 23, 27, 28, 61, 62, 66, 67, 68, 69, 83, 86, 87, 102, 103, 239, 243, 275

Colobos, John, Abba (the Dwarf), 237

Cyril of Alexandria, St. 37

Diadochos of Photiki, St. 33, 34, 150, 160, 161, 166, 192, 194, 220, 275

Dionysios the Areopagite 47, 48, 72, 73, 76, 79, 144, 354

Dorotheos of Gaza. St. 41, 85, 176, 213, 224, 227, 248, 251, 266

Evagrius, Abba 217, 248

Gregory of Nyssa, St. 101, 111, 129, 130

Gregory Palamas, St. 34, 37, 48, 52, 80, 93, 100, 101, 130, 142, 143, 147, 195, 204, 205, 209, 210, 246, 247, 252, 255, 262, 263, 264, 267, 279, 280, 298, 307, 316, 322, 324

Gregory of Sinai, St. 49, 89, 107, 112, 200, 208, 215, 258

Gregory the Theologian, St. 31, 61, 69, 143, 248, 312, 313, 327, 336

Hesychios the Priest, St. 113, 134, 141, 192, 199, 215, 224, 262

Ilias, Abba 129

Ilias the Presbyter 218, 257

Isaac, Abba 268

Isaac the Syrian, St. 51, 85, 181, 183, 194, 217, 268

Isidore of Pelusium 78, 86

John of Damascus 100, 101, 102, 103, 106, 119, 126

John of Karpathos, St. 297

John of the Ladder, St. (John of Sinai, Klimakos) 3, 38,

Index of subjects

Bibliography

The Art of Prayer. An Orthodox Anthology, comp. Igumen Chariton of Valamo. ET London, Faber, 1966.

Barsanuphius and John. Questions and Answers. Greek text ed. Nicodemus of the Holy Mountain/S. Schoinas (Volos, 1960); ET (selections) St. Herman of Alaska Brotherhood, 1990.

Cyril of Jerusalem and Nemesius of Emesa. The Nature of Man. LCC vol. 4. London, SCM Press, 1955.

Dorotheos of Gaza. Discourses and Sayings. ET Eric P. Wheeler. Cistercian Studies 33, Kalamazoo, Mich. 1977. French tr. SC 92, 1963.

Early Fathers from the Philokalia. Tr. from Russian by E. Kadloubovsky and G.E.H. Palmer. London, Faber, 1954.

Gregory Palamas. Triads in Defence of the Holy Hesychasts. Greek text and French tr. J.Meyendorff (Spicilegium Sacrum Lovaniense) 30-31: Louvain, 1973. ET of Triads (selections by N.Gendle), CWS London, SPCK, 1983.

The One Hundred and Fifty Chapters. ET Robert E. Sinkewicz. Toronto, Pontifical Institute of Mediaeval Studies, 1988. Homilies. EPE Vols. 9,10,11. Thessaloniki 1985-6.(Gk.)

Isaac the Syrian. The Ascetical Homilies. ET Holy Transfiguration Monastery, Boston, 1884.

John Chrysostom. Six Books on the Priesthood. ET Graham Neville. London, SPCK, 1964.

John Climacus, The Ladder of Divine Ascent. ET C.Luibheid and N.Russell. CWS 1982. ET (including The Shepherd) Archimandrite Lazarus Moore. Boston, Holy Transfiguration Monastery, 1978.

Mantzaridis, Georgios I. Palamika. Thessaloniki, Pournara, 1973.

Nicholas Cabasilas. The Life in Christ. ET C.J. de Catanzaro, St. Vladimir's Seminary Press, 1974.

Nicodemos of the Holy Mountain. A Handbook of Spiritual Counsel. Greek text ed. S. Schoinas (Volos 1969). ET Peter A. Chamberas. CWS 1989.

Philokalia Vols.1-5. Greek text (Athens 1980 etc.) Modern Greek tr. (Thessaloniki 1987 etc.) ET Vols 1-3. London, Faber 1979- 1984.

Pseudo-Dionysius the Areopagite. Complete Works. CWS 1987.

Pseudo-Macarius. The Fifty Spiritual Homilies and the Great Letter. CWS, ET George A. Maloney, S.J. 1992.

Rantosavlievits, Artemiou: The Mystery of Salvation according to St. Maximus the Confessor. Athens, 1975. (in Gk.)

Rantovits, Amphilochiou. The Mystery of the Holy Trinity according to St. Gregory Palamas. Thessaloniki, 1973. (In Gk.) Romanides, John. Dogmatic and Symbolic Theology of the Orthodox Catholic Church. Thessaloniki 1973. (In Gk.)

The Sayings of the Desert Fathers. ET Benedicta Ward. London, Mowbrays, 1975.

Archimandrite Sophrony. Saint Silouan the Athonite. ET Rosemary Edmonds. Monastery of St. John the Baptist, Essex, 1991.

His Life is Mine. ET Rosemary Edmonds. London, Mowbrays, 1977.

The Monk of Mount Athos: Staretz Silouan 1866-1938. ET Rosemary Edmonds. London, Mowbrays, 1973.

Symeon the New Theologian. The Discourses. CWS, 1980.

The Practical and Theological Chapters and The Three Theological Discourses. ET Paul McGuckin. Cistercian Studies 41, Kalamazoo, 1982.

Hymns. SC 96 and 174.

Theological and Ethical Treatises. SC 129.

Writings from the Philokalia on Prayer of the Heart. ET from
the Russian, E. Kadloubovsky and G.E.H. Palmer, London, Faber, 1951.

Yannaras, Christos. Elements of Faith. Greek ed. 1983. ET
Keith Schram. Edinburgh, T&T Clark, 1991.

Other works by the same author

1. A night in the desert of the Holy Mountain, first edition 1991, reprinted 1994, second edition 1995, Birth of the Theotokos monastery, p. 200

2. The illness and cure of the coul in the Orthodox Tradition, first edition 1993, reprinted 1994, 1997 Birth of the Theotokos Monastery, p. 202

3. Orthodox Spirituality, first edition 1994, reprinted 1996, Birth of the Theotokos Monastery, p.112

4. Life after death, Birth of the Theotokos Monastery, 1996, p. 392

★ ★ ★

5. Mia vradia stin erimo tou agiou Orous, editions A´ 1978, B´ 1979, Γ´ 1982, Δ´ 1984, E´ 1985, ΣΤ´ 1986, Z´ 1987, H´ 1989, Θ´ 1990, I´ 1992, IA´ 1993, IB´ 1994, IΓ´ 1995, IΔ´ 1997, Birth of the Theotokos Monastery

6. Osmi Gnoseos, editions "Tertios", Katerini 1985

7. Martiria zois, 1985

8. To Mistirion tis paedias tou Theou editions A´ 1985, B´ 1987, Γ´ 1991, Birth of the Theotokos Monastery

9. Paraklitika, editions "Tertios", Katerini 1986

10. Orthodoxi Psychotherapia (Pateriki therapeutiki agogi) editions A´ 1986, B´ 1987, Γ´ 1989, Δ´ 1992, E´ 1995, Birth of the Theotokos Monastery

11. Piotita zois, editions A´ 1987, B´ 1989, Birth of the Theotokos Monastery

12. Apokalipsi tou Theou, editions A´ 1987, B´ 1992, Γ´ 1996, Birth of the Theotokos Monastery

13. Therapeutiki agogi, editions A´ 1987, B´ 1989, Γ´ 1993, Δ´ 1997, Birth of the Theotokos Monastery

14. Sizitisis gia tin Orthodoxi Psychotherapia, editions A´ 1988, B´ 1992, Birth of the Theotokos Monastery

15. Psychiki asthenia kai igia, editions A´ 1989, B´ 1991, Γ´ 1995, Birth of the Theotokos Monastery

16. Anatolika I, editions A´ 1989, B´ 1993, Birth of the Theotokos Monastery

17. Keros tou piisai, Birth of the Theotokos Monastery, 1990

18. To politevma tou Stavrou, editions A´ 1990, B´ 1992, Birth of the Theotokos Monastery

19. Ecclesiastiko fronima, editions A´ 1990, B´ 1993, Birth of the Theotokos monastery

20. Prosopo kai Eleftheria, Birth of the Theotokos Monastery, 1991

21. O Vlepon, editions A´ 1991, B´ 1992, Birth of the Theotokos Monastery

22. Orthodoxos kai ditikos tropos zois, editions A´ 1992, B´ 1994, Birth of the Theotokos Monastery

23. Mikra isodos stin Orthodoxi pnevmatikotita, Athens 1992

24. O Agios Grigorios o Palamas os Agioritis, editions A´ 1992, B´ 1996, Birth of the Theotokos Monastery

25. Katichisi kai Baptisi ton enilikon, Athens 1993

26. Romeoi se Anatoli kai Disi, Birth of the Theotokos Monastery, 1993

27. Paremvasis stin sychroni kinonoia A´, Birth of the Theotokos Monastery, 1994

28. Paremvasis stin sychroni kinonoia B´, Birth of the Theotokos Monastery, 1994

29. AIDS, enas tropos zois, 1994

30. To prosopo stin Orthodoxi Paradosi, editions A´ 1994, B´ 1997, Birth of the Theotokos Monastery

31. Epoptiki Katichisi, Birth of the Theotokos Monastery, 1994

32. I zoi meta ton thanato, editions A´ 1994, B´ 1995, Γ´ 1996, Δ´ 1997, Birth of the Theotokos Monastery

33. I Despotikes eortes, Birth of the Theotokos Monastery, 1995

34. Iparxiaki psychologia kai Orthodoxi Psychotherapia, Birth of the Theotokos Monastery, 1995

35. Osoi pistoi, Birth of the Theotokos Monastery, 1996

36. Gennima kai thremma Romeoi, Birth of the Theotokos Monastery, 1996

37. Entefxis kai synentefxis, Birth of the Theotokos Monastery, 1997

★ ★ ★

38. Secularism in church, theology and pastoral care, "The truth", αρ. φύλ. II, 29 Μαϊου - 5 Ιουνίου, 1994, W. Australia and "Alive in Christ", the magazine of the Diocese of Eastern Pennsylvania, Orthodoxy Church in America, Volume X, No l, 2, 1994

39. Die Autorität in der orthodoxen Kirche (Kurzfassung der Einführung für deutsche Theologiestudenten am 29.9.1996), εις Philia, Zeitschrift für wissenschaftliche, ökumenische und kulturelle Zusammenarbeit der Griechisch-Deutschen Initiative, II/1996